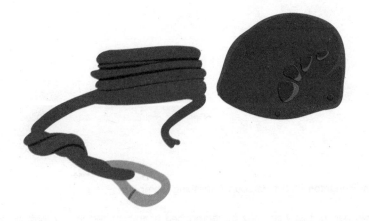

my Book 1

Authors and Advisors

Alma Flor Ada • Kylene Beers • F. Isabel Campoy

Joyce Armstrong Carroll • Nathan Clemens

Anne Cunningham • Martha C. Hougen

Elena Izquierdo • Carol Jago • Erik Palmer

Robert E. Probst • Shane Templeton • Julie Washington

Contributing Consultants

David Dockterman • Mindset Works®

Jill Eggleton

HMH

into Reading™

*my*Book 1

Welcome to myBook!

Do you like to read different kinds of texts for all kinds of reasons? Do you have a favorite genre or author? What can you learn from a video? Do you think carefully about what you read and view?

Here are some tips to get the MOST out of what you read and view:

Set a Purpose. What is the title? What is the genre? What do you want to learn from this text or video? What about it looks interesting to you?

Read and Annotate. As you read, underline and highlight important words and ideas. Make notes about things you want to figure out or remember. What questions do you have? What are your favorite parts? Write them down!

Make Connections. How does the text or video connect to what you already know? To other texts or videos? To your own life or community? Talk to others about your ideas. Listen to their ideas, too.

Wrap It Up! Look back at your questions and annotations. What did you like best? What did you learn? What do you still want to know? How will you find out?

As you read the texts and watch the videos in this book, make sure you get the MOST out of them by using the tips above.

But, don't stop there . . . decide what makes you curious, find out more about it, have fun, and never stop learning!

MODULE 1

Eyes on the Prize

MODULE 2

Here's the Story

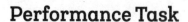

MODULE 3

Designing the Future

MODULE 4

On a Journey

MODULE 5

Good Times, Bad Times

🌱 **SOCIAL STUDIES CONNECTION:** THE GREAT DEPRESSION

9

EYES ON THE PRIZE

"Let us make our future now, and let us make our dreams tomorrow's reality."

—Malala Yousafzai

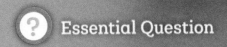
What is the path to success?

Get Curious

Video

Words About Paths to Success

The words in the chart will help you talk and write about the selections in this module. Which words about paths to success have you seen before? Which words are new to you?

Add to the Vocabulary Network on page 13 by writing synonyms, antonyms, and related words and phrases for each word about paths to success.

After you read each selection in this module, come back to the Vocabulary Network and keep building it. Add more boxes as needed.

WORD	MEANING	CONTEXT SENTENCE
eminent (adjective)	An *eminent* person is well-known and respected.	Jane Goodall is an eminent animal scientist who is best known for her work with chimpanzees.
dedication (noun)	*Dedication* is extreme devotion or commitment to a task or purpose.	Our drama teacher won a teaching award for her dedication to her students.
attain (verb)	When you *attain* something, you achieve it.	My little sister was happy to attain her goal of school spelling champion.
initiatives (noun)	An *initiative* is an important program or plan that's intended to solve a problem.	The recycling initiative at school has resulted in fewer items going into the garbage.

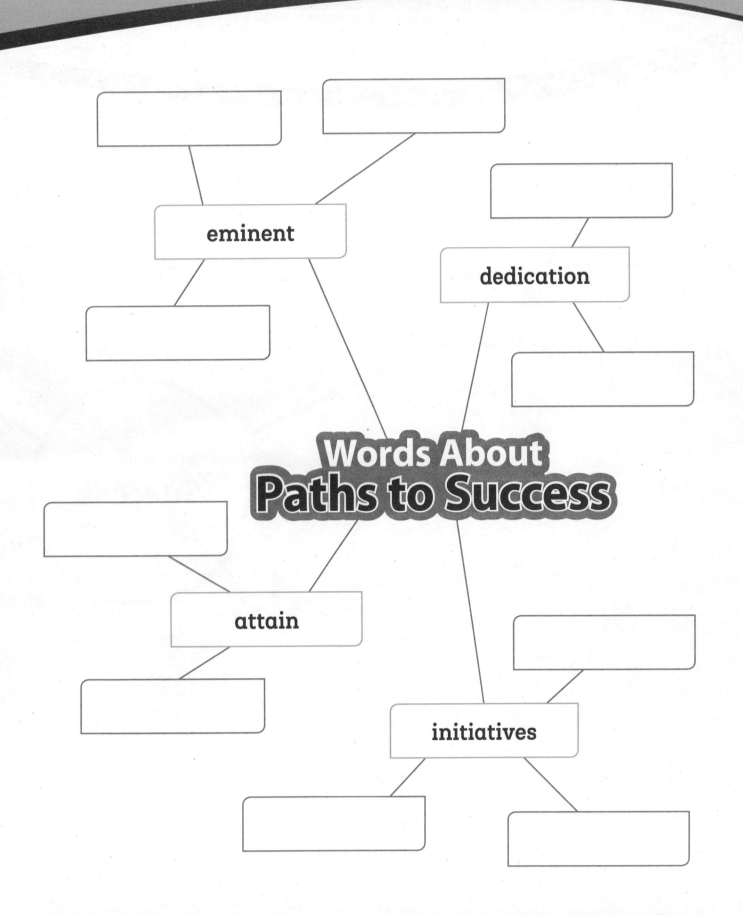

Words About
Paths to Success

eminent

dedication

attain

initiatives

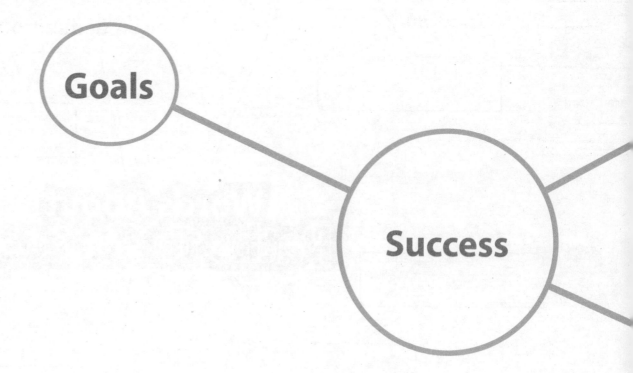

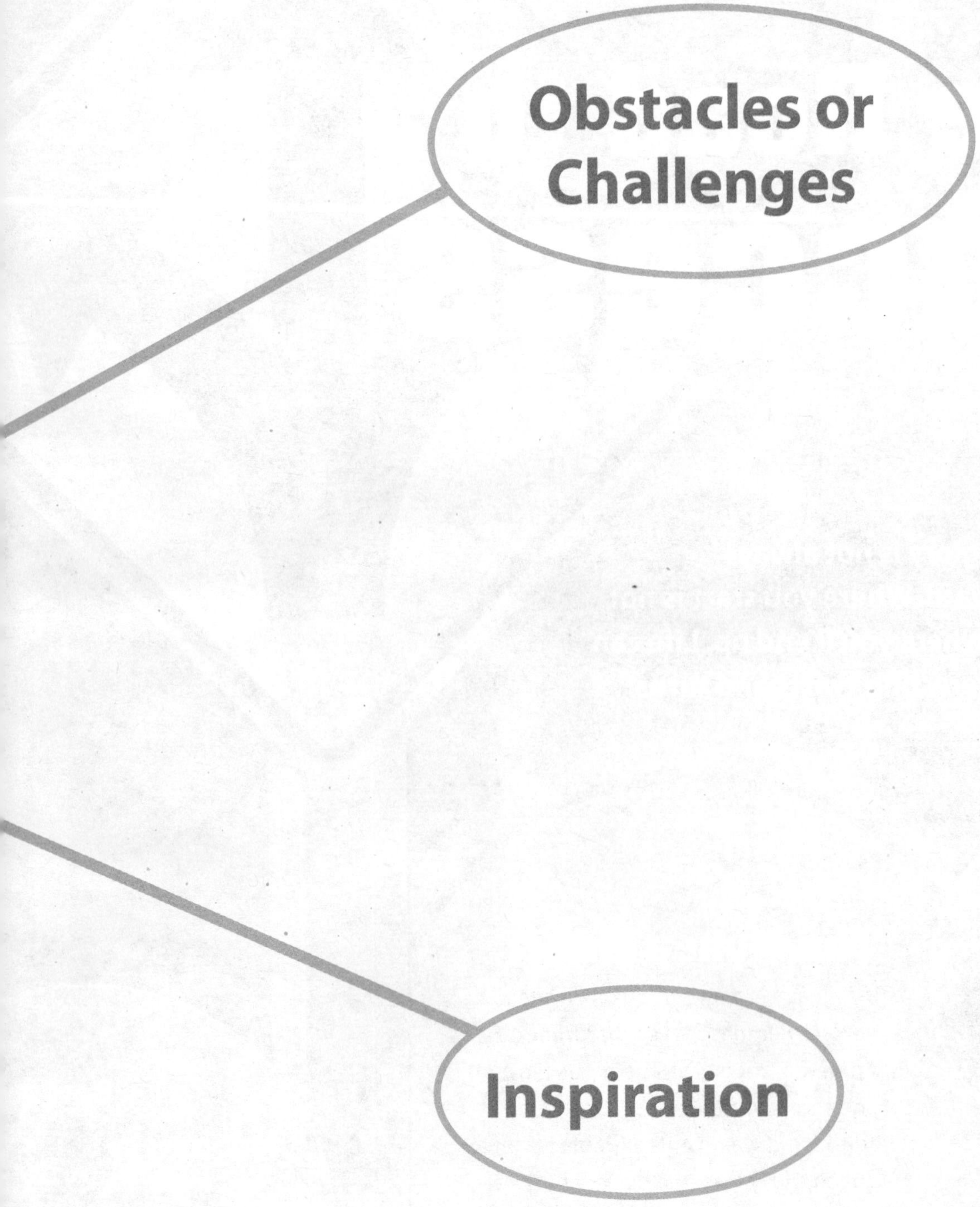

Obstacles or Challenges

Inspiration

Short
Read

The Road to Success

The path to glory is not always straightforward. Where you start is not necessarily where you'll end up. Life can be full of interesting twists and turns!

1 The Money Maker

If your aim is to get rich, you will need to get lucky or to work very hard, or both. Andrew Carnegie was born poor, in a one-room home. He started working at age 13 and was eventually able to get a good job. He invested his money in steel and became the richest man in the world! Carnegie gave away most of his money to charities before he died.

The Switch Hitter 2

Many people start out doing one thing, and then excel at something completely different. Julia Child was a secret intelligence officer with top-level security clearance before she wrote her first cookbook at age 50. She wrote *Mastering the Art of French Cooking* and became one of the most eminent chefs of all time.

The Helper 3

Mother Teresa is one of the most beloved figures in world history. She didn't make money, invent anything, or become "Internet famous"; rather, she was known for her lifelong dedication to helping the poor and sick in India. She worked with orphans, leper colonies, and people with HIV/AIDS. Sometimes just being a loving and giving person can bring you fame and admiration.

4 The Planet Saver

Helping people is very important, but so is helping our planet. As the first woman in East and Central Africa to earn a doctoral degree (the highest academic degree possible), Wangari Muta Maathai founded the Green Belt Movement that empowers communities to conserve environmental resources. Her group has planted more than 51 million trees in Kenya, among other environmental initiatives.

The Slow Burn 5

George Dawson didn't learn how to read until age 98. He grew up poor in the southern United States and was not able to attend school as a child. After Dawson learned how to read, he wrote a book, *Life Is So Good*, which became a bestseller. It's never too late to attain success in a way that matters to you.

Prepare to Read

GENRE STUDY **Realistic fiction** tells a story about characters and events that are like those in real life.

- Authors of realistic fiction tell the story through the plot—the main events of the story. The plot includes a conflict, or problem, and the resolution, or how the problem is solved.

- Authors of realistic fiction might tell the story through first-person point of view. In first-person point of view, the narrator is a character in the story.

SET A PURPOSE **Think about** the title and genre of this text. What are some different meanings of the word *push*? Based on the title, what do you predict the story will be about? Write your ideas below.

Meet the Author: Walter Dean Myers

CRITICAL VOCABULARY

executive

equipped

harnesses

stabilizing

exhaled

dejected

congestion

fundamentals

Sometimes a ★Dream★ Needs a Push

by Walter Dean Myers

illustrated by Benjamin Wachenje

1   You might have heard of my dad, Jim Blair. He's six five and played a year of good basketball in the pros before tearing his knee up in his second year. The knee took forever to heal and was never quite the same again. Still, he played pro ball in Europe for five years before giving it up and becoming an executive with a high-tech company.

2   Dad loved basketball and hoped that one day I would play the game. He taught me a lot, and I was pretty good until the accident. It was raining and we were on the highway, approaching the turnoff toward our house in Hartsdale, when a truck skidded across the road and hit our rear bumper. Our little car spun off the road, squealing as Dad tried to bring it under control. But he couldn't avoid the light pole. I remember seeing the broken windows, hearing Mom yelling, amazingly bright lights flashing crazily in front of me. Then everything was suddenly dark. The next thing I remember is waking up in the hospital. There were surgeries and weeks in the hospital, but the important thing was that I wasn't going to be walking again.

3   I didn't like the idea, but Mom and I learned to live with it. Dad took it hard, real hard. He was never much of a talker, Mom said, but he talked even less since I was hurt.

4   "Sometimes I think he blames himself," Mom said. "Whenever he sees you in the wheelchair he wants to put it out of his mind."

executive   An executive in a business decides what should be done.

5   I hadn't thought about that when Mr. Evans, an elder in our church, asked me if I wanted to join a wheelchair basketball team he was starting.

6   "We won't have the experience of the other teams in the league," he said. "But it'll be fun."

7   When I told Mom, she was all for it, but Dad just looked at me and mumbled something under his breath. He does that sometimes. Mom said that he's chewing up his words to see how they taste before he lets them out.

8   Our van is equipped with safety harnesses for my chair, and we used it on the drive to see a game between Madison and Rosedale. It was awesome to see guys my age zipping around in their chairs playing ball. I liked the chairs, too. They were specially built with rear stabilizing wheels and side wheels that slanted in. Very cool. I couldn't wait to start practicing. At the game, Mom sat next to me, but Dad went and sat next to the concession stand. I saw him reading a newspaper and only looking up at the game once in a while.

9   "Jim, have you actually seen wheelchair games before?" Mom asked on the way home.

10   Dad made a little motion with his head and said something that sounded like "Grumpa-grumpa" and then mentioned that he had to get up early in the morning. Mom looked at me, and her mouth tightened just a little.

equipped If you equip yourself for a job or experience, you make sure you have what is necessary to do it well.
harnesses A harness is a strap used to fasten or control something.
stabilizing Something that's stabilizing keeps other things steady.

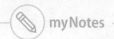

11   That was okay with me because I didn't want him to talk about the game if he didn't like it. After washing and getting into my pjs, I wheeled into my room, transferred to the bed, and tried to make sense of the day. I didn't know what to make of Dad's reaction, but I knew I wanted to play.

12   The next day at school, tall Sarah told me there was a message for me on the bulletin board. Sarah is cool but the nosiest person in school.

13   "What did it say?" I asked.

14   "How would I know?" she answered. "I don't read people's messages."

15   "Probably nothing important," I said, spinning my chair to head down the hall.

16   "Just something about you guys going to play Madison in a practice game and they haven't lost all season," Sarah said. "From Nicky G."

17   The school has a special bus for wheelchairs and the driver always takes the long way to my house, which is a little irritating when you've got a ton of homework that needs to get done, and I had a ton and a half. When I got home, Mom had the entire living room filled with purple lace and flower things she was putting together for a wedding and was lettering nameplates for them. I threw her a quick "Hey" and headed for my room.

18   "Chris, your coach called," Mom said.

19   "Mr. Evans?"

20   "Yes, he said your father had left a message for him," Mom answered. She had a big piece of the purple stuff around her neck as she leaned against the doorjamb. "Anything up?"

21 "I don't know," I said with a shrug. My heart sank. I went into my room and started on my homework, trying not to think of why Dad would call Mr. Evans.

22 With all the wedding stuff in the living room and Mom looking so busy, I was hoping that we'd have pizza again. No such luck. Somewhere in the afternoon she had found time to bake a chicken. Dad didn't get home until nearly seven-thirty, so we ate late.

23 While we ate Mom was talking about how some woman was trying to convince all of her bridesmaids to put a pink streak in their hair for her wedding. She asked us what we thought of that. Dad grunted under his breath and went back to his chicken. He didn't see the face that Mom made at him.

24 "By the way"—Mom gave me a quick look—"Mr. Evans called. He said he had missed your call earlier."

25 "I spoke to him late this afternoon," Dad said.

26 "Are the computers down at the school?" Mom asked.

27 "No, I was just telling him that I didn't think that the Madison team was all that good," Dad said. "I heard the kids saying they were great. They're okay, but they're not great. I'm going to talk to him again at practice tomorrow."

28 "Oh," Mom said. I could see the surprise in her face and felt it in my stomach.

29 The next day zoomed by. It was like the bells to change classes were ringing every two minutes. I hadn't told any of the kids about my father coming to practice. I wasn't even sure he was going to show up. He had made promises before and then gotten called away to work. This time he had said he was coming to practice, which was at two-thirty, in the middle of his day.

30   He was there. He sat in the stands and watched us go through our drills and a minigame. I was so nervous, I couldn't do anything right. I couldn't catch the ball at all, and the one shot I took was an air ball from just behind the foul line. We finished our regular practice, and Mr. Evans motioned for my father to come down to the court.

31   "Your dad's a giant!" Kwame whispered as Dad came onto the court.

32   "That's how big Chris is going to be," Nicky G said.

33   I couldn't imagine ever being as tall as my father.

34   "I was watching the teams play the other day." Dad had both hands jammed into his pockets. "And I saw that neither of them were running baseline plays and almost all the shots were aimed for the rims. Shots off the backboards are going to go in a lot more than rim shots if you're shooting from the floor."

35   Dad picked up a basketball and threw it casually against the backboard. It rolled around the rim and fell through. He did it again. And again. He didn't miss once.

36   "I happen to know that you played pro ball," Mr. Evans said, "and you're good. But I think shooting from a wheelchair is a bit harder."

37   "You have another chair?" Dad asked.

38   Mr. Evans pointed to his regular chair sitting by the watercooler. Dad took four long steps over to it, sat down, and wheeled himself back onto the floor. He put his hands up and looked at me. I realized I was holding a ball and tossed it to him. He tried to turn his chair back toward the basket, and it spun all the way

around. For a moment he looked absolutely lost, as if he didn't know what had happened to him. He seemed a little embarrassed as he glanced toward me.

39   "That happens sometimes," I said. "No problem."

40   He nodded, exhaled slowly, then turned and shot a long, lazy arc that hit the backboard and fell through.

41   "The backboard takes the energy out of the ball," he said. "So if it does hit the rim, it won't be so quick to bounce off. Madison made about twenty percent of its shots the other day. That doesn't win basketball games, no matter how good they look making them."

42   There are six baskets in our gym, and we spread out and practiced shooting against the backboards. At first I wasn't good at it. I was hitting the underside of the rim.

43   "That's because you're still thinking about the rim," Dad said when he came over to me. "Start thinking about a spot on the backboard. When you find your spot, really own it, you'll be knocking down your shots on a regular basis."

44   Nicky G got it first, and then Kwame, and then Bobby. I was too nervous to even hit the backboard half the time, but Dad didn't get mad or anything. He didn't even mumble. He just said it would come to me after a while.

45   Baseline plays were even harder. Dad wanted us to get guys wheeling for position under and slightly behind the basket.

46   "There are four feet of space behind the backboard," Dad said. "If you can use those four feet, you have an advantage."

exhaled   If you exhaled, you breathed out.

25

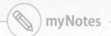

47   We tried wheeling plays along the baseline but just kept getting in each other's way.

48   "That's the point," Dad said. "When you learn to move without running into each other you're going to have a big advantage over a team that's trying to keep up with you."

49   Okay, so most of the guys are pretty good wheeling their chairs up and down the court. But our baseline plays looked more like a collision derby. Dad shook his head and Mr. Evans laughed.

50   We practiced all week. Dad came again and said we were improving.

51   "I thought you were terrible at first," he said, smiling. I didn't believe he actually smiled. "Now you're just pretty bad. But I think you can play with that Madison team."

52   Madison had agreed to come to our school to play, and when they arrived they were wearing jackets with their school colors and CLIPPERS across the back.

53   We started the game and Madison got the tip-off. The guy I was holding blocked me off so their guard, once he got past Nicky G, had a clear path to the basket. The first score against us came with only ten seconds off the clock.

54   I looked up in the stands to see where Mom was. I found her and saw Dad sitting next to her. I waved and she waved back, and Dad just sat there with his arms folded.

55   Madison stopped us cold on the next play, and when Bobby and Lou bumped their chairs at the top of the key, there was a man open. A quick pass inside and Madison was up by four.

56   We settled down a little, but nothing worked that well. We made a lot of wild passes for turnovers, and once, when I was actually leading a fast break, I got called for traveling when the ball got ahead of me, and I touched the wheels twice before dribbling. The guys from Madison were having a good time, and we were feeling miserable. At halftime, we rolled into the locker room feeling dejected. When Dad showed up, I felt bad. He was used to winning, not losing.

57   "Our kids looked a little overmatched in the first half," Mr. Evans said.

58   "I think they played okay," Dad said, "just a little nervous. But look at the score. It's twenty-two to fourteen. With all their shooting, Madison is just eight points ahead. We can catch up."

59   I looked at Dad to see if he was kidding. He wasn't. He wasn't kidding, and he had said "we." I liked that.

60   We came out in the second half all fired up. We ran a few plays along the baseline, but it still seemed more like bumper cars than basketball with all the congestion. Madison took twenty-three shots in the second half and made eight of them plus three foul shots for a total score of forty-one points. We took seventeen shots and made eleven of them, all layups off the backboard, and two foul shots for a total of thirty-eight points. We had lost the game, but everyone felt great about how we had played. We lined up our chairs, gave Madison high fives before they left, and waited until we got to the locker room to give ourselves high fives.

dejected   To feel dejected is to feel sad and hopeless.
congestion   Congestion is crowding.

27

61   Afterward, the team voted, and the Hartsdale Posse all agreed that we wanted to play in the league. Dad had shown us that we could play, and even though we had lost we knew we would be ready for the next season.

62   Dad only comes to practice once in a while, but he comes to the games when they're on the weekend. At practice he shows us fundamentals, stuff like how to line your wrist up for a shot, and how the ball should touch your hand when you're ready to shoot. That made me feel good even if he would never talk about the games when he wasn't in the gym. I didn't want to push it too much because I liked him coming to practice. I didn't want to push him, but Mom didn't mind at all.

63   "Jim, if you were in a wheelchair," she asked, "do you think you could play as well as Chris?"

64   Dad was on his laptop and looked over the screen at Mom, then looked over at me. Then he looked back down at the screen and grumbled something. I figured he was saying that there was no way he could play as well as me in a chair, but I didn't ask him to repeat it.

fundamentals Fundamentals are the simplest ideas or parts of something.

Collaborative Discussion

Look back at what you wrote on page 18. Tell a partner something new that the story made you think about. Then work with a group to discuss the questions below. Refer to details and examples in *Sometimes a Dream Needs a Push* to explain your answers. Take notes for your responses. When you speak, use your notes.

1 How would you describe the main character, Chris, to a friend? Use details from the text to support your description.

Listening Tip

Give your full attention to what each member of your group says. Show you are listening by making eye contact with the speaker.

2 This story is told from Chris's point of view, so readers know only his thoughts and feelings. How would the story be different if it was told from Chris's father's point of view?

Speaking Tip

When sharing your responses, say each word clearly and at a pace that isn't too fast or too slow.

3 Chris's team, the Hartsdale Posse, lost the basketball game to Madison. Why do you think the author chose to have them lose?

Write a Personal Note

PROMPT ....

In *Sometimes a Dream Needs a Push*, you read about a boy named Chris who joins a
wheelchair basketball team. Chris and his father—a former basketball player—have a
complicated relationship.

Basketball brings Chris and his father closer together. Write a note that Chris might
give to his father on Father's Day to show his appreciation. Use evidence from the text
to help you write details about Chris's father.

PLAN ....

Make notes about Chris's father and his relationship with Chris.
Include Chris's thoughts and feelings about his dad.

WRITE

Now write your note in a Father's Day card from Chris to his father from *Sometimes a Dream Needs a Push*.

Make sure your card
☐ is personal—from Chris to his father.
☐ is written from Chris's point of view.
☐ includes details from the text about Chris's father.
☐ uses transition words to connect ideas.
☐ uses appropriate verb tenses.

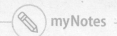

Prepare to View

GENRE STUDY **Documentaries** present facts and information to support a view about a topic in visual and audio form.

- A narrator explains a particular topic as images on the screen change to support the narration.

- The purpose of a documentary might be to inform the viewers about a topic.

- Real people, places, and events are used in the video to help viewers understand the topic.

- Like informational texts, documentaries include more formal, authoritative language to explain the topic.

SET A PURPOSE **Think about** the title and genre of this text. Have you ever played the game of chess? How hard do you think it would be to become a chess champion? Write your ideas below.

**Build Background:
The Game of Chess**

CRITICAL VOCABULARY

slums

principles

represent

The Queen of Chess

As you watch *The Queen of Chess*, take note of details that show Phiona's life in Katwe, Uganda, and how learning to play chess changed her life for the better. Take notes in the space below.

Listen for the Critical Vocabulary words *slums, principles*, and *represent*. Pay attention to how each word is used in the video and listen for clues to the word's meaning. Take notes in the space below about how each word is used.

slums A slum is an overcrowded urban area where poor people live.

principles The principles of a game are its basic rules.

represent If you represent your country in a competition, you participate in it on behalf of the country.

Collaborative Discussion

Look back at what you wrote on page 32. Tell a partner something you learned from this video. Then work with a group to discuss the questions below. Refer to details and examples in *The Queen of Chess* to explain your answers. Take notes for your responses. When you speak, use your notes.

1 What was life like for Phiona before she learned to play chess? What did her future look like at that time?

Listening Tip

If you can't hear someone in your group easily, ask that person to speak a little louder.

2 How did learning to play chess change Phiona's life? Use evidence from the video to support your response.

Speaking Tip

Build your ideas on what speakers have said before you. If you agree with what a speaker has said, say so, and then add your ideas.

3 What is Phiona like as a person? Pick a trait that she displays (bravery, determination, etc.). Support your choice with evidence.

Write About a Trait

PROMPT ....

In *The Queen of Chess,* you meet Phiona, a young Ugandan girl who learns to play chess. Through the video, you learn about Phiona's life in Uganda and how the game changes her life.

Pick one trait, or special characteristic, that is good to have as a chess player and that also helps a person overcome challenges in life. Explain how Phiona shows this trait.

PLAN ....

Make a list of Phiona's traits and how each one helped her succeed in chess and deal with her life in Uganda.

WRITE

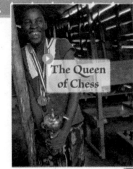

The Queen of Chess

Now write about one of Phiona's traits, based on information from *The Queen of Chess.*

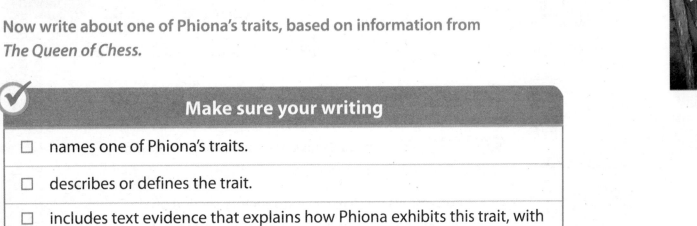

✓	Make sure your writing
☐	names one of Phiona's traits.
☐	describes or defines the trait.
☐	includes text evidence that explains how Phiona exhibits this trait, with specific examples from the video.
☐	uses some Critical Vocabulary words.
☐	uses correct capitalization of proper nouns.

Notice & Note
Numbers and Stats

Prepare to Read and View

GENRE STUDY **Photo Essays** are a series of photos and captions that tell about a true event or a theme.

- Photo essays can have an introductory section of informational text that puts the photos in context.

Meet the Climbers

Video Interviews present the point of view of real people on an event or a topic.

- The people being interviewed can share their thoughts in a first-person voice.

SET A PURPOSE **Think about** the titles of the photo essay and video interview. Explain what you would like to learn about rock climbing in the box below.

Build Background:
Tommy Caldwell and Kevin Jorgeson

CRITICAL VOCABULARY

sheer

ascending

rank

analysis

variations

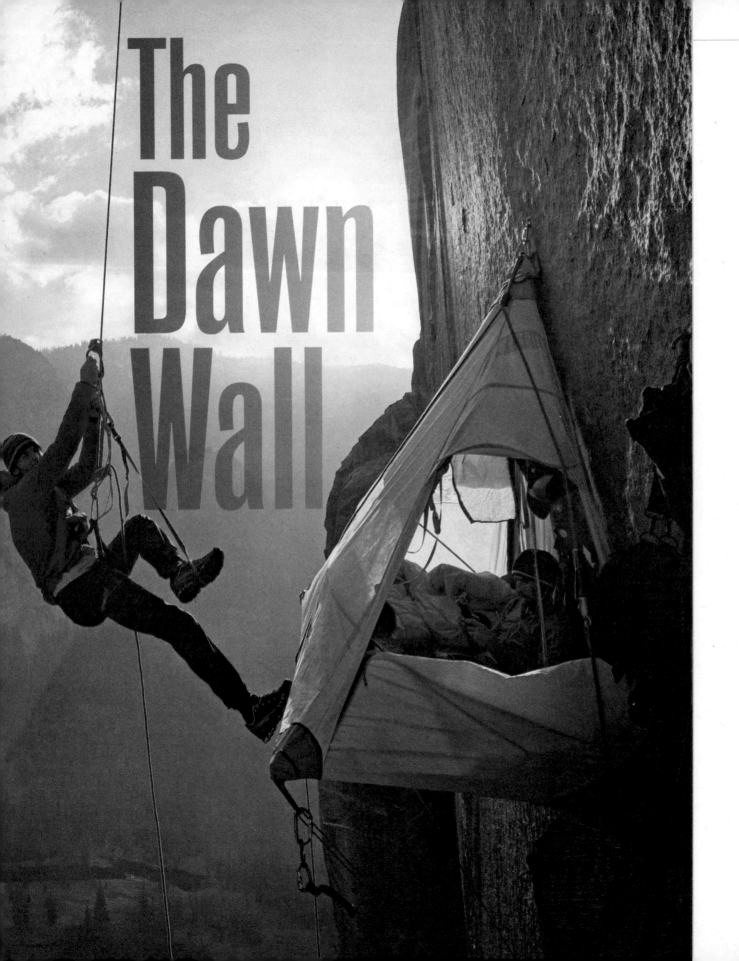

The Dawn Wall

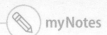

The Challenge of El Capitan

1 If you visit Yosemite National Park in California, you can hike to the top of El Capitan, a cliff that stands about 3,000 feet high. With no technical gear, you can walk up the incline on the back side of the cliff, on a route through forests and meadows, to El Capitan from the Tamarack Campground. You'll walk for 5.3 miles, ascending about 2,000 feet with a 9% average grade (that's how steep it is compared to flat ground). At the top, you can look out over the Yosemite Valley.

2   However, there's another way to get to the top of El Capitan—climbing straight up the sheer rock face of the granite cliff. Climbers have been ascending the rock formations of Yosemite since the 1940s. El Capitan was always seen as the ultimate challenge. It wasn't until 1958 that a climber, Warren Harding, was able to make it from the base to the top of the cliff over the course of 18 months. That happened five years *after* Edmund Hillary and Tenzing Norgay summited Mount Everest!

3   Harding's route up El Capitan was along the middle of the cliff, called the Nose. Today, expert climbers can ascend that route in less than a day.

El Capitan, Yosemite, CA 3,000 ft. (914 m)

One World Trade Center, New York, NY 1,776 ft. (541 m)

The Willis Tower, Chicago, IL 1,450 ft. (442 m)

The Bank of America Plaza, Dallas, TX 921 ft. (281 m)

These skyscrapers look tiny compared to the massive El Capitan.

sheer   A sheer cliff is extremely steep or completely vertical.
ascending   If you are ascending a hill or cliff, you are climbing it.

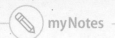

The Dawn Wall

4 There are now many routes for climbers to ascend El Capitan in addition to the Nose—the Snake Dike, the Astroman, the Southeast Buttress, and more. One of the most challenging routes is called the Dawn Wall.

Jorgeson and Caldwell reach the summit.

31 Pitches
30
29
28
27
26
25
24
23
22
21
20
19
18
17
16
15
14
13
12
11
10
9
8
7
6
5
4
3
2
1

The numbers show the pitches—or points at which ropes had to be retied—as Jorgeson and Caldwell climbed.

5   The Dawn Wall is a mostly smooth granite face. Experts rank it as the most challenging free climb in the world. In 2005, an expert climber named Tommy Caldwell rappelled down the Dawn Wall. He spent time studying the wall, trying to figure out if it could be free climbed successfully.

6   What is a "free climb"? It's a style of climbing in which climbers use only their hands, feet, and body for support and climbing. A rope can be attached to a free climber, but it isn't used to help the climber up the wall. The rope is strictly for safety, to catch the climber if he or she slips or falls.

7   When using a rope for safety on a climb, the rope must be continually untied and re-secured as the climbers move up the wall. The length of the rope—which limits how far a climber may move without stopping to untie and re-secure—is called a pitch. A long climb with a safety rope is called a "multi-pitch" climb.

Jorgeson and Caldwell

8   In 2009, Tommy Caldwell teamed up with climber Kevin Jorgeson to plan their climb of the Dawn Wall. After working on an analysis of the wall for almost five years, the athletes began their climb on December 27, 2014. They would stay on the wall for 19 days, relying on a few key tools and plans to keep them alive.

9   The infographics on the preceding pages and the photo essay that follow show what it took for these men to accomplish their wildly ambitious goal.

rank   If you rank something, you give it a position or grade in relation to others of its type.
analysis   An analysis is a detailed study of something.

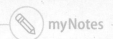

Every afternoon, Caldwell and Jorgeson leave their tents as the sun moves across the sky and no longer shines directly on the cliff. After climbing up a series of rigged ropes, they attempt the next pitch.

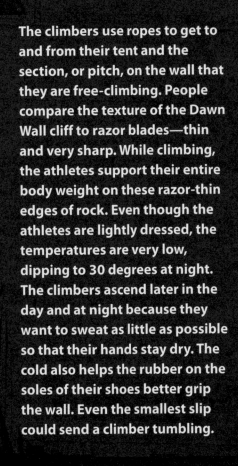

The climbers use ropes to get to and from their tent and the section, or pitch, on the wall that they are free-climbing. People compare the texture of the Dawn Wall cliff to razor blades—thin and very sharp. While climbing, the athletes support their entire body weight on these razor-thin edges of rock. Even though the athletes are lightly dressed, the temperatures are very low, dipping to 30 degrees at night. The climbers ascend later in the day and at night because they want to sweat as little as possible so that their hands stay dry. The cold also helps the rubber on the soles of their shoes better grip the wall. Even the smallest slip could send a climber tumbling.

During the day, the climbers return to their tents to eat, sleep, and recover. Their hands are blistered and bruised from the climb. They need time to heal. The climbers make coffee on a small stove, update their social media accounts on their phones, and accept food deliveries.

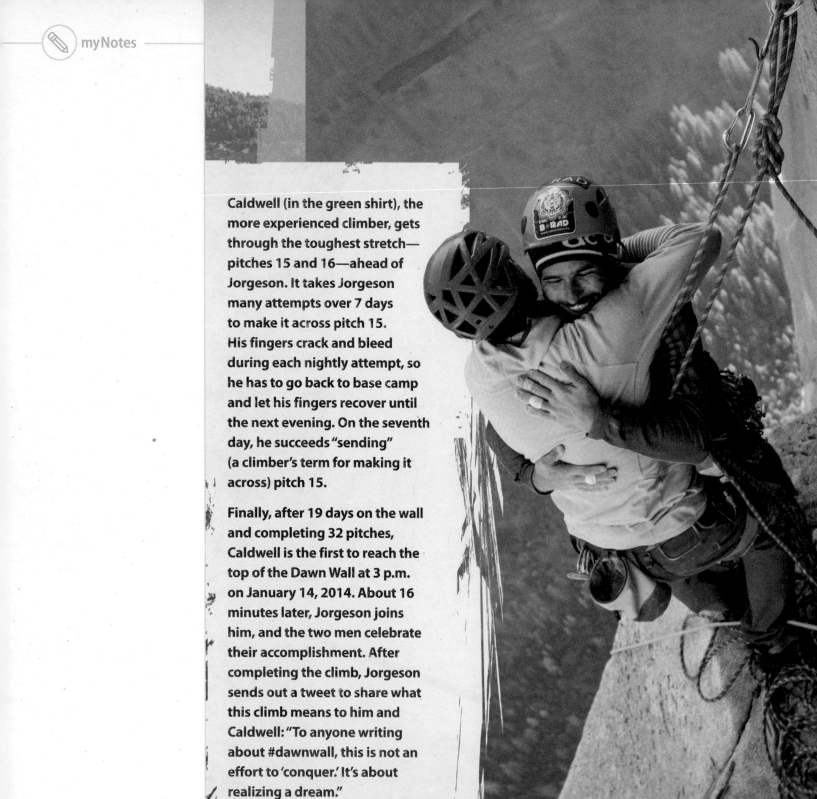

Caldwell (in the green shirt), the more experienced climber, gets through the toughest stretch—pitches 15 and 16—ahead of Jorgeson. It takes Jorgeson many attempts over 7 days to make it across pitch 15. His fingers crack and bleed during each nightly attempt, so he has to go back to base camp and let his fingers recover until the next evening. On the seventh day, he succeeds "sending" (a climber's term for making it across) pitch 15.

Finally, after 19 days on the wall and completing 32 pitches, Caldwell is the first to reach the top of the Dawn Wall at 3 p.m. on January 14, 2014. About 16 minutes later, Jorgeson joins him, and the two men celebrate their accomplishment. After completing the climb, Jorgeson sends out a tweet to share what this climb means to him and Caldwell: "To anyone writing about #dawnwall, this is not an effort to 'conquer.' It's about realizing a dream."

Meet the Climbers

As you watch *Meet the Climbers Who Made Yosemite's Toughest Ascent*, notice how Caldwell and Jorgeson describe their feelings about their historic climb. How does the video help you better understand the importance of this climbing accomplishment? Write your ideas below.

Listen for the Critical Vocabulary word *variations*. Pay attention to how the word is used to see if you hear clues to the word's meaning. Take notes in the space below about how the word is used.

variations   Variations are changes in the condition, level, or quantity of something.

Meet the Climbers

Collaborative Discussion

Look back at what you wrote on page 38. Tell a partner something you learned from the photo essay and video interview. Then work with a group to discuss the questions below. Refer to details and examples in *The Dawn Wall* and *Meet the Climbers Who Made Yosemite's Toughest Ascent* to explain your answers. Take notes for your responses. When you speak, use your notes.

1 On page 40, the text says you can easily climb to the top of El Capitan if you follow a certain route. Why do you think some climbers want to climb the cliff on more difficult routes?

 Listening Tip

Look at group members as they speak and notice the facial expressions or gestures they use to help explain their thoughts and ideas.

2 Pick one photo in the photo essay. What information does it add to your understanding of the climbers' ascent of the Dawn Wall?

 Speaking Tip

Make eye contact with group members as you speak to help you tell whether they understand your ideas.

3 In the video, the interviewer asks Caldwell and Jorgeson how they feel about being an inspiration for kids. Are you inspired to climb El Capitan or any other cliff? Use evidence to explain why or why not.

Write a News Report

PROMPT

In *The Dawn Wall* selections, you learned about climbers Tommy Caldwell and Kevin Jorgeson, the first to free climb the Dawn Wall route to reach the top of El Capitan. The video and photo essay described El Capitan and the climb, and introduced these two history-making climbers.

Imagine that you are a news reporter and were there when the climbers reached the top of the cliff face. Write a news report about the historic event. In your report, summarize what the climbers accomplished and why it was important.

PLAN

Record details about El Capitan and the Dawn Wall. Then make notes about what Tommy Caldwell and Kevin Jorgeson did to plan and prepare for their climb, what they endured along the way, and how they felt about reaching the top of El Capitan along the Dawn Wall route.

Meet the Climbers

WRITE

Now write your news report about Tommy Caldwell and Kevin Jorgeson from *The Dawn Wall.*

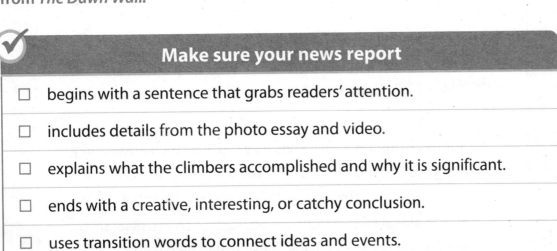

Make sure your news report

☐	begins with a sentence that grabs readers' attention.
☐	includes details from the photo essay and video.
☐	explains what the climbers accomplished and why it is significant.
☐	ends with a creative, interesting, or catchy conclusion.
☐	uses transition words to connect ideas and events.

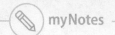

Prepare to Read

GENRE STUDY **Informational texts** give facts and examples about a topic.

- Authors of informational texts may organize their ideas using headings and subheadings. The headings and subheadings tell readers what the next section of text will be about.

- Informational texts include visuals, such as charts, diagrams, graphs, timelines, and maps. These visuals help readers better understand when, how, and where certain events took place.

SET A PURPOSE **Think about** the title and genre of this text. Look at the photos and skim the headings to see which young people are featured. How do you think these young people changed the world? Write your ideas below.

> Because inspired People.

Build Background: Timeline

CRITICAL VOCABULARY

descent

propaganda

deport

viewpoints

phenomenon

endorsement

hurdles

dubious

indigenous

Young People
WHO CHANGED THE WORLD

1   Around the world and through history, young people have used their unique talents to impact the way people think, to inspire social change, to work to save the planet, and even to help define eras. Age is no obstacle for young people like these nine who have changed the world.

This Phillis Wheatley statue is part of the Boston Women's Memorial sculpted by Meredith Bergmann.

Phillis Wheatley

18TH CENTURY AMERICAN POET

A Child Slave—and a Brilliant Mind

2 The girl who would become known as Phillis Wheatley was only seven years old in August of 1761, when she was sold into slavery after being kidnapped from her home in West Africa. Susanna Wheatley, a wealthy Boston resident, purchased the child from a ship captain, intending the girl to work as a domestic laborer. Susanna named her "Phillis" after the ship that carried the child into bondage.

3 Susanna Wheatley and her husband soon became aware of Phillis's deep intelligence. Although Phillis was still expected to be a servant, the Wheatleys permitted her to learn to read and write. Phillis was soon studying the Bible, reading British authors John Milton and Alexander Pope, and reading Greek and Latin classics by Virgil, Ovid, and Homer.

Worldwide Fame

4 Phillis became world famous at age 17, when she published a poem in honor of a recently departed reverend, George Whitefield. The poem was printed in Boston, Newport, Philadelphia, and London.

5   By age 18, Phillis had written 28 poems, but due to discrimination against people of African descent in the colonies, she could not find a publisher. She published her poems as a volume in London, when she was 20 years old, in 1773.

6   Phillis was celebrated by many important figures of her time. She corresponded with the first president of the United States, George Washington, and she was also supported by the governor of Massachusetts, John Hancock.

An Early Death—and an Eternal Voice

7   Susanna Wheatley granted Phillis her freedom at age 21, several years before Mrs. Wheatley died. Phillis married four years later, and she continued to write until her death at age 31. Many of her poems were not published, and, unfortunately, she died in abject poverty.

8   Today, Phillis Wheatley's poems still bring her voice and message from the past into the present.

from "To the Right Honorable William, Earl of Dartmouth"

> Should you, my lord, while you peruse my song,
> Wonder from whence my love of Freedom sprung,
> Whence flow these wishes for the common good,
> By feeling hearts alone best understood,
> I, young in life, by seeming cruel fate
> Was snatch'd from Afric's fancy'd happy seat:
> What pangs excruciating must molest,
> What sorrows labour in my parent's breast?
> Steel'd was that soul and by no misery mov'd
> That from a father seiz'd his babe belov'd:
> Such, such my case. And can I then but pray
> Others may never feel tyrannic sway?
>
> —Phillis Wheatley

descent   A person's descent is a person's family background or ancestors.

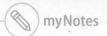

Louis Braille

INVENTOR OF WRITTEN LANGUAGE FOR THE BLIND

A Childhood Accident

9 Louis Braille was the youngest of four siblings growing up in a small town in France when, at age three, Louis was blinded in an accident. He was playing with an awl, a sharp tool that can poke holes in leather, and he struck himself in the eye. The injury became infected, and by the time Louis was five years old, he was completely blind in both eyes.

A Need for Books

10 Louis's parents sent him to the local school with the other children. Young Louis was able to keep up with his schoolwork despite his blindness. When he was 10 years old, he was awarded a scholarship at the Royal Institute for Blind Youth in Paris. (The institute still exists today, and is called the National Institute for Blind Youth.)

11 At the institute, children were expected to learn how to read using paper embossed with letters that look like the ones you are reading now, only with raised lines. It was a slow process to read this way, and the books were large and bulky, fragile, and expensive. For the entire school, there were only three books. In addition, it was impossible for children to write anything that they would be able to read later.

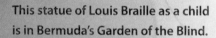
This statue of Louis Braille as a child is in Bermuda's Garden of the Blind.

58

Young Inventor

12 Louis got the idea for his new written alphabet for the blind from a military captain, Charles Barbier. Barbier's "night writing" system was comprised of raised dots and dashes on paper that could be felt by one's fingertips. This method of writing was used by soldiers who needed to communicate silently and without a source of light.

13 Barbier's system, however, was too complex. The number of dots and dashes needed to communicate made it laborious to read quickly and understand. Louis knew he could do better. From ages 12 to 15, he worked on developing his own system of written language that could be read by touch.

A Lasting Impact

14 The braille system uses only six dots for each letter, and the dots are placed in columns so that the reader is able to quickly and easily comprehend them. The most important aspect of the system that Braille created is that each letter can be felt with just one fingertip. From the start, Braille's system could be written as well as read — simply by poking raised bumps into paper.

15 Louis's system of writing is still used today. You can find it on signs in subway stations and airports, and braille users today can even read computer screens using refreshable braille displays. For writing, people can use a computer that prints with an embossed printer so that they and others can read their work. Thanks to Louis Braille, many people who are blind have access to the world of reading and writing for pleasure, education, work, and life in general.

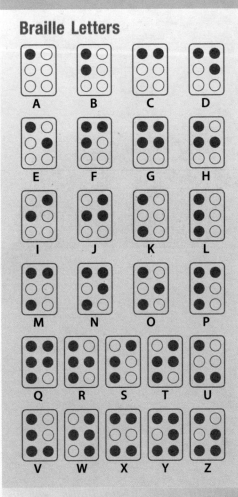

Braille Letters

This is the braille system that Louis Braille invented. Each letter can be completely felt with just the tip of one finger.

Sophie Scholl

HERO OF THE RESISTANCE

A Girl in Hitler's Germany

16 Sophie Scholl was born in Germany in 1921. She grew up surrounded by the propaganda of the rising Nazi party, and when she was 12 years old, she joined the Hitler Youth movement with many of her friends. Soon, however, Sophie began to realize that Hitler and his Nazi party were bad for Germany—and the world.

Standing Up Against Hitler

17 In 1942, the Nazis began to deport German Jews to concentration camps where they were forced to labor under inhumane conditions, or were murdered outright. Soon after, Sophie, then in her early 20s, and her brother and a friend, began to publish leaflets critical of Hitler throughout Germany.

18 Sophie and her group called themselves The White Rose, and they kept their identities secret. The work of The White Rose was incredibly dangerous because Germany at the time was tightly controlled by the state police. Anyone found speaking out against the government would be jailed—or worse.

A Symbol of Courage

19 Unfortunately, Sophie and her fellow members of The White Rose were reported and captured. Sophie was brutally interrogated, convicted of treason, and then killed on February 22, 1943.

20 Today, Sophie is remembered as a hero who stood up to one of history's worst dictators.

> **propaganda** Propaganda is information, especially of a misleading nature, used to promote a particular point of view.
>
> **deport** Governments deport people by removing them from the country in which they are living.

Anne Frank

HOLOCAUST DIARIST

A Family in Hiding

21 Anne Frank grew up in a happy and loving Jewish home in Germany. As her parents saw Hitler become more powerful, they knew that it wasn't safe to be Jewish in Europe, and they tried to escape to England or the United States. When they failed to receive permission to immigrate, they instead moved to the Netherlands, which was soon occupied by Nazi Germany. As Anne's family realized that they couldn't escape Hitler's reach, they went into hiding when Anne was ten years old. Anne and her family moved into what was called the Secret Annex. Non-Jewish friends brought them food and hid their location.

The Voice of a Writer

22 Shortly before her family went into hiding, Anne received a diary for a birthday present. She began writing, giving details of her life in hiding. She captured the moments of fear, longing, and humor that she and her family experienced. She also wrote about her dreams for the future.

23 Anne's family was discovered by the Nazis after two years in hiding and sent to a concentration camp. Anne was only 15 years old when she died. After the war, her father discovered her journal and was so moved by her writing that he chose to publish it. Soon, *The Diary of Anne Frank* became one of the most widely read books in the world. Over the years, there have been more than 30 million copies in print.

Maria Tallchief

FIRST AMERICAN PRIMA BALLERINA

An Osage Dancer

24 Maria Tallchief was born in 1925 in Fairfax, Oklahoma, which is on the Osage Indian Reservation. Her father was a wealthy real estate executive. Her grandmother's name was Eliza Big Heart, and, as a child, Maria would attend tribal dances with her.

25 Maria's training in ballet and piano began when she was three years old. She and her sister Marjorie were very talented, and her parents decided to move to Beverly Hills, California, to give the girls more opportunities for artistic development. By age 12, Maria was studying with some of the most respected ballet instructors in the nation.

26 At age 15, Maria gave a solo performance at the Hollywood Bowl, and two years later, after high school, she joined a Russian ballet troupe based in New York City.

Worldwide Fame

27 Maria was not treated well by her fellow dancers in the troupe because of her Native American heritage, but they soon changed their viewpoints. Maria became the first American of any background to break barriers in ballet. She became the first American ever to dance at the Paris Opera. And at age 22, when she joined the New York City Ballet, she became the first ever American prima ballerina, or chief dancer, of a ballet company.

28 Maria lived to age 88, and after an accomplished career with the New York City Ballet, went on to found the Chicago City Ballet and serve as its artistic director. Among her many honors, she received the National Medal of Arts, the highest award given by the U.S. government for contributions to the arts.

viewpoints   Viewpoints are ways of looking at things.

Pelé

WORLD-RENOWNED ATHLETE

A Childhood in Poverty

29 Edson Arantes do Nascimento, the soccer phenomenon better known as Pelé, was born in 1940. Although his father was a minor league soccer player, the family still lived in abject poverty. For children in Pelé's neighborhood there was little entertainment other than playing soccer barefoot in the street, kicking a soccer ball made from a rolled-up sock stuffed with rags.

Pride of Brazil

30 Pelé's father coached him, and when Pelé was 11 years old he joined his first soccer team. Pelé soon became a star player. At age 15, he joined a professional team, Santos. Then, at age 17, he made it onto Brazil's national squad to play in the 1958 World Cup.

31 The young star became world-famous quickly, as he scored three goals in a 5-2 semifinal game against France, and then two more goals in the final match against the host country, Sweden. Brazil's World Cup victory of 1958 was its first ever—and Pelé was the undisputed star. Teams from all over Europe offered him positions. Pelé continued to play on the Brazilian pro team Santos, and for a time, he was the highest paid athlete in the world because he made additional money from numerous endorsement deals.

32 In 2001, Pelé, along with Argentina's Diego Maradona, were named by the international soccer organization FIFA as the most important men's players of the 20th Century. Pelé also worked as a United Nations ambassador for environmental issues.

phenomenon A phenomenon is someone who is very impressive because of a special ability or wide popularity.

endorsement An endorsement deal is when a person publicly says that he or she likes a product or service in exchange for money.

Easton LaChappelle

TEEN INVENTOR

From Boredom to Inspiration

33 Easton LaChappelle was just an ordinary 14-year-old student, bored in class, when he came up with an idea for something remarkable. He wanted to do something special with a 3D printer he had at home, and he decided to try to make a robotic arm. His creation, made from fishing line and plastic blocks, using his 3D printer, was displayed at the 2011 Colorado state science fair, and Easton received the third-place prize.

34 The prize wasn't the most memorable part of the fair for Easton, though. While at the fair, he met a 7-year-old girl who had a prosthetic arm. The hand on this arm could only open and close in a single kind of grip, and it cost $80,000. Easton was shocked—and determined to overcome these hurdles of cost and functionality. He made it his goal to create a prosthetic arm that would cost less than $1,000.

A Helpful Invention

35 Easton hoped to make a prosthetic arm that could be controlled by the user's mind. It's not science fiction to imagine that this is possible; in fact, there was a children's game that Easton was aware of in which the player could move a foam ball up and down using a headset that measured his or her brain waves. Easton bought the game, took it apart, and figured out how it worked. He applied the same principles to the prosthetic arm he built.

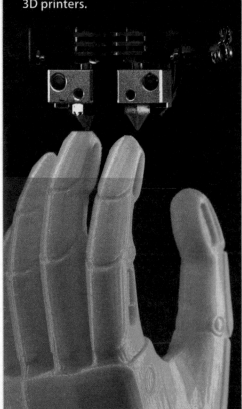

Today, many manufacturers can create prostheses using 3D printers.

> **hurdles** Hurdles are barriers or obstacles to success.

36 Easton's prosthetic arm cost only $350 to produce, and he made it open source. That means that anyone can download the design from the internet and build it with their own materials.

Prosthetic limbs are made by many companies, using many different methods.

Continued Improvements

37 At age 17, Easton founded Unlimited Tomorrow, a company dedicated to developing assistive technology. The company has a program that digitally scans an amputee's residual limb, or the part of his or her limb that remains, as well as the person's other, complete, limb. Then, Easton's software analyzes the scans to create a design for a custom-fit prosthesis. The designs can then be printed on a 3D printer anywhere in the world.

38 Easton plans to continue inventing and developing prostheses, with the goal of bringing them to anyone in the world who needs them.

Malala Yousafzai

YOUNGEST NOBEL PEACE PRIZE WINNER

A Girl's Right to Education

39 As a girl growing up in the Swat Valley region of Pakistan, Malala wasn't aiming to be anyone's hero. She was born in 1997 and had a happy childhood with a loving family— her mother, her father, and her younger brother. She was a girl who just wanted to go to school and learn with her friends. An excellent student, she was encouraged by her parents in her education.

40 When the Taliban, an ultraconservative armed religious group, began to take control of the Swat Valley, they began attacking girls' schools and promoting the idea that girls should not be allowed to receive an education. When Malala was 11 years old, she began blogging about her experience trying to get an education despite the pressure from the Taliban. She gave a speech in Peshawar, Pakistan, entitled "How dare the Taliban take away my basic right to education?"

41 Malala continued working as an activist for girls' education. She was awarded Pakistan's National Youth Peace Prize in 2011. Soon after, her family discovered that the Taliban had issued a death threat against her. Malala and her father were dubious that even the Taliban would actually attempt to assassinate a child. They were soon proved wrong.

dubious If you are dubious you are doubtful and disbelieving.

Attacked by the Taliban

42   On October 9, 2012, when Malala was 15 years old, she was riding home from school in a small bus with her friends. She was chatting with the other girls when their bus was stopped. Gunmen came onto the bus and asked which one of the girls was Malala. The other girls didn't say anything, but their glances in Malala's direction gave away her identity. The gunman shot her in the face, and then fled.

43   Malala was flown to a hospital in Peshawar, and was eventually flown to the United Kingdom, where she had multiple surgeries to repair the damage done by the bullet. While she required surgery to fix paralysis on the left side of her face, Malala's brain was not injured.

A Global Leader—and a Student

44   Within six months of the attack, Malala was attending school again, in Birmingham, England. A year later, she published her autobiography, *I am Malala: The Girl Who Stood Up for Education and Was Shot by the Taliban.* She also, along with her father, founded the Malala Fund, which is a global group promoting girls' education around the world. The Malala Fund has opened schools in many areas where girls have limited opportunities to attend school.

45   In 2014, Malala was awarded the Nobel Peace Prize for her work. Malala leads by example—besides running her foundation, she also studied in one of the world's most challenging university programs. As of 2018, she was a student of politics, philosophy, and economics at University of Oxford, in England.

At top, Malala's family includes her parents and two younger brothers. Below, the inset map shows the Swat Valley, the area where Malala grew up in Pakistan.

Xiuhtezcatl Martinez

ENVIRONMENTAL ACTIVIST

A Youth in the Spotlight

46 One of the many special things about this young environmental activist is his name—Xiuhtezcatl—which is pronounced "shoo-tez-cat." On his father's side of the family, Xiuhtezcatl is descended from the Aztec people, an indigenous people of the Americas. His name means "turquoise mirror" in the Nahuatl [nah-wa-tull] language.

47 Xiuhtezcatl has been in the spotlight from a young age. After watching a nature documentary as a child, he realized that what humans do has a profound effect on our environment. He became involved in a group founded by his mother, called Earth Guardians. Earth Guardians is a global network of environmental activists. Xiuhtezcatl became the youth director of the organization and spoke out globally to help people understand the youth perspective on the environment.

Fighting for a Safer Future

48 As part of their work, the Earth Guardians support 21 young people who, as of 2018, filed a lawsuit claiming that the U.S. government, by not doing enough to help the environment, is infringing on the rights of young people to clean air and water and a healthy future.

49 Xiuhtezcatl spoke at the United Nations Summit in Rio de Janeiro that addressed environmental issues. He's also addressed the United Nations General Assembly in New York. He has put his message to music in a hip-hop music album he made with his sister, and he also wrote a book, *We Rise,* which he sees as a toolkit for other young activists.

indigenous Indigenous people are native to an area.

Collaborative Discussion

Young People
WHO CHANGED THE WORLD

Look back at what you wrote on page 54. Tell a partner something that surprised you about the young people you read about. Then work with a group to discuss the questions below. Refer to details and examples in *9 Young People Who Changed the World* to explain your answers. Take notes for your responses. When you speak, use your notes.

1 What is one way that one of these young people changed the world? Support your response with evidence from the text.

Listening Tip

Give your full attention to what each member of your group says. Show you are listening by making eye contact with the speaker.

2 Choose two people featured in this informational text. How are the two alike and different?

Speaking Tip

When sharing your responses, say each word clearly and at a pace that isn't too fast or too slow.

3 If you could meet one of the young people featured in the text, whom would you choose and why? What would you say to this person?

Write a Letter

In *9 Young People Who Changed the World*, you learned about young people who faced a problem and decided to do something about it. They used courage, compassion, brain power, and creativity to seek a solution and ultimately change the world for the better.

Choose one of the nine people featured and write a letter to a younger friend explaining what is special about the person you chose.

Reread the text about the person you chose. Record details about him or her. Then make notes about the person's background, the problem this person saw or faced, and what the person did to address it.

WRITE

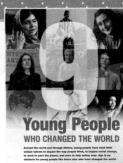

Now write your letter about one of the people from *9 Young People Who Changed the World.*

✓
Make sure your letter

☐	begins with a salutation to the person you are writing to
☐	includes language and ideas appropriate for a younger person
☐	identifies the person you are writing about and explains why that person is special
☐	ends with a conclusion that describes what the younger person can learn from the person you chose
☐	uses transition words to connect ideas

(?) Essential Question

What is the path to success?

Write an Informational Motivational Speech

PROMPT Think about what you learned about success in this module.

Imagine you've been asked to give a speech to a group of younger students. Your purpose is to explain to your listeners how they can achieve a goal no matter how difficult or impossible it may seem. You will use evidence from the texts and videos to give examples of people who have been successful in overcoming great challenges to achieve their goals.

I will write a speech about _____.

✓ Make sure your speech

- ☐ provides an introduction that explains your topic and grabs your audience's attention.

- ☐ includes examples of motivational words and the people who have achieved difficult goals from the texts and videos.

- ☐ uses facts and details to explain how these people achieved their goals.

- ☐ is organized into paragraphs connected by transition words.

- ☐ ends with a conclusion that encourages your audience to set and achieve their own goals.

To support your idea, identify people in the texts and videos who have overcome challenges to achieve their goals. Look back at your notes and revisit the texts and videos as necessary.

In the chart below, write the main idea of your speech in the top box. Then use evidence from the texts and videos to jot down ideas for each paragraph in your speech. Be sure that each paragraph supports your main idea. Use Critical Vocabulary words where appropriate.

My Topic: _____

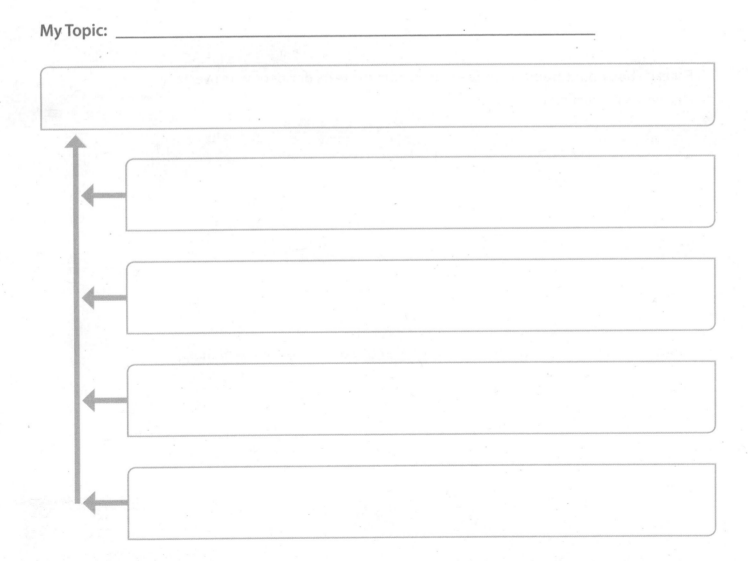

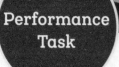

DRAFT ·· Write your speech.

Write an **introduction** that will grab your audience's attention and state your topic.

For each **body paragraph,** identify a person from the texts or videos who overcame challenges to meet his or her goal.

For the **conclusion,** restate your main idea and end with a motivating sentence.

The revision and editing steps give you a chance to look carefully at your writing and make changes. Work with a partner to determine whether you have successfully supported your main ideas with evidence from the texts and videos. Use these questions to help you evaluate and improve your speech.

PURPOSE/ FOCUS	ORGANIZATION	EVIDENCE	LANGUAGE/ VOCABULARY	CONVENTIONS
☐ Does my speech explain how people can achieve their goals? ☐ Does my speech stay on topic?	☐ Will my introduction grab my audience's attention? ☐ Does my conclusion inspire my listeners to set and achieve their own goals?	☐ Do I use at least two stories from the texts and videos as examples of how to achieve success? ☐ Do the examples I've chosen help support my main idea?	☐ Did I use transition words to create a smooth flow of ideas? ☐ Did I use language appropriate for my topic and audience?	☐ Did I use correct spelling? ☐ Have I used commas correctly? ☐ Did I use correct capitalization?

Create a Finished Copy Make a final copy of your speech. You may wish to include photographs of the people you discuss in your speech. Consider these options to share your speech.

1 Deliver your speech to your class or a younger class.

2 Record your speech on a school website and ask viewers for feedback.

3 Publish your speech in a school newsletter.

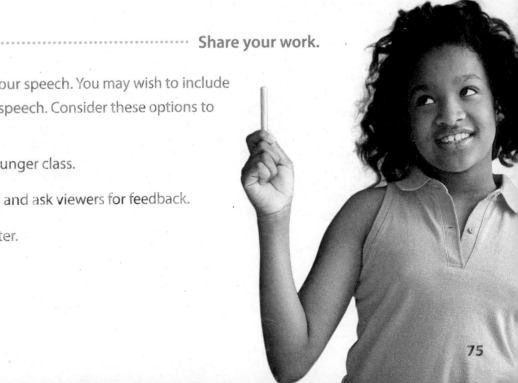

Here's the Story

"Some books are to be tasted, others to be swallowed, and some few to be chewed and digested."

—Francis Bacon

? Essential Question

What makes a story worth reading?

Get Curious
Video

Words About Great Stories

The words in the chart will help you talk and write about the selections in this module. Which words about stories have you seen before? Which words are new to you?

Add to the Vocabulary Network on page 79 by writing synonyms, antonyms, and related words and phrases for each word about stories.

After you read each selection in this module, come back to the Vocabulary Network and keep building it. Add more boxes if you need to.

WORD	MEANING	CONTEXT SENTENCE
voracious (adjective)	If you describe a person as voracious, you mean that the person is extremely eager about reading.	A voracious reader can read two books or more a month.
discipline (noun)	Discipline is self-control.	My cousin has the discipline to write in his journal each evening.
persevere (verb)	When you persevere with something, you continue to do it, even when you face difficulties.	The runners persevere through the muddy conditions to finish the race.
intrepid (adjective)	An intrepid person is fearless and adventurous.	My cousin and her family are intrepid travelers who love hiking trails during any season—even winter.

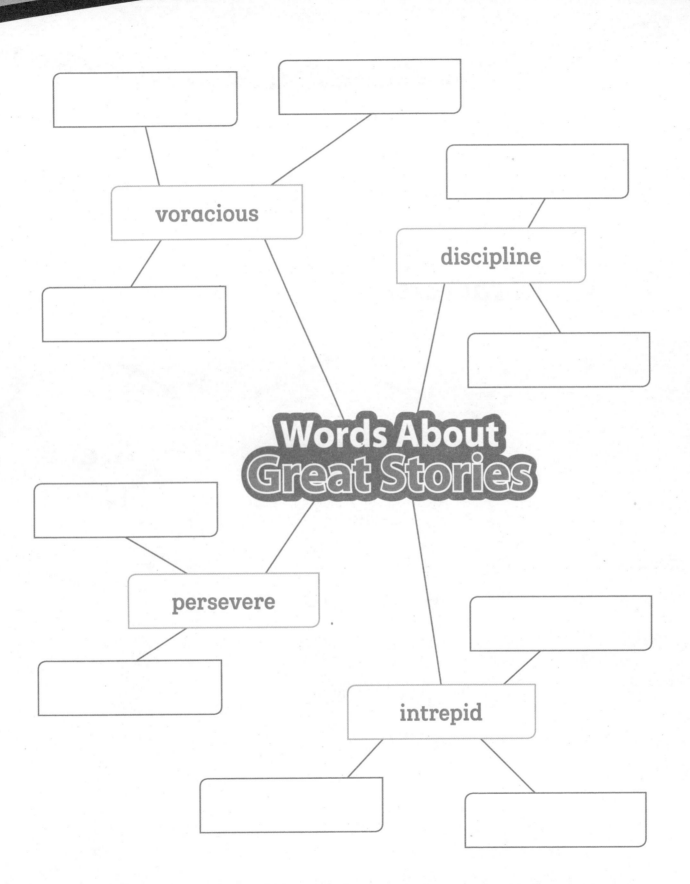

voracious

discipline

persevere

intrepid

Words About Great Stories

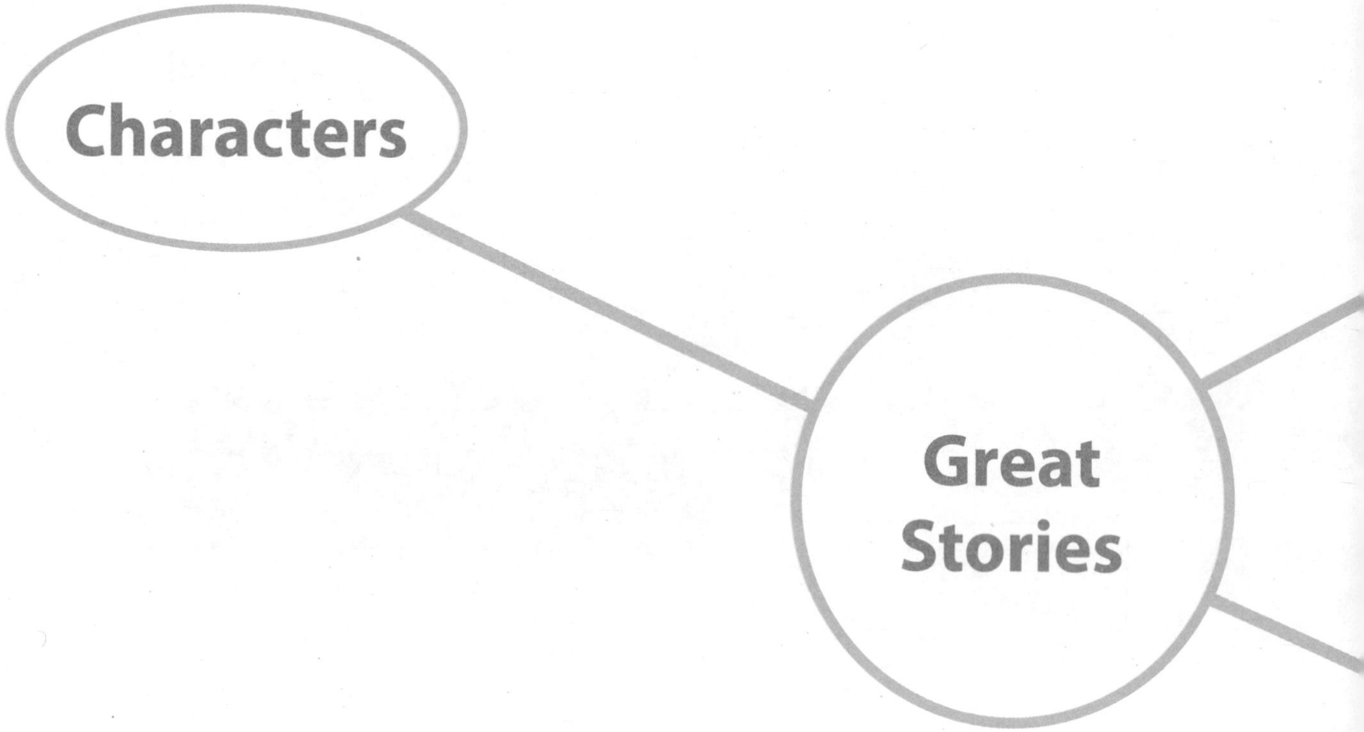

Characters

Great
Stories

Setting

Plot

Short
Read

How to Succeed as a Storywriter

What does it take to write books people want to read?

J.K. Rowling

Read, Read, Read

The world's best writers are usually voracious readers themselves. J.K. Rowling, the author of the *Harry Potter* series, is a big fan of classic English author Jane Austen. Rowling has read Austen's many books countless times.

1

Stay Focused

Good writing starts with good habits. Carry a notebook with you to write down story ideas as they occur to you. Block out a half-hour every day to focus on your writing. Just like playing a sport or a musical instrument, discipline and lots of practice will improve your skills.

Keep Writing

Writer's block, often caused by stress or anxiety, is a real phenomenon that affects even some of the best writers. To overcome this obstacle, it's important to relax and just allow your ideas to flow. Going for walks, listening to music, or just changing your environment can help.

3

Ray Bradbury

4

Be Ready for Rejection

Madeleine L'Engle's *A Wrinkle in Time* was rejected 26 times before it was published. Ray Bradbury was one of the most acclaimed science fiction writers of all time, but he said he fielded thousands of rejections. These authors—and many others—persevere and become hugely successful.

5

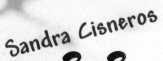

Sandra Cisneros

Be Brave, Be Yourself

The most beloved authors have an intrepid voice that belongs only to them. Sandra Cisneros's bestseller, *The House on Mango Street,* has sold over six million copies. Cisneros says that she found the style that makes her writing unique by trying to write like herself instead of like her classmates or teachers. The world needs more brave voices telling original stories—maybe someday we will read yours!

Prepare to Read

> **GENRE STUDY** **Realistic Fiction** tells a story about characters and events that are like those in real life.

- Authors of realistic fiction might tell the story through a third-person point of view, such as an observer, using pronouns *he, she, him, her, his, hers, they, them,* and *their*.

- Realistic fiction includes characters who act, think, and speak like real people.

- Realistic fiction is set in a place that seems real.

> **SET A PURPOSE** **Think about** the chapter title and genre of this text. How would you define the word "identity"? What do you think the title means? Write your ideas below.

CRITICAL VOCABULARY
imitation
indifference
spitefully
pondered
fumed
confided
escorting
habitually
surmised

Meet the Author:
Gary Soto

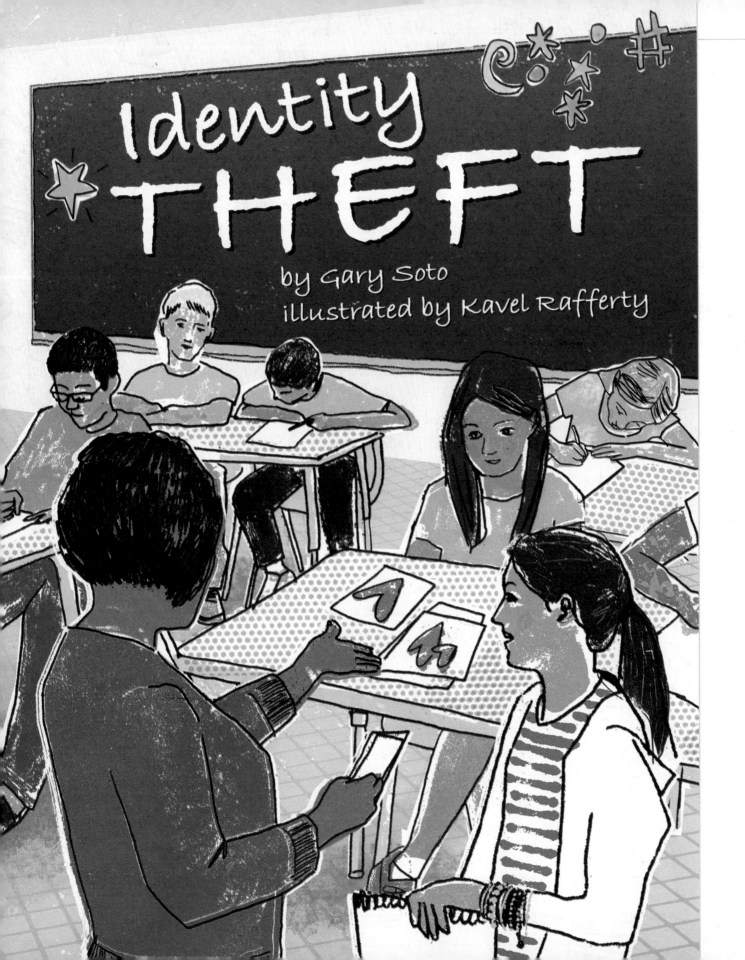

Identity THEFT

by Gary Soto

illustrated by Kavel Rafferty

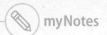

1　**The Day After** Valentine's Day Ana Hernandez arrived at school early intending to sort through her batch of cards. They read BE MINE, YOU'RE THE MOST, SWEETIE, CUTIE-PIE. If only they were true. No one had ever said, "Be mine," or called her "cutie-pie," an expression from her grandmother's generation. These days, the bolder sixth-grade boys would scream, "You like me, huh?" Still, Ana felt popular as she sorted through her cards, her mouth sweetened by the cinnamon candy a boy had dropped into one of the envelopes. She suspected it was from Peter, but she couldn't be sure.

2　She was still reading her valentines when her teacher entered the classroom with a new girl. The teacher's smile made Ana curious—was it possible that Ms. Welty had received a valentine's card from another teacher? There were rumors that she and Mr. Saks, the third-grade teacher, liked each other.

3　"Ana," Ms. Welty called. "Ana, I want you to meet . . . " The teacher stalled, then smiled, a little color flushing her cheeks. "I want you to meet Ana Hernandez."

4　Confused, Ana put down a large valentine.

5　"What I mean," Ms. Welty started to explain, "is that *this* is Ana Hernandez. You two have the same name!"

6　The original Ana Hernandez glared at the imitation Ana Hernandez. She didn't like it: someone else with *her* name. Also, she had to admit that the *other* Ana Hernandez was pretty, an inch or two taller, and nicely dressed. And was that a cell phone tucked in the pocket of her stylish jeans? And were those *really* the most on-trend shoes of the year?

7　But the original Ana quickly replaced the glare in her eyes with something like indifference.

8　"You got so many valentines," the new Ana sang. She picked one up and sniffed it, her pretty little nose wrinkling in a cute way.

> **imitation**　Something described as imitation looks like the real thing but is only a copy.
>
> **indifference**　Indifference is a lack of interest.

9   *Dang, even her voice is nicer than mine,* the original Ana thought spitefully. "These are some of them," she explained. "Most of them I had to carry home in a sack yesterday." She wished she could bite her tongue off and let it crawl away like a snake. That was such an obvious lie!

10   The new Ana smiled, and the original Ana wondered, *Is she laughing at me?*

11   It was a weird experience, like looking at a twin sister you had never seen before. The original Ana Hernandez pondered her ill will toward this new girl and felt that she was being unfair. *She can't help it,* Ana figured, *that she has my name.*

12   The new Ana fit right into school life. She volunteered to be a crossing guard and helped raise the flag. She helped at a fundraising car wash and was rumored to have played her flute at an assisted-living complex across the street from school. Within a week she was chosen to say the Pledge of Allegiance on the intercom, a special honor usually assigned to students with good grades. She recited it so well that she was assigned to read the school bulletin, which always started with the menu for the day.

13   The original Ana steamed. She had recited the Pledge of Allegiance on the intercom before, but she had never been asked to read the bulletin. Boldly she approached the principal in the hallway outside the office.

14   "Mr. Ortiz," she asked, "when can I read the bulletin?"

15   "But you just did," he countered in surprise.

16   They soon discovered the error. The reader was supposed to have been the original Ana, not the new Ana. The secretary, they guessed, had made a mistake. When Mr. Ortiz offered the original Ana the chance to read the school bulletin, she grabbed the opportunity. But she felt slighted, and the bulletin she read to the entire school was unimportant. She reported two missing basketballs and a restroom that was going to be closed for the week.

> **spitefully**   To do something spitefully is to do it in a deliberately mean, hurtful way.
> **pondered**   If you pondered something, you thought deeply about it.

17   Original Ana observed that new Ana received lots of attention. Ms. Welty would call, "Okay, who can remember when President Lincoln—" and before the teacher could finish her sentence, new Ana would fling her arm up, bracelets jangling. The new Ana didn't do this *all* the time, only at moments when the original Ana knew the answers.

18   One day when soccer teams were chosen during recess, Becky Ramirez, the star athlete of the school, said, "I'll take Ana Hernandez." The original Ana stepped forward, and Becky snapped, "No, not you—the other Ana. The new girl!" That day Ana was chosen last, and on the field the ball was never passed to her.

19   In a classroom spelling bee the original Ana had to sit down almost immediately, after she stumbled on *rhinoceros*. The spelling bee became hotly contested between the new Ana and Peter, the boy the original Ana had hoped sent her a special valentine.

20   "Spell *triangular*," Ms. Welty called to Peter.

21   He spelled it, wincing as he struggled to get the letters in the proper order. He clenched his fists in victory when Ms. Welty said, "That's correct." In turn, the new Ana eased through the word *magnetic*.

22   The battle lasted ten minutes. The boys rooted for Peter, and the girls screamed their heads off for the new Ana. In the end Peter prevailed, but the new Ana clapped for the victor and even held up his hand like a champ.

23   This made the original Ana mad. *She, the newcomer, a fraud, a mere imitation—how dare she touch the hand that put the cinnamon candy in my valentine card!* Ana fumed.

No, not you— the other Ana.

fumed   A person who fumed was very angry.

24   Ana confided in her mother while they were in the kitchen peeling potatoes at the sink. Two onions that would bring tears to their eyes sat on the counter. The daughter was ready for tears, even if they were forced to her eyes by big bloated onions.

25   "There's nothing wrong," her mother argued softly. Her lined brow expressed her concern for her daughter. "When I was at school, there was another Beatriz Mendoza."

26   Mendoza was her mother's maiden name, and Beatriz her childhood name. Now she was known as Betty, though some of her friends called her Lu-Lu. Why, Ana could never figure out, but it was a name that her mother responded to.

27   The original Ana considered being called Annie. She then thought about using her middle name, Maria. But there were two Marias in the other sixth-grade class, and a third, Ana felt, would be one too many. She then decided, "I'll change my name," and considered Michelle, a pretty name, one that sounded French.

28   "Michelle Hernandez," she said to her mirror. "My name is Michelle." She giggled and then remembered that her grandmother had a Chihuahua named Michelle, a frighteningly ugly dog with bulging eyes and crooked teeth.

29   In class Ms. Welty would call, "Ana," and both girls would answer yes. Most times Ms. Welty was seeking out the new Ana.

30   Then the original Ana concluded, "I shouldn't be stuck-up. I should be friends with her." But by the time the original Ana decided to warm up to the new Ana, she discovered that the newcomer was so popular that they couldn't hang. She just couldn't manage to establish a friendship with the new Ana, even when the original Ana confided, "You know, I have a birthmark on my thigh."

31   Then a new fad—jangling bracelets first worn by the new Ana— spread throughout the school. "I don't want to wear them," the original Ana fumed, but in the end she, too, wore bracelets and was not above jangling them for no reason except to show she was one of the crowd.

---

confided If you've confided in someone, you've told that person something personal or secret.

32   As spring advanced, bringing flowers and freshness to the air, the original Ana drifted away from her classmates. She spent time alone, eating her sandwich, potato chips, and cookies by herself. She began to revel in this quiet time, though occasionally she would look up and see the new Ana at the center of activity. There she was playing four-square or soccer, and escorting guests around school. She was responsible for starting a school garden—tomato and eggplant seeds were first planted in egg cartons. After they'd sprouted, mothers and fathers came to dig up the soil on a Saturday morning. That day the original Ana saw a television crew approaching the new girl.

33   "Now she's going to be on TV," the original Ana cried. She was. The new Ana was given ten seconds on camera. She posed with Peter near the garden, displaying an egg carton of tomato plants.

34   And what could the original Ana do but watch the new Ana play her flute during a talent show? She had to swallow her jealousy—yes, that was it—when Peter joined her to sing a song in French!

35   The original Ana felt like the Invisible Girl. She would walk around school, and no one seemed to see her. One day in the girls' room, she looked at the mirror over the sink, and her reflection was not there.

36   The mirror was gone, its broken shards gathered up in a dustpan and thrown away, but the symbolism was clear.

37   "She's stolen my identity," the original Ana lamented after reading an article in the newspaper about criminals stealing information about another person. She chewed a fingernail. Could this *really* happen to her? She was only twelve, but perhaps years from now when she got her first credit card, this new Ana would steal it. Or maybe this new Ana would get in a car wreck and say *she* had been at fault. Then she swallowed from fear. She imagined having a baby that was claimed by the new Ana!

escorting   If you are escorting someone, you are going somewhere with that person.

38   That night she hardly slept. She listened to a dog overturn the garbage can—or was it the new Ana digging through the trash, gathering information about their family? She peered outside but saw no one.

39   During spring break the original Ana learned that her family would be moving. Her father and mother had spoken many times about a new house and often went to open houses on the weekend. Now it was really going to happen—and soon. Her father had gotten a promotion at work, and they were moving to Escondido, thirty miles north of their house in Chula Vista.

40   "The new place has a pool," her father said.

41   A pool! Ana pictured herself diving into the water and fetching a dime on the bottom. She pictured having friends over for a swim party. *I'll be the new girl!* she thought. *I can make a fresh start, and that Ana can have my stupid old school.*

42   "It's going to be nice," she mumbled in bed at night, and wondered about the stick-on stars on her ceiling. They'll have to stay, she assumed, and the girl who lives in my bedroom will have something to look at at night.

43   On the first day at her new school Ana was nervous. *Will they like me?* she wondered. She dressed in her new clothes and pocketed a cell phone, her first, which she habitually opened and closed.

44   Her mother escorted her to the office, where Ana was introduced to a counselor, a woman with a face like a pretty flower and who smelled like a flower when she extended her hand. Two girls, office helpers, said hi. A boy, seated in a chair and with a bloodied elbow—he was still hugging his skateboard—managed to put a smile on his face.

45   *It's nice here*, Ana told herself as the counselor led her from the office. Ana could see that the school was clean and modern. The flower beds were flush with yellow and red flowers, and a custodian was mopping up a spill in the hallway.

---

habitually   To do something habitually is to do it repeatedly, out of habit.

46   "Here she is, Ms. Carroll," the counselor announced lightly.

47   Ana's new teacher approached. Ana liked her right away, and liked how she took her hand in hers.

48   "I hear you're a very good reader," Ms. Carroll encouraged.

49   "I guess," Ana answered simply.

50   Together they entered the classroom, Ms. Carroll prodding her gently. Another girl was hunkered down at her desk, holding a pair of large scissors. *What is she cutting?* Ana wondered, then surmised that she was making a collage.

51   Ms. Carroll said to the girl, "Ana, I want to you to meet . . . " She stalled, uncertain how to continue. Then she said it: "I want you to meet Ana Hernandez, our new student. Funny, you both have the same name."

52   The girl glared at Ana, and her scissors chopped at the air. That day, the original Ana became the new Ana. The *new* new Ana couldn't help but falsely praise, "What a nice collage." She brought her hand to her hair, and the bracelets on her wrists jangled. The students entering the classroom asked, "Who's she? What's her name?"

53   "Me?" She turned around in a neat pirouette. "I'm Ana Hernandez."

---

surmised   If you surmised something, you guessed it was true.

Collaborative Discussion

Look back at what you wrote on page 84. Tell a partner two things that interested you about the characters in the story. Then work with a group to discuss the questions below. Refer to details and examples in *Identity Theft* to explain your answers. Take notes for your responses. When you speak, use your notes.

1 Skim page 86. How do you know that popularity is important to the original Ana? Find examples in the reading.

Listening Tip

Listen for the specific details the speaker uses to answer a question. Which details or examples can you add?

2 Reread page 88. Which words and phrases in the passage about the spelling bee refer to a contest or a battle? Why do you think the author chose these words?

Speaking Tip

Wait for your group's leader to call on you. Then, speak clearly and make eye contact with each member of your group.

3 Skim pages 86 and 88. The character Peter appears several times within the text. How is Peter part of the conflict in the plot of *Identity Theft*?

Write a News Article

PROMPT ....

At the end of *Identity Theft,* Ana Hernandez moved from Chula Vista to Escondido, California.

Imagine you are a student reporter for the Escondido school newspaper. Write an article introducing Ana to students at her new school. Include details about why she moved and her interests.

PLAN ....

Use details from the text to answer *Who, What, When, Where,* and *Why* questions about Ana's move and activities that she likes to do.

WRITE

Now write your news article about Ana from *Identity Theft*.

Make sure your news article

- ☐ introduces Ana in the first paragraph.

- ☐ states a clear purpose for why you are writing the article.

- ☐ contains details that answer *Who, What, When, Where,* and *Why* questions.

- ☐ uses word choices that make the article interesting to read.

- ☐ ends with a concluding statement about Ana.

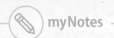

Prepare to Read

GENRE STUDY **Fantasies** are imaginative stories with characters and events that are not real.

- Authors of fantasy tell the story through the plot—the main events of the story. The plot includes a conflict, or problem, and the resolution, or how the problem is solved.
- The events in fantasy stories might defy time or logic.
- Authors of fantasy stories use sensory details and figurative language to develop the setting and the characters.

SET A PURPOSE **Think about** the title and genre of this text. Imagine living on a planet where you see the sun for only one hour every seven years. How would you feel about living on that planet? How would you feel about summer? Write your ideas below.

Meet the Author:
Ray Bradbury

CRITICAL VOCABULARY

slackening

frail

drenched

savagely

resilient

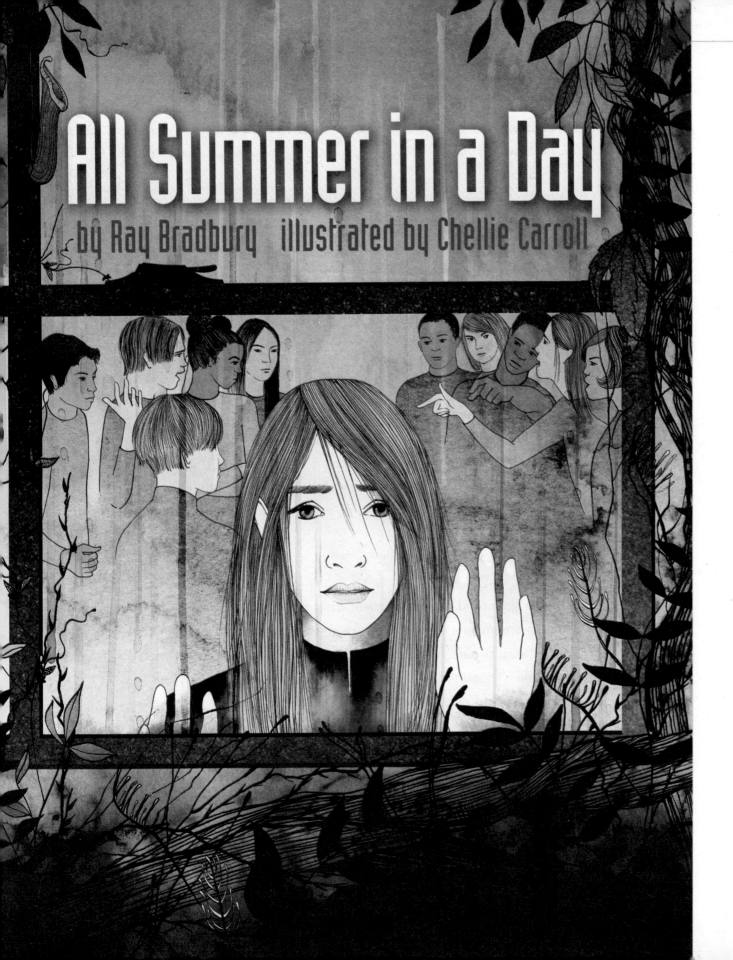

All Summer in a Day

by Ray Bradbury   illustrated by Chellie Carroll

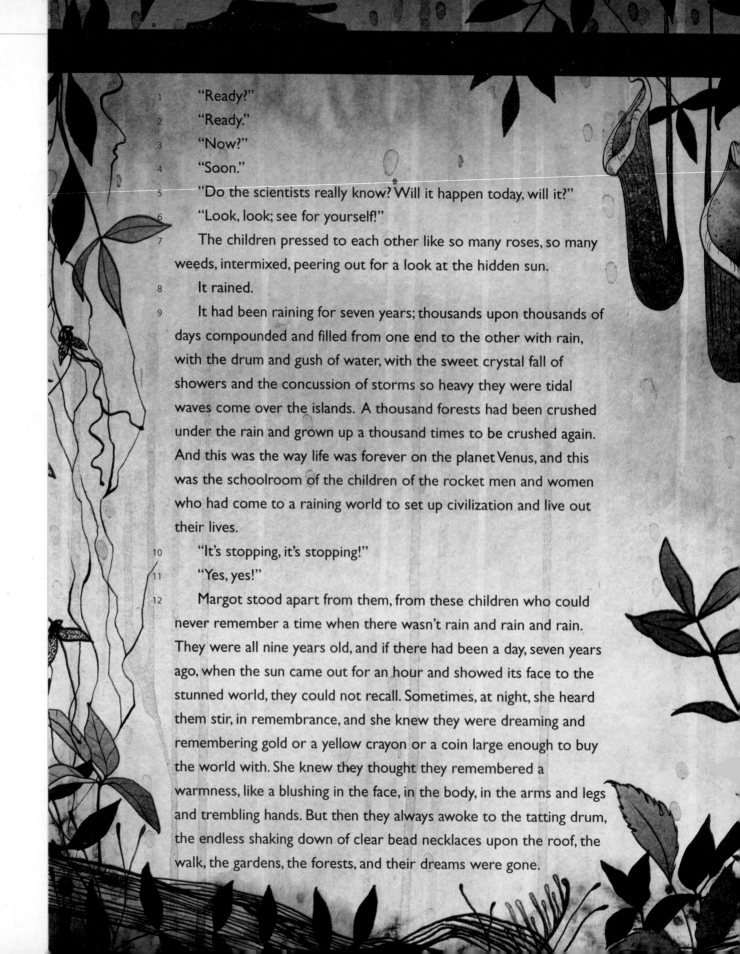

 myNotes

1 "Ready?"

2 "Ready."

3 "Now?"

4 "Soon."

5 "Do the scientists really know? Will it happen today, will it?"

6 "Look, look; see for yourself!"

7 The children pressed to each other like so many roses, so many weeds, intermixed, peering out for a look at the hidden sun.

8 It rained.

9 It had been raining for seven years; thousands upon thousands of days compounded and filled from one end to the other with rain, with the drum and gush of water, with the sweet crystal fall of showers and the concussion of storms so heavy they were tidal waves come over the islands. A thousand forests had been crushed under the rain and grown up a thousand times to be crushed again. And this was the way life was forever on the planet Venus, and this was the schoolroom of the children of the rocket men and women who had come to a raining world to set up civilization and live out their lives.

10 "It's stopping, it's stopping!"

11 "Yes, yes!"

12 Margot stood apart from them, from these children who could never remember a time when there wasn't rain and rain and rain. They were all nine years old, and if there had been a day, seven years ago, when the sun came out for an hour and showed its face to the stunned world, they could not recall. Sometimes, at night, she heard them stir, in remembrance, and she knew they were dreaming and remembering gold or a yellow crayon or a coin large enough to buy the world with. She knew they thought they remembered a warmness, like a blushing in the face, in the body, in the arms and legs and trembling hands. But then they always awoke to the tatting drum, the endless shaking down of clear bead necklaces upon the roof, the walk, the gardens, the forests, and their dreams were gone.

13   All day yesterday they had read in class about the sun. About how like a lemon it was, and how hot. And they had written small stories or essays or poems about it: *I think the sun is a flower, That blooms for just one hour.* That was Margot's poem, read in a quiet voice in the still classroom while the rain was falling outside.

14   "Aw, you didn't write that!" protested one of the boys.

15   "I did," said Margot. "I did."

16   "William!" said the teacher.

17   But that was yesterday. Now the rain was slackening, and the children were crushed in the great thick windows.

18   "Where's teacher?"

19   "She'll be back."

20   "She'd better hurry, we'll miss it!"

21   They turned on themselves, like a feverish wheel, all tumbling spokes. Margot stood alone. She was a very frail girl who looked as if she had been lost in the rain for years and the rain had washed out the blue from her eyes and the red from her mouth and the yellow from her hair. She was an old photograph dusted from an album, whitened away, and if she spoke at all her voice would be a ghost. Now she stood, separate, staring at the rain and the loud wet world beyond the huge glass.

22   "What're *you* looking at?" said William.

23   Margot said nothing.

24   "Speak when you're spoken to."

slackening   Something that is slackening is slowing down.
frail   Something frail is weak and easily broken.

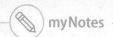

25 He gave her a shove. But she did not move; rather she let herself be moved only by him and nothing else. They edged away from her, they would not look at her. She felt them go away. And this was because she would play no games with them in the echoing tunnels of the underground city. If they tagged her and ran, she stood blinking after them and did not follow. When the class sang songs about happiness and life and games her lips barely moved. Only when they sang about the sun and the summer did her lips move as she watched the drenched windows. And then, of course, the biggest crime of all was that she had come here only five years ago from Earth, and she remembered the sun and the way the sun was and the sky was when she was four in Ohio. And they, they had been on Venus all their lives, and they had been only two years old when last the sun came out and had long since forgotten the color and heat of it and the way it really was.

26 But Margot remembered.

27 "It's like a penny," she said once, eyes closed.

28 "No it's not!" the children cried.

29 "It's like a fire," she said, "in the stove."

30 "You're lying, you don't remember!" cried the children.

31 But she remembered and stood quietly apart from all of them and watched the patterning windows. And once, a month ago, she had refused to shower in the school shower rooms, had clutched her hands to her ears and over her head, screaming the water mustn't touch her head. So after that, dimly, dimly, she sensed it, she was different and they knew her difference and kept away. There was talk that her father and mother were taking her back to Earth next year; it seemed vital to her that they do so, though it would mean the loss of thousands of dollars to her family. And so, the children hated her for all these reasons of big and little consequence. They hated her pale snow face, her waiting silence, her thinness, and her possible future.

drenched If something is drenched, it is soaking wet.

32   "Get away!" The boy gave her another push. "What're you waiting for?"

33   Then, for the first time, she turned and looked at him. And what she was waiting for was in her eyes.

34   "Well, don't wait around here!" cried the boy savagely. "You won't see nothing!"

35   Her lips moved.

36   "Nothing!" he cried. "It was all a joke, wasn't it?" He turned to the other children. "Nothing's happening today. *Is* it?"

37   They all blinked at him and then, understanding, laughed and shook their heads.

38   "Nothing, nothing!"

39   "Oh, but," Margot whispered, her eyes helpless. "But this is the day, the scientists predict, they say, they *know*, the sun . . ."

40   "All a joke!" said the boy, and seized her roughly. "Hey, everyone, let's put her in a closet before the teacher comes!"

41   "No," said Margot, falling back.

42   They surged about her, caught her up and bore her, protesting, and then pleading, and then crying, back into a tunnel, a room, a closet, where they slammed and locked the door. They stood looking at the door and saw it tremble from her beating and throwing herself against it. They heard her muffled cries. Then, smiling, they turned and went out and back down the tunnel, just as the teacher arrived.

43   "Ready, children?" She glanced at her watch.

44   "Yes!" said everyone.

45   "Are we all here?"

46   "Yes!"

47   The rain slacked still more.

48   They crowded to the huge door.

49   The rain stopped.

> **savagely** To do something savagely is to do it in a forceful and unfriendly way.

50   It was as if, in the midst of a film concerning an avalanche, a tornado, a hurricane, a volcanic eruption, something had, first, gone wrong with the sound apparatus, thus muffling and finally cutting off all noise, all of the blasts and repercussions and thunders, and then, second, ripped the film from the projector and inserted in its place a beautiful tropical slide which did not move or tremor. The world ground to a standstill. The silence was so immense and unbelievable that you felt your ears had been stuffed or you had lost your hearing altogether. The children put their hands to their ears. They stood apart. The door slid back and the smell of the silent, waiting world came in to them.

51   The sun came out.

52   It was the color of flaming bronze and it was very large. And the sky around it was a blazing blue tile color. And the jungle burned with sunlight as the children, released from their spell, rushed out, yelling into the springtime.

53   "Now, don't go too far," called the teacher after them. "You've only two hours, you know. You wouldn't want to get caught out!"

54   But they were running and turning their faces up to the sky and feeling the sun on their cheeks like a warm iron; they were taking off their jackets and letting the sun burn their arms.

55   "Oh, it's better than the sun lamps, isn't it?"

56   "Much, much better!"

57   They stopped running and stood in the great jungle that covered Venus, that grew and never stopped growing, tumultuously, even as you watched it. It was a nest of octopi, clustering up great arms of fleshlike weed, wavering, flowering in this brief spring. It was the color of rubber and ash, this jungle, from the many years without sun. It was the color of stones and white cheeses and ink, and it was the color of the moon.

58   The children lay out, laughing, on the jungle mattress, and heard it sigh and squeak under them resilient and alive. They ran among the trees, they slipped and fell, they pushed each other, they played hide-and-seek and tag, but most of all they squinted at the sun until the tears ran down their faces; they put their hands up to that yellowness and that amazing blueness and they breathed of the fresh, fresh air and listened and listened to the silence which suspended them in a blessed sea of no sound and no motion. They looked at everything and savored everything. Then, wildly, like animals escaped from their caves, they ran and ran in shouting circles. They ran for an hour and did not stop running.

59   And then—

60   In the midst of their running one of the girls wailed.

61   Everyone stopped.

62   The girl, standing in the open, held out her hand.

63   "Oh, look, look," she said, trembling.

64   They came slowly to look at her opened palm.

65   In the center of it, cupped and huge, was a single raindrop. She began to cry, looking at it. They glanced quietly at the sun.

66   "Oh. Oh."

67   A few cold drops fell on their noses and their cheeks and their mouths. The sun faded behind a stir of mist. A wind blew cold around them. They turned and started to walk back toward the underground house, their hands at their sides, their smiles vanishing away.

68   A boom of thunder startled them and like leaves before a new hurricane, they tumbled upon each other and ran. Lightning struck ten miles away, five miles away, a mile, a half mile. The sky darkened into midnight in a flash.

69   They stood in the doorway of the underground for a moment until it was raining hard. Then they closed the door and heard the gigantic sound of the rain falling in tons and avalanches, everywhere and forever.

---

resilient Something that is resilient is strong and recovers quickly.

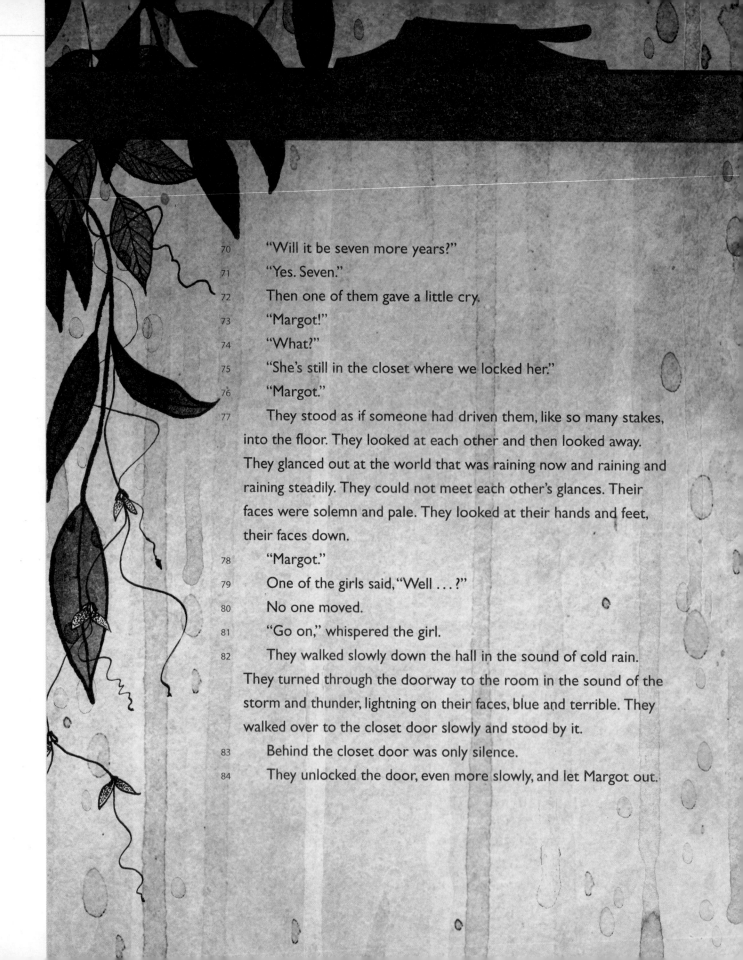

70   "Will it be seven more years?"

71   "Yes. Seven."

72   Then one of them gave a little cry.

73   "Margot!"

74   "What?"

75   "She's still in the closet where we locked her."

76   "Margot."

77   They stood as if someone had driven them, like so many stakes, into the floor. They looked at each other and then looked away. They glanced out at the world that was raining now and raining and raining steadily. They could not meet each other's glances. Their faces were solemn and pale. They looked at their hands and feet, their faces down.

78   "Margot."

79   One of the girls said, "Well . . . ?"

80   No one moved.

81   "Go on," whispered the girl.

82   They walked slowly down the hall in the sound of cold rain. They turned through the doorway to the room in the sound of the storm and thunder, lightning on their faces, blue and terrible. They walked over to the closet door slowly and stood by it.

83   Behind the closet door was only silence.

84   They unlocked the door, even more slowly, and let Margot out.

Collaborative Discussion

Look back at what you wrote on page 96. Tell a partner about two elements of the story that helped you identify *All Summer in a Day* as a fantasy. Then work with a group to discuss the questions below. Refer to details and examples in the text to explain your answers. Take notes for your responses. When you speak, use your notes.

1 Reread the first few paragraphs on page 98. In paragraph 7, the text says the children are "like so many roses, so many weeds." Why does the author make this comparison?

Listening Tip

Give your full attention to what each member of your group says. Show you are listening by looking at the speaker.

2 Reread page 100–101. Why are the other children cruel to Margot? Use details from the text in your answer.

Speaking Tip

As you speak, look at the others in your group. Does anyone look confused? Invite that person to ask you a question.

3 Explain how the children in the story react when the sun comes out.

Write a Letter of Apology

....

In *All Summer in a Day* you read about how William and the other children bullied Margot. William locked Margot in a closet and caused her to miss her only chance in seven years to see the sun.

Imagine you are William and you feel terrible about how you treated Margot. Write a short but heartfelt apology letter to Margot. State two or three reasons why you feel bad for what you did to her. Use details from the story to support your reasoning.

PLAN ....

Make a list of reasons William can give in his letter of apology.

WRITE

Now write the letter of apology to the character Margot in *All Summer in a Day*.

✓ Make sure your letter of apology

- ☐ begins with a heading that gives the writer's address and a date.

- ☐ includes a greeting, such as *Dear Margot*.

- ☐ gives three reasons in the body of the letter why you feel bad about what you did.

- ☐ explains what you have learned from the experience.

- ☐ closes with *Sincerely*, and a signature.

Prepare to Read

GENRE STUDY **Persuasive texts** give an author's opinion about a topic and try to convince readers to believe that opinion.

- Persuasive texts include evidence such as facts and examples to support the author's viewpoint.

- Authors of persuasive texts may organize their ideas by using parallel structures. Parallelism can help authors emphasize a strong point in their argument.

- Persuasive texts can include repetition to emphasize an argument.

SET A PURPOSE **Think about** the title and genre of this text. What meanings could rain, snow, or seasons have in a story? Make a prediction about what this persuasive essay might be about.

Meet the Author:
Thomas C. Foster

CRITICAL VOCABULARY

Victorian

atmosphere

democratic

transformed

associate

108

IT'S MORE THAN JUST RAIN OR SNOW OR SPRINGTIME

by Thomas C. Foster

It was a dark and stormy night.

¹

² What, you've heard that one? Right, Snoopy. And Charles Schulz had Snoopy write it because it was a cliché. It had been one for a very long time back when your favorite beagle decided to become a writer. Edward Bulwer-Lytton, a famous Victorian novelist, actually did begin a (bad) novel with "It was a dark and stormy night." And now you know everything you need to know about dark and stormy nights. Except for one thing.

³ Why?

⁴ You wondered that too, didn't you? Why would a writer want the wind howling and the rain pouring down?

⁵ You may say that every story needs a setting and that weather is part of the setting. That is true, by the way, but it isn't the whole deal. There's much more to it. Here's what I think: weather is never just weather. **It's never just rain.** And that goes for snow, sun, warmth, cold, and sleet too.

⁶ But let's think about rain for a moment.

⁷ Rain can be a plot device; it can make the characters seek shelter, get stranded or lost or stuck somewhere, waiting for it to end. This can be very handy for an author. Rain can also bring along tons of atmosphere. It's more mysterious, murkier, more isolating than most other weather conditions. (Fog is good too, of course.) Then there is the

---

Victorian If something is Victorian, it is in the romantic style of England's 19th-century Victorian era.

atmosphere Atmosphere is the overall tone or mood of a place or situation.

misery factor. Rain can make you more wretched than anything else you'll meet in the outside world. With a little rain and a bit of wind, you can die of hypothermia on the Fourth of July. And there's also something democratic about it. Rain falls on *everybody*. You can be rich or poor, guilty or innocent, male or female, young or old, powerful or weak, and it doesn't matter. Everybody gets wet.

8   What else can rain do? For one thing, it's clean. So if you want a character to be cleansed, let him walk through the rain to get somewhere. He can be quite transformed when he gets there. (He might also have a cold, but that's another matter.) He can be less angry, less confused, more sorry— whatever you want.

9   Rain can also bring new life and hope. This is partly because we associate it with spring. (April showers do in fact bring May flowers.) But also think of the story of Noah. Lots of rain, major flood, ark, cubits, dove, olive branch, rainbow. This flood is the big eraser. It destroys life on Earth but also allows a brand-new start. Rain can bring the world back to life.

10   So an author can use rain to do just about anything he or she wants. Other kinds of weather, too. Fog is good. It almost always means some kind of confusion. Authors use fog to suggest that people can't see clearly. Charles Dickens starts out *A Christmas Carol* with fog filling the streets of London—a good setting for Ebenezer Scrooge, who has lost his way and needs ghostly help to find it again.

democratic   Something that is democratic is available to everyone.

transformed   Something that is transformed is changed in a meaningful way.

associate   If you associate one idea with another, you are connecting the two ideas.

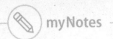
11   Snow? It can mean as much as rain. Snow is clean, plain, warm (if it covers you like a blanket), threatening, inviting, playful, suffocating. You can do just about anything you want with snow.

12   But an author doesn't have a quick shower of rain, or a flurry of snow, or a flood or a blizzard, for no reason at all. Like I said, it's never just rain.

13   **And it never just happens to be spring, or fall, or winter, either.**

14   Here's my favorite snippet of poetry:

15
> *That time of year thou mayst in*
>   *me behold*
> *When yellow leaves, or none, or*
>   *few, do hang*
> *Upon those boughs which shake*
>   *against the cold:*
> *Bare ruined choirs, where late the*
>   *sweet birds sang.*

16   (Oh, sorry, you need a translation? Try this: "If you look at me, you'll see a particular season. It's the season when only a few yellow leaves, or maybe none at all, are hanging on branches that are shaking in the wind, as if they're cold. Those branches are like bare and ruined balconies for choirs where, a while ago, sweet birds used to sing." But it sounds a lot better the way Shakespeare says it.)

17   That's Shakespeare's Sonnet 73. I like it for a lot of reasons. But the thing that really works here is the meaning. The speaker of the poem is seriously feeling his age, and making us feel it too. He's talking about getting old, and he's talking about a particular season: fall. November in the bones. It makes my joints ache just to think about it.

18   Now to the nuts and bolts. Shakespeare didn't invent this metaphor. Fall = middle age was a cliché long before he got hold of it. What he does is *use* this old metaphor in a new way, getting so specific and detailed (yellow leaves, branches shivering in the wind, missing birds) that it forces us to really *see* two things. One is what he's actually describing: the end of autumn and the coming of winter. The other is the thing he's really talking about: standing on the edge of old age.

19   For as long as anyone's been writing, the seasons have stood for the same set of meanings. Maybe it's written into our brains that spring has to do with childhood and youth. Summer is adulthood and romance and passion and satisfaction. Autumn is failing health, weakness, and middle age and tiredness (but also harvest, which makes us think of eating our fill and having lots stored up for the winter). And then winter is old age and resentment and death.

20   Writers know that this is how we naturally think about the seasons, and they make use of that. When Shakespeare asks his beloved, "Shall I compare thee to a summer's day?" we know without thinking about it that this is much more flattering than if he'd compared her to, say, January eleventh. The White Witch doesn't make it eternal spring in Narnia, does she? The idea is practically funny. She makes it always winter (and never Christmas) because, well, she's evil, and so she hates the very idea of new life, new growth, happiness, and forgiveness. It takes Aslan to bring all of those things. And, of course, the spring.

21   Or take Henry James. He wants to write a story in which America (youth, enthusiasm) comes into contact with Europe (stuffy, dull, bound by rules and traditions). So he comes up with a girl, American, young, fresh, direct, open, naive, and something of a flirt. And he comes up with a man, also American but who's lived for a long time in Europe. The man is slightly older, bored, worldly, shut off to his emotions. She's all spring and sunshine; he's all frosty stiffness. Names, you ask? *Daisy* Miller and Frederick *Winterbourne*. Really, it's just too perfect. Once you notice the names, you pretty much know things will end badly, since daisies can't survive in winter. And end badly they do.

22   Every writer can use the seasons, and every writer does so in a slightly different way. What readers learn, finally, is that it's not simple. We can't assume that "summer" means X and "fall" means Y. But writers know there's a set of patterns that can be used in different ways. Sometimes a writer uses the patterns straight, and winter means what we expect it to mean—cold, death. Sometimes a writer turns our expectations around, and summer isn't warm and rich and happy; instead it's dusty and hot and miserable. The patterns are still the same, though, no matter how the writer uses them. And they've been around for a very long time.

23   So when you open up a book, check the weather, and the calendar too. If it's raining or snowing, if it's winter or summer, if the characters are shivering or sweating—it all matters.

Collaborative Discussion

Look back at what you wrote on page 108. Tell a partner two things you learned from this text. Then work with a group to discuss the questions below. Refer to details and examples in *It's More Than Just Rain or Snow or Springtime* to explain your answers. Take notes for your responses. When you speak, use your notes.

1. Find two sentences that include the words "It's never just . . ." Why does the author repeat those words?

2. How can writers use rain in multiple ways and give it multiple meanings? Use examples from the text to support your response.

3. On page 111, paragraph 8, the author says in an aside, "(He might also have a cold, but that's another matter.)" How can you tell that this comment is intended to be funny?

Listening Tip

Listen closely to the speaker. Wait until the speaker has finished before you share your ideas.

Speaking Tip

Before you speak, wait for your group's leader to call on you. Then, speak clearly and make eye contact with everyone in your group.

Write a List of Character Names

In *It's More Than Just Rain or Snow or Springtime*, you learned about how writers use word choices to convey messages about characters and themes.

Imagine you are writing a play or story. Come up with three character names and write a sentence explaining how each name sends a message to the reader about the character. Use advice from *It's More Than Just Rain or Snow or Springtime* to make your choices.

PLAN

Make a list of three to five names that can represent an important idea or message within a text. Make notes to explain what each name represents and tells about the character.

WRITE

Now write your list of character names using advice from *It's More Than Just Rain or Snow or Springtime.*

IT'S MORE
THAN JUST
RAIN OR
SNOW OR
SPRINGTIME
by Thomas C. Foster

✓ **Make sure your list of character names**

☐ includes names for at least three different characters.

☐ uses words that represent a significant trait of each character.

☐ contains a variety of different meanings.

☐ explains why each name sends a message to the reader about the character.

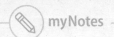

Notice & Note
Tough Questions

Prepare to Read

GENRE STUDY A **play** is a story that can be performed for an audience.

- Plays are made up of a cast of characters whose lines of dialogue reveal the plot. Dialogue is the conversation between characters. Authors use informal language to make the conversation seem real.

SET A PURPOSE **Think about** the title and genre of this text. How might the title *Upside-Down and Backward* be related to the word "dream" in *A Midsummer Night's Dream*? What sort of problems could arise if someone was living as if in a dream?

**Meet the Author:
William Shakespeare**

CRITICAL VOCABULARY

overcome

fleeting

miserable

demeaning

elope

conspiring

garland

outraged

Upside-Down and Backward

by Louise Rozett, adapted from the play
A Midsummer Night's Dream by William Shakespeare

illustrated by Ayesha Lopez

myNotes

Characters

PUCK
A mischievous sprite who lost his glasses

THESEUS
[THEE-see-us]
The duke of Athens

EGEUS
[Ee-JEE-us]
Hermia's father

HERMIA
[HUR-mee-uh]
Lysander's girlfriend and Helena's bestie

HELENA
[HELL-eh-na]
Demetrius's ex-girlfriend and Hermia's bestie

LYSANDER
[ligh-SAN-der]
Hermia's boyfriend

DEMETRIUS
[dih-MEE-tree-us]
Helena's ex-boyfriend, now in love with Hermia (oops!)

Prologue

1 *(The setting is the city of Athens, in ancient Greece. Puck stands on stage, squinting at the audience.)*

2 **PUCK:** Well *hello* there, I'm Puck! I'm the "mischievous sprite" mentioned in the list of characters. *(Winks.)* No, I'm not winking at *you*—I lost my glasses and can't see too well. But enough about me! I'm here to introduce you to Shakespeare's *Midsummer Night's Dream* by telling you about our four main characters. Their names are Hermia, Lysander, Demetrius, and Helena, and they're in a pickle. So I help them by making things even worse! Ha! But that comes later. First, here's what you need to know. Hermia's father, Egeus, wants her to marry Demetrius, but she's in love with Lysander, and guess what? Lysander loves her, too. Lucky, right? Meanwhile, to boost his case, Lysander tries to cast Demetrius in a bad light. He tells Egeus that Demetrius once loved Hermia's best friend Helena, but dumped her for Hermia, proving himself to be a "spotted and inconstant man" (aka, a total jerk). Hermia has a few days to think about things, and then she will have to choose her fate. And that's where we start! I'll leave you to it—I have to find my glasses.

3 *(Puck leaves as Lysander and Hermia come in. Lysander is holding Hermia, who looks like she might faint.)*

Scene 1

4 **LYSANDER:** Hermia, my love, are you all right? You look so pale . . .

5 *(Hermia can barely speak, she is so overcome with tears.)*

6 **LYSANDER:** Please don't cry! Every book I have ever read tells of true love being a rough road. All sorts of things go wrong. Sometime couples are from different walks of life, or are too different in age, or their families want them to marry someone else—

7 **HERMIA:** It is torture, having your love chosen for you by someone else!

8 **LYSANDER:** Even if two people *do* get together, other things can tear them apart, making their love as brief as lightning in the sky. *(Lysander wipes away Hermia's tears.)* Beautiful things can be fleeting, my love. But they're still beautiful.

9 **HERMIA:** *(trying to smile at him)* If that's the way it is, then I suppose we must be patient and bear our struggle. Pain and sorrow is part of true love.

---

overcome   Someone who is overcome is experiencing a deep level of emotion.

fleeting   Something that is fleeting passes by very quickly.

10 **LYSANDER:** (*taking her hands*) But that doesn't mean we can't take matters into our own hands. (*He looks around, lowering his voice.*) Let us leave Athens, Hermia, and I will marry you! Tomorrow night, sneak out of your father's house and meet me in the woods at that spot with the roses where you and Helena like to go. So? Will you? Will you marry me?

11 (*Hermia is so excited, she can't help but throw her arms around Lysander.*)

12 **HERMIA:** Oh, Lysander, I swear on every arrow Cupid has ever shot, on the doves of the Goddess of Love, and on every vow that has been broken by a man—and men have broken more vows than women have made—I will be there tomorrow!

13 **LYSANDER:** (*laughing*) I will not break my vow. Will you keep yours? Look! Here comes Helena.

14 (*The lovers break their hug as Hermia's friend Helena enters, looking miserable.*)

15 **HERMIA:** Lovely Helena! Where are you off to?

16 **HELENA:** Really? You're calling me "lovely"? Take that back, Hermia. I know Demetrius loves you, not me—you, with your starry eyes and your sweet voice. I wish some of your beauty would rub off on me. I'd give anything to look like you, sound like you—to *be* you. What did you do to win him over? What are your tricks? You have to tell me!

17 **HERMIA:** Helena, I did nothing. I *scowl* at the man and he still loves me.

18 **HELENA:** Clearly my smile could learn a few things from your frown!

19 **HERMIA:** I *yell* at him, and he still loves me.

> **miserable** Someone who is miserable is very unhappy.

122

20 **HELENA:** I wish my kind words would have that effect.

21 **HERMIA:** The *ruder* I am, the more he follows me around.

22 **HELENA:** And the nicer I am, the more he hates me.

23 **HERMIA:** (*getting frustrated with her friend*) Helena, it's not my fault he's being an idiot!

24 **HELENA:** You're right. It's not. It's your *beauty's* fault. I should be so lucky.

25 **HERMIA:** Look, don't worry! Demetrius is never going to see me again because Lysander and I are leaving. (*She looks around at her city in sadness.*) Before I fell for Lysander, I loved Athens. But this place is no longer home to me. I have no choice but to go.

26 **LYSANDER:** Helena, don't tell *anyone* our secret. Tomorrow night, when the moonlight shines on the dewy grass— that time of night when we can flee without getting caught—Hermia and I will leave Athens for good.

27 **HERMIA:** We're meeting in the woods, where you and I always go to tell each other our secrets, Helena. Then Lysander and I will go somewhere new, and meet new people, start a new life. Goodbye, my childhood friend. Pray for us, will you? And I wish you luck with Demetrius. He would be lucky to have you. Lysander, I'll see you tomorrow night. Until then, let's make sure we aren't seen together.

28 **LYSANDER:** Goodbye, my love. And goodbye, Helena—I hope Demetrius falls for you the way you have for him.

29 (*Lysander blows Hermia a kiss, which she catches. Helena rolls her eyes as the couple exits in opposite directions.*)

30 **HELENA:** Some people have all the luck! In Athens, I'm considered as pretty as Hermia, but what good does that do me? None. Because Demetrius only has eyes for her—he's obsessed! Of course, I'm obsessed too. Love does crazy things to people. It makes us see what we want to see, not what's actually there. It's blind, just like Cupid with his blindfold in paintings! Love also has terrible judgement, and makes people behave badly. Before Demetrius saw Hermia, he promised me he was mine. But then, he decided he wanted her and his promises to me melted like snow in the hot sun. (*Helena is suddenly defiant.*) Well, his promises are not the only ones that melt. I'm *not* going to keep Hermia's secret—I'm going to tell Demetrius that she is running off with Lysander tomorrow night. He'll follow her into the woods, and then he'll thank me for telling him, which will make breaking my word to my friend worth it . . . won't it? It'll hurt to see him chase after her, but at least there's a chance that when he sees her devotion to Lysander, he'll come back to me!

31 (*As Helena dashes off to find Demetrius and spill her secret, Puck returns.*)

Scene 2

32 **PUCK:** Ah, so cute, and *such* hot messes, am I right? So, while all this was going on, I was chatting with my boss, Oberon. He told me about a special flower that has magic nectar which is actually a love potion. If the nectar is put on the eyelids of a sleeping person, the person will fall in love with the first person they see when they wake up. *Cool!* Oberon wanted me to find this flower so he could use it for his own purposes, but then *this* happened . . .

33 *(Puck ducks behind a tree as Demetrius comes into the woods, followed by Helena.)*

34 **DEMETRIUS:** Helena, how many times must I say it? I don't love you! And I thought you said Lysander and Hermia were here. Just wait until I get my hands on that guy. *Arghhhh!* I'm going crazy in these woods without my love, and it's your fault! Get out of my sight!

35 **HELENA:** If you stop being so attractive, I'll stop following you!

36 **DEMETRIUS:** *How* can you still find me attractive? Am I nice to you? No. Am I telling you as clearly as I know how that I *don't, can't, and won't* love you? Yes!

37 **HELENA:** Somehow, that just makes me love you more. The more you push me away, the more I want to be with you! Look, just think of me as your pet. I know, I know—sounds demeaning, right? And yet, I'd consider it an honor if you thought of me that way.

38 **DEMETRIUS:** Helena, I can't even look at you!

39 **HELENA:** And I can't *not* look at you!

> **demeaning** Behaving in a demeaning way may show a lack of self-respect.

40 **DEMETRIUS:** You know you're putting yourself at risk by going into a deserted forest at night, right?

41 **HELENA:** I know you'll look after me. And the wood is not deserted because *you* are here, and you're all I need! How many other ways can I say it?

42 **DEMETRIUS:** That's it. You're on your own. Good luck fighting off the hungry wild animals!

43 **HELENA:** You can't escape me, Demetrius! I have the power of love on my side.

44 **DEMETRIUS:** If you follow me, I can't be held responsible for what I might do. Consider this fair warning!

45 *(Demetrius stomps off.)*

46 **HELENA:** I'm not giving up yet!

47 *(Helena chases after him as Puck pops out from behind the tree.)*

48 **PUCK:** So *now*, my boss wants me to help Helena by putting that potion I mentioned on Demetrius's eyes while he sleeps. Then he'll wake up, see her, and fall in love instantly. Gotta run— if I lose track of Demetrius, the plan will be ruined and I'll be in trouble. As usual.

49 *(Puck dashes off just as . . .)*

Scene 3

50 *(. . . Lysander and Hermia enter, stumbling through the dark forest, exhausted.)*

51 **LYSANDER:** My love, you're about to fall down with exhaustion. And I have to admit I'm not exactly sure where we are. Let's stop and rest. We can start again in the daylight.

52 **HERMIA:** Good idea. I'll sleep over here on this bank. Where will you sleep?

53 **LYSANDER:** Right next to you, of course. *(Hermia gives him a look.)* I promise I will do nothing other than protect you. On my honor!

54 **HERMIA:** Despite your sweet promises, and the fact that I believe you, we have to do what's proper. You sleep over there, I'll sleep here, and our love will be the stronger for it.

55 **LYSANDER:** Of course. Sleep well, my love.

56 **HERMIA:** You, too.

57 *(As the two sleep, Puck returns.)*

58 **PUCK:** Did I just go in a circle? I can't tell. It is *dark* in this forest! I'm sure my glasses would help . . . Wait, isn't that Demetrius sleeping on the ground there? It is! And that's Helena, over there! What is she doing with this guy? He totally doesn't deserve her. *(Puck squints into the darkness, not realizing that he is looking at Lysander and Hermia, not Demetrius and Helena.)*

59 **PUCK:** But all will be different in the morning. Just a few drops of this and Demetrius will fall so deeply in love with Helena, he won't know what hit him. Ha! *(Puck puts the drops on Lysander's eyelids. Pleased with himself, he scampers off, smacking right into a tree.)* Ow! I really have to find those glasses . . .

60 *(Puck disappears into the forest. Moments later, Helena appears. She's out of breath, having lost sight of Demetrius, which of course is exactly what Demetrius hoped would happen.)*

61 **HELENA:** This is ridiculous—I can't chase him anymore. Hermia is so lucky—men run *toward* her, not *away* from her. How did I ever think she and I were the same? *(Helena practically trips over Lysander, asleep on the ground.)* Oh, Lysander! Is that you? Are you all right? Are you injured? Wake up!

62 *(Lysander opens his eyes . . . and it's like Cupid's arrow has pierced him through. He takes one look at Helena and his heart nearly explodes with love! He leaps to his feet.)*

63 **LYSANDER:** Helena! Gorgeous creature! What can I do for you? Shall I run through fire? Shall I seek revenge on Demetrius? Tell me! I'll do anything!

64 **HELENA:** Huh? No, that's okay. You don't have to worry about him. It doesn't matter that he loves Hermia because she only has eyes for you.

65 **LYSANDER:** Hermia? I couldn't care less about Hermia. She bores me! It's *you* I love. You are the beautiful, gentle woman of my dreams! I have finally seen the light. How could I have been so blind and clueless?!

66 *(Helena is stunned for a moment. Then, furious, she stomps her foot.)*

67 **HELENA:** Stop mocking me, Lysander! All of this is cruel enough as it is! I thought you were nice.

68 *(Helena runs off into the woods. Lysander glances at Hermia, who is still asleep.)*

69 **LYSANDER:** I can't believe I ever loved you, Hermia. Just looking at you makes me feel ill, like I've had too many sweets. Stay right there, asleep, while I go after Helena, my *true* love. Goodbye forever!

70 *(No sooner has Lysander run off than Hermia calls out in her sleep, in the middle of a nightmare.)*

71 **HERMIA:** Lysander! Help! There's a snake, a snake! *(Hermia bolts upright, gasping for breath as she realizes she was just dreaming.)* I had the *worst* dream! There was this— *(Hermia looks around to see that Lysander is gone.)* Lysander? Where have you gone? Why would you leave me here by myself? Please, answer me! *(There is no answer. Frightened, she gets up.)* I must find him before death finds me in this dark forest . . . *(Off she goes into the dark forest . . .)*

Scene 4

72 *(Puck enters, frustrated.)*

73 **PUCK:** I admit to my boss that I ran into a tree because I lost my glasses, and what does he do? He sends me back here to double-check that I put the love potion on the right person. *Annoying,* right? Now where are those two? *(He hears voices and strains to see.)* Is that them?

74 *(Puck ducks behind a tree as Demetrius and Hermia appear.)*

75 **DEMETRIUS:** Hermia, you know how much I love you. Must you be so unkind to me?

76 **HERMIA:** What have you done with Lysander? Have you harmed him in any way? That's the only reason I can think of for him to leave me while I *slept!* If you hurt him, Demetrius, you will be very sorry indeed.

77 **PUCK:** *(to audience)* Uh-oh. *That's* Demetrius. And he's still in love with Hermia, which means . . . *(Puck starts giggling)* . . . I *did* put the love potion on the wrong person! I put it on Lysander! I wonder who—or *what*—he saw first when he woke up! *Hahahaaaaa!*

78 **DEMETRIUS:** Beautiful Hermia, you hurt me with your cruel words!

79 **HERMIA:** Where *is* Lysander? Tell me right now!

80 **DEMETRIUS:** I would rather elope with Helena than tell you where he is.

81 **HERMIA:** *(gasping)* So you *did* harm him! What did you do to him? Did you do it while he was sleeping, you coward? You're no better than a snake, you with your lying tongue!

82 **DEMETRIUS:** I didn't hurt him. All right? Calm down. He's fine, as far as I know. *(Under his breath.)* Unfortunately.

83 **HERMIA:** But where is he? *(Demetrius shrugs, annoyed.)* I'm done with you, Demetrius. You are, quite simply, *the worst.*

84 *(Hermia stomps off to search for Lysander.)*

> **elope** To elope means to run away secretly to get married.

127

85 **DEMETRIUS:** I'd better let her cool off before I go after her. This whole thing is a depressing disaster—it makes me so tired . . .

86 *(Demetrius throws himself in a heap on the ground and closes his eyes. Puck comes out from behind the tree.)*

87 **PUCK:** Well, I'm not going to lie—this was a *bad* mistake. *(He giggles.)* It's a funny one, though! Instead of turning false love into true love, I turned a good love bad! That's the way the cookie crumbles—some vows stick, some don't, whether a love potion is involved or not. Regardless, this mess is fixed easily enough. *(He takes out the potion and puts some on Demetrius's eyes.)*

Now to find Helena, to make sure I get it right this time. *(Puck is about to leave when he hears arguing.)* I can't trust my eyes but I *can* trust my ears! That sounds like Lysander and Helena, making enough racket to wake the dead!

88 **LYSANDER:** For the last time, my love, my beauty, I am *not* making fun of you! I love you! These tears that stream down my cheeks should tell you that I'm not lying!

89 **HELENA:** How can you be telling me the truth? You've already made these vows—to Hermia! So the vows you made to me are a lie.

90 **LYSANDER:** I wasn't in my right mind when I made my vows to her.

91 **HELENA:** And you're not in your right mind now, you jerk.

92 **LYSANDER:** Look at it this way. Demetrius loves her, not you, and—

93 *(At the sound of his name, Demetrius wakes. His eyes land on Helena and he is instantly in love with her.)*

94 **DEMETRIUS:** Helena! You gorgeous thing! Perfect in every way! Allow me to kiss your beautiful hand.

95 *(For a moment, Helena just looks at him like he's crazy. And then . . .)*

96 **HELENA:** Is this a joke to you?! Are my feelings worth so little? You two have banded together to humiliate me for sport! You call yourselves men, treating a lady this way? I know you both love Hermia!

97 **LYSANDER:** You're right on one count. Demetrius, we all know you love Hermia. Well, she is yours—I give her up to you. Now you must give up your claim to Helena, who is *my* true love.

98 **DEMETRIUS:** Keep Hermia, I want Helena. She's *my* true love! I barely even remember who Hermia is.

99 **LYSANDER:** Don't believe him, Helena. He lies.

100 **DEMETRIUS:** You don't understand a thing, you—Oh, look! Here comes Hermia, *your* love.

101 *(Hermia enters, scratched up from running through the forest in terror.)*

102 **HERMIA:** Is that you, Lysander? Oh thank goodness! I thought I heard your voice. Why did you leave me like that?

103 **LYSANDER:** Love sent me off in another direction. I had to heed its call.

104 **HERMIA:** Love? I don't understand.

105 **LYSANDER:** I had to find my beloved Helena, who shines like a star in the heavens! I no longer want you, Hermia. It's Helena I love.

106 **HERMIA:** I—you—wait, what?

107 *(Helena looks at her friend, astonished.)*

108 **HELENA:** Hermia! You're in on this, too? All *three* of you are conspiring against me? I can't believe you would do this, after everything we've shared. We're best friends—no—more like sisters! We've been close for so long, and now you're going to throw away what we have just to help these jerks play a prank on me? Women everywhere would disapprove.

109 **HERMIA:** What are you talking about? I'm not doing anything to you!

110 **HELENA:** Oh, please. You put Lysander up to this! You told him to call me beautiful. And then you sent your other love—*my* ex-boyfriend who can't stand the sight of me—to woo me with words like "gorgeous" and "perfect"! Who says those things to someone they hate? Demetrius and Lysander wouldn't do this unless *you* asked them to! You are the one who is beloved, not me. You should feel sorry for me, not hate me.

111 **HERMIA:** Helena, truly, I have no idea what you're talking about.

112 **HELENA:** Fine. Keep pretending. Mock me as soon as my back is turned. See if I care. This is a prank for the history books! I'm leaving. Goodbye to *all* of you.

---

conspiring Conspiring is teaming up with someone to make a plan against someone else.

113 **LYSANDER:** No, Helena, my love, don't go!

114 **HERMIA:** Stop toying with her like that, Lysander.

115 **DEMETRIUS:** Yes, stop, or I shall have to stop you myself.

116 **LYSANDER:** I should like to see you try, Demetrius. Helena, I love you, and will die just to prove it!

117 **DEMETRIUS:** As will I!

118 **LYSANDER:** Will you? Well then! Let's have a duel and *end* this!

119 **DEMETRIUS:** A duel it is!

120 **HERMIA:** Lysander, stop this nonsense!

121 *(Hermia reaches for Lysander and he yanks his arm away as if she had scalded him.)*

122 **LYSANDER:** Don't touch me. You are vile to me, you snake!

123 **HERMIA:** How can you talk to me that way?

124 **LYSANDER:** Enough! Get away from me! How many times must I say it?

125 **HERMIA:** Are you kidding right now?

126 **HELENA:** He *is* kidding! Just like *you* are!

127 **HERMIA:** Lysander, I am still me! You are still you! We are *in love*! Have you forgotten? We were in love before you fell asleep and then when you woke up . . . *(She falters as he simply stares at her.)* So, this is real? You're actually leaving me?

128 **LYSANDER:** Finally, she gets it! Yes, we are done. I love Helena. The. End.

129 *(Very slowly, Hermia turns to Helena with fury in her eyes.)*

130 **HERMIA:** *Youuuuu* . . . How did you do this? How did you steal him away from me?

131 **HELENA:** And *still* you continue this game? Nice. *Real* nice. You are so fake!

132 **HERMIA:** Fake? Me? How can you say that? If I didn't know better, I'd think I was still having a nightmare . . .

133 *(Helena takes a step back.)*

134 **HELENA:** *(To the young men)* This joke has gone far enough. Are you going to let her hurt me? I'm not a fighter—please! I'm no match for her. *(To Hermia)* Believe me, I've never done anything to you. Never! Well, I'll admit that I *did* tell Demetrius that you and Lysander were running away together so I could follow him into the forest. But all I want now is to go back to Athens and get away from *all* of you. I won't follow you anymore.

135 **LYSANDER:** No! Helena, you stay; Hermia, you go!

136 **DEMETRIUS:** Lysander! Come! We will settle this once and for all!

137 *(The young men exit, to have their duel.)*

138 **HERMIA:** Do you see what you've done now?

139 **HELENA:** I don't trust any of you anymore, least of all you! Some friend you are.

140 *(Helena runs out. After watching her go, Hermia heads in the opposite direction. A thick fog begins to roll in.)*

141 **PUCK:** Well, I have to say, that was better than reality TV! But I've had my fun. It's time to set this right before those foolish boys hurt each other. First I have to climb this tree and find the flower that will undo what the first flower did! Then I'll use the cover of the fog that's coming in to keep the boys from finding each other. Don't worry—we'll get this all settled soon enough.

142 *(Puck disappears up the tree to find the flower.)*

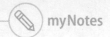

Scene 5

143 (Lysander enters, struggling to see through the fog.)

144 **LYSANDER:** Demetrius! Where did you go? Say something so I can find you!

145 (Puck peeks his head out from the branches of the tree. He is now wearing a garland of flowers around his head. He looks down at Lysander and grins.)

146 **PUCK:** Here is my chance! (Calling down to Lysander, disguising his voice as Demetrius.) I'm right here, Lysander! Can't you see my sword glinting in the moonlight?

147 (Lysander looks around but can't see a thing.)

148 **LYSANDER:** I can't see through this fog! Where are you?

149 **PUCK:** (as Demetrius) Over here!

150 **LYSANDER:** Enough of this nonsense, Demetrius. I'm going to sit right here. When you're ready to do this, come get me. Until then, I'll be napping. That's how not scared I am.

151 (Lysander sits with his back against Puck's tree and promptly falls asleep. Demetrius enters.)

> **garland** A garland is a wreath of leaves and flowers worn on the head or around the neck.

152 **DEMETRIUS:** Hey! Coward! Where did you go? Are you shaking in your boots? Get out here!

153 (Puck, still in the tree, pretends to be Lysander.)

154 **PUCK:** (as Lysander) Who are you calling a coward? You're the one who's hiding like a little kid! Should I fight you with a stick instead of a sword, kid?

155 **DEMETRIUS:** (furious) Where are you?!

156 **PUCK:** (as Lysander) Just follow my voice!

157 **DEMETRIUS:** This is ridiculous! I'm going to sit right here. Come and get me when you're ready to fight, coward!

158 (Demetrius sits down on the other side of Puck's tree and promptly falls asleep. Slowly, quietly, Puck starts to climb down, but then Helena shows up. He freezes, clinging to the tree.)

159 **HELENA:** This fog—I have no idea which way Athens is. It doesn't matter— I'm so tired, I can't take another step. I'll sleep for a while. Maybe everything will be clearer in the morning.

160 (Helena lies down just a few feet away from the tree, and sleeps.)

161 **PUCK:** Annnnd wait for it . . . wait for it . . .

162 (Hermia enters, equally exhausted.)

163 **HERMIA:** I'm upset, filthy, scratched, and scraped. I can't go any further. All I can do now is rest, and hope that Lysander survives this duel. How did it come to this?

164 (Hermia lies down and sleeps. Puck climbs the rest of the way down the tree.)

165 **PUCK:** Finally! Here is the moment to right these hilarious wrongs. Now. This is Lysander, right? *(He double checks, leaning in close, squinting.)* Yes! Great. *(He plucks a flower from the garland on his head and dabs it on Lysander's eyes.)* And just to be safe . . . *(He rolls Lysander onto his side, so he is facing Hermia.)* There! When you wake, you will see your love, and all will be right with your world once again.

166 *(Puck skips off, tossing his garland into the air, quite pleased with himself.)*

Scene 6

167 *(Finally, morning has come. The fog has disappeared. Theseus, who is duke of Athens, and Hermia's father, Egeus, come into the clearing.)*

168 **THESEUS:** Who are these people sleeping here?

169 **EGEUS:** Why, that's . . . my daughter? And Lysander? And Demetrius and Helena? I don't understand!

170 **THESEUS:** I nearly forgot. Isn't today the day Hermia must make her decision? Let's wake them up! *(Theseus blows his hunting horn, startling the young people awake.)* Explain yourselves!

171 *(Lysander opens his eyes to see Hermia, and feels a rush of love for her.)*

172 **LYSANDER:** Hermia? *(Then, groggy and confused, he sees Theseus and Egeus.)* My lord, I . . . I'm not sure what to say. I don't quite know how we all ended up here. But, in all honesty, I know that Hermia and I were planning to run away—

173 **EGEUS:** *(outraged)* And for that you must be punished. Did you hear that, Demetrius? He wanted to take away your wife!

174 **DEMETRIUS:** *(to Lysander)* Are we . . . awake? Is this actually happening?

175 **LYSANDER:** I believe it is but I feel so . . . odd.

176 **DEMETRIUS:** *(to Egeus)* I'm sorry, sir, but I don't want to marry your daughter after all. I mean, I did love her at one point, but that was a strange moment in time when I was not myself. I am back to my old self now, and I love Helena. As I did. Before. A while ago, I mean.

177 **HELENA:** *(wary)* You *do* love me?

178 **DEMETRIUS:** I do!

179 **EGEUS:** But—

180 **THESEUS:** Egeus, today is for celebrating! Let's allow these couples to love who they love, and let them marry! Let us all go to the temple!

181 *(Lysander stands, extending his hand to help up his former rival, then turns to Hermia.)*

> **outraged** If you are outraged about something, you're angry and shocked.

182 **LYSANDER:** Shall we go to the temple, my love, and marry as we planned?
(*He pulls her up, and she throws herself into his arms.*)

183 **HERMIA:** Oh, Lysander! Yes, yes, yes! I want nothing more than to forget the strange dream I had! You no longer loved me, and it was terrible . . .

184 (*As they exit, Demetrius reaches out to Helena. She slowly takes his hand. He pulls her to her feet and kisses her cheek. She looks at him, not sure she's ready to trust all this yet.*)

185 **DEMETRIUS:** Shall we go to the temple as well, beautiful Helena?

186 **HELENA:** Uh, let's just take this one step at a time . . .
(*As they wander off, Puck pops up from behind a rock.*)

187 **PUCK:** And there you have it! Everyone is reunited with the person they're supposed to be with, thanks to me. Or no thanks to me, depending on how you look at it. And check this out! I was also reunited . . . with my glasses!

188 (*He pulls them out of his pocket and holds them up, admiring them. Then he drops them on the ground and steps on them. He looks up with a grin.*) Life's more fun without them, wouldn't you say?

The End

Collaborative Discussion

Look back at what you wrote on page 118. Describe the message of the play to a partner. Then work with a group to discuss the questions below. Refer to details and examples in *Upside-Down and Backward* to explain your answers. Take notes for your responses. When you speak, use your notes.

1. When does Puck show up in this play? How is he different from the other characters in the play?

Listening Tip

If someone in your group is not speaking loudly enough, ask that person to speak a little louder.

2. Scene 5 takes place in the fog. Why is this important to the story?

Speaking Tip

When it is your turn to share your thoughts and ideas about the text, make sure you speak clearly and at a moderate pace.

3. Reread Scene 6. Why did the characters think they were in a dream? Use examples from the play in your answer.

Write a Review

PROMPT ....

Upside-Down and Backward is a modern adaptation of William Shakespeare's 16th-century play *A Midsummer Night's Dream*.

Did you enjoy this adaptation of Shakespeare's play? Did it make you laugh? Were the characters and plot of the play interesting and engaging? Did the play make you think about your own life? Write a review that might appear in your town's local newspaper or magazine. State your opinion about the play, using examples from the text.

PLAN ....

Make notes about the elements of the play you liked or disliked. Think about the characters, the setting, and the plot.

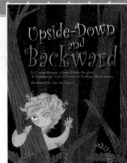

WRITE

Now write your review about *Upside-Down and Backward*.

Make sure your review

☐ begins with an opening statement that includes the title of the play and the play from which it was adapted.

☐ explains at least two elements of the play you liked and disliked, and why.

☐ uses examples or details from the play to support your opinion.

☐ concludes with an overall evaluation of the play.

Essential Question

What makes a story worth reading?

Write a Story Sequel

PROMPT Think about what you learned in this module about how writers construct their stories.

Imagine you write for a literary magazine. Your editor asks you to write a short sequel to *All Summer in a Day*. What will happen next to Margot, William, and the class? As you craft your sequel, use what you have learned about including references to weather from *It's Never Just Rain or Snow or Springtime*.

I will write about _____.

✓ Make sure your story sequel
☐ has an appropriate setting that uses weather to convey a message about the characters or plot.
☐ uses dialogue that provides details about the characters and their struggles.
☐ uses transition words to connect ideas.
☐ has a conflict, or problem, that connects to the plot from *All Summer in a Day*.
☐ has a satisfying resolution to the problem you presented.

PLAN .... **Gather information.**

Find the weather references in *All Summer in a Day*. How does each reference relate to ideas you learned about in *It's Never Just Rain or Snow or Springtime*? Look back at your notes and revisit the texts as necessary.

Then think about how the weather and setting might affect the characters, conflict, plot events, and resolution of your sequel. Fill out the chart below with details about your sequel.

My story title is: ______________________________

Setting	**Characters**

Plot
Problem (Conflict)
Events
Solution (Resolution)

DRAFT ·· Write your sequel.

Write an **introduction** that provides a setting for the sequel and connects to the original text.

Develop the **plot**. Include the main events of the sequel and a conflict from the notes in your story map.

Make sure the **resolution** flows logically from the conflict in your sequel.

The revision and editing steps give you a chance to look carefully at your writing and make changes. Work with a partner to determine whether you have explained your ideas clearly to readers. Use these questions to help you evaluate and improve your article.

PURPOSE/ FOCUS	ORGANIZATION	EVIDENCE	LANGUAGE/ VOCABULARY	CONVENTIONS
☐ Does my sequel idea make sense? ☐ Does my sequel's problem connect logically to the original story?	☐ Does the introduction describe the setting and the characters? ☐ Have I provided a logical resolution?	☐ Have I used what I learned about weather references to convey a message about the characters or plot?	☐ Have I included transition words that connect ideas?	☐ Do all sentences have subject-verb agreement? ☐ Do pronouns match the nouns they modify? ☐ Have I used commas correctly with prepositional phrases?

PUBLISH .... Share your work.

Create a Finished Copy Make a final copy of your sequel. You may wish to include an illustration. Consider these options to share your sequel.

1. Record a Story Sequel Podcast. Record yourself and your classmates reading their sequels aloud; then play it for other classes.

2. Publish the sequels in a class online newsletter.

3. Start a blog in which you read and comment on other sequels.

Designing the Future

"To invent, you need a good
imagination and a pile of junk."

—Thomas Edison

What inspires the most amazing inventions?

Get Curious
Video

Words About Inventions

The words in the chart will help you talk and write about the selections in this module. Which words about designing the future have you seen before? Which words are new to you?

Add to the Vocabulary Network on page 145 by writing synonyms, antonyms, and related words and phrases for each word about designing the future.

After you read each selection in this module, come back to the Vocabulary Network and keep building it. Add more boxes if you need to.

WORD	MEANING	CONTEXT SENTENCE
innovations (noun)	An innovation is a new idea or way of doing something.	In the late 1940s, the television and the LP record were considered innovations.
blueprint (noun)	A blueprint is a plan or model of something.	A 3D printer requires a blueprint before it can create a product.
manufacturer (noun)	A manufacturer is a business that makes goods for sale.	A textile manufacturer makes cloth for clothing and furniture.
advances (noun)	Advances in a particular area of study, such as technology or medicine, are improvements in that area.	Huge advances in information technology, such as laptop computers and smartphones, were made during the 1990s and 2000s.

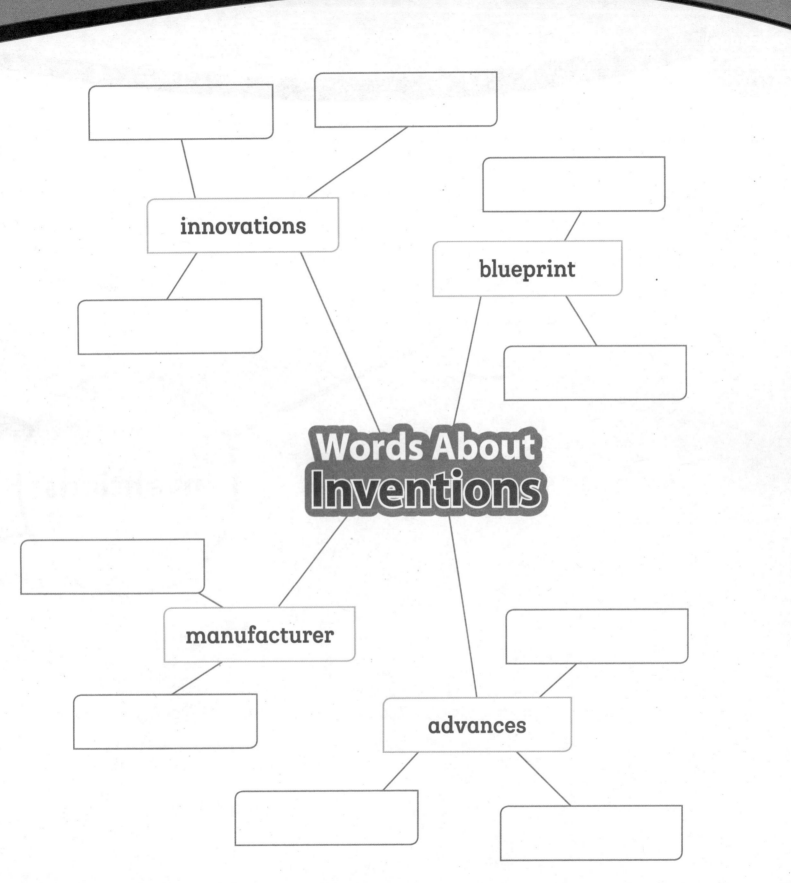

innovations

blueprint

Words About Inventions

manufacturer

advances

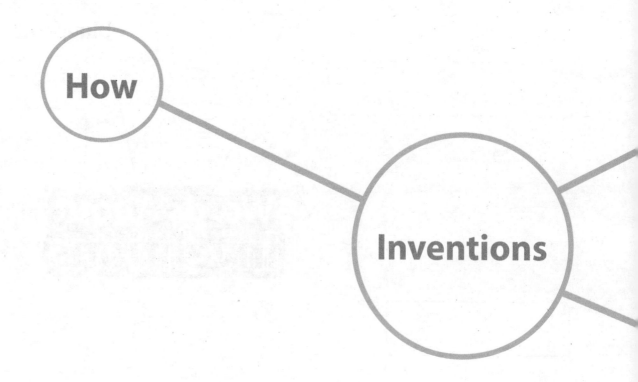

What

Why

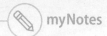

Design Innovations

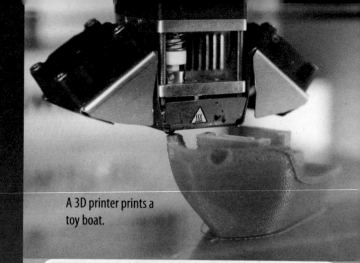

A 3D printer prints a toy boat.

You may have heard the expression "necessity is the mother of invention." What does it mean? When we need something that doesn't exist, we invent it! Here are three (of many) recent innovations that are helping people around the world.

3D Printing

Also known as additive manufacturing, 3D printing is the process of making a three-dimensional object by adding one layer at a time.

It works like this. First, a designer uses software to create a blueprint, or plan, for the object. (You can also find existing blueprints online.) Next, the blueprint and the materials—such as plastics or metals—are loaded into a 3D printer. The materials are heated to a liquid state, then hardened one layer at a time to form the object.

What's so great about 3D printing? Using this process, almost anybody can become a manufacturer. Makers can design and print objects quickly, at a fraction of the usual cost.

For example, the 3D printing process has allowed volunteers to create custom-made artificial limbs. The limbs go to people who could not afford expensive conventional prostheses.

In another example, a San Francisco startup printed an entire "tiny house" in just 24 hours. It cost about $10,000. Now, various organizations have proposed printing tiny houses to shelter the homeless.

A rescue robot helps an emergency crew.

Drones

A drone is an unmanned aerial vehicle (UAV) or, in essence, a flying robot. Drones come in many shapes and sizes and can be used to transport anything from weapons to pizzas.

The increasing use of drones is controversial, for reasons of both safety and ethics. Some naysayers worry about midair collisions or drone crashes on busy streets. Others object to the way drones are used in warfare.

Despite these legitimate concerns, drones have many positive uses. In the wildfire-prone western United States, for example, drones are used to spot and fight fires. Not only can drones battle forest fires, but they can also replant deforested areas. One company plans to use drones to plant one billion trees per year.

Drones are also helping to protect endangered wildlife. In Indonesia, drones monitor the Sumatran orangutan population. And, in East Africa, drones spot poachers who illegally hunt elephants and rhinos.

Perhaps drones' most useful purpose is helping sick and injured people. About eight million people worldwide lack access to basic medical care. Now, several organizations are making plans to use drones to deliver emergency and medical supplies to communities in need.

Rescue Robots

Robots aren't a new invention, but recent advances in robotic technology have allowed new types of robots to perform a variety of search-and-rescue functions.

For example, in Japan, where massive earthquakes are a constant risk, rescue robots use ultrasonic sensors that detect sounds beyond the limits of human hearing, and infrared cameras that can detect body heat to locate humans trapped at disaster sites. The bots then load the victims onto carts and transport them to safety.

As their name suggests, snakebots are robots that look and move like snakes. They have been used at various disaster sites around the world, slithering through difficult terrain to search for victims, gather information, and even deliver emergency supplies.

A snakebot can explore difficult terrain.

**Notice
& Note**
Contrasts and
Contradictions

Prepare to Read

GENRE STUDY A **biography** is the story of a real person's life written by someone other than that person.

- Authors of biographies present events in sequential, or chronological, order. This helps readers understand what happened in the person's life and when.

- Biographers may use literary language to present major events in a person's life. For example, the author may use similes to describe how the person is feeling.

- Biographies include third-person pronouns, such as *he, she, him, her, his, hers, they, them,* and *their.*

SET A PURPOSE **Think about** the title and genre of this text. What do you think life was like for a boy inventor living on a farm in the early 1900s? What questions would you ask him? Write your ideas below.

CRITICAL VOCABULARY

haphazardly

captivated

appealing

orderly

bombarded

stimulated

crude

dissect

precision

revolutionary

Meet the Author:
Kathleen Krull

The Boy Who Invented TV
The Story of Philo Farnsworth

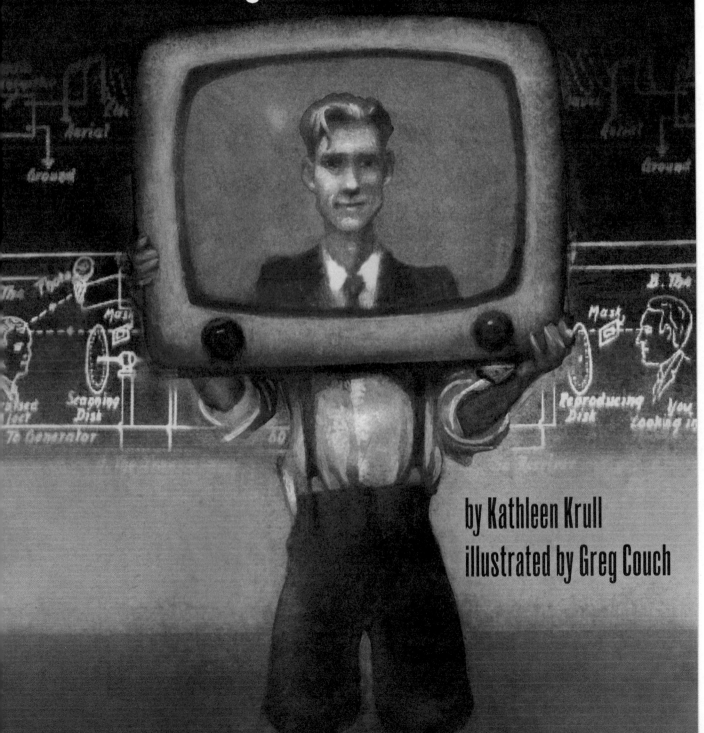

by Kathleen Krull

illustrated by Greg Couch

Life Before Philo

1 Imagine what it was like growing up on a farm in the American West of 1906. With electricity rare out in the country, chores took up most of your day. No refrigerators, no cars, few phones, hardly any indoor bathrooms. Long distances separated you from friends and relations. Meeting up with others took some effort—you rode a horse or walked. There were trains, but riding or even seeing one was a big deal.

2 Getting news was another challenge. What government leaders were doing in Washington, the latest in the arts and sciences, whether sports teams were winning or losing, new information of any kind—it trickled in haphazardly by mail. Not many people had books, and libraries were few and far between.

3 It was all a bit lonely.

4 What about fun? Movies—no. Radio—no (it was only on military ships). There was music, if you played your own instruments. There were no malls to go hang out at. When you had enough money saved up to buy a bicycle or roller skates, you ordered from the "wish book"—the Sears, Roebuck mail-order catalog.

5 And there was no television. That's right. **NO TV.**

6 In 1906, inside a log cabin on a farm in Utah, a boy was born who would change things. His name was Philo Taylor Farnsworth.

haphazardly   Things that are arranged haphazardly are not organized and are perhaps out of order.

7 No sooner did Philo Farnsworth learn to talk than he asked a question. Then another, and another. His parents answered as best they could.

8 Noticing Philo's interest in anything mechanical, his father took the three-year-old boy to see a train at a station. At first Philo was afraid this huge, noisy thing might be a monster. But the nice engineer invited the boy up into the cab with him, explaining a bit about how steam-powered trains worked.

9 That night Philo sat at the kitchen table and drew detailed pictures of what went on inside the motor of a train.

10   Two new machines captivated Philo as he grew up. One was a hand-cranked telephone, purchased by a neighbor. Holding the phone one day, hearing the voice of his beloved aunt, six-year-old Philo got goose bumps. After all, she lived a long ways away!

11   Another neighbor brought a hand-cranked phonograph to a dance. Music swirling out of a machine—it was almost impossible to believe.

12   "These things seemed like magic to me," Philo said later. Besides being incredibly clever, the inventions brought people together in whole new ways.

13   Philo's father shared his wonder. On clear summer nights, as they lay in the grass and gazed at the stars, his father told him about Alexander Graham Bell and the telephone, Thomas Edison and the phonograph. Inventors—these became Philo's heroes.

14   Away on a temporary job, his father appointed Philo, the oldest of five children, the "man" in the family. Philo was eight. His many chores included feeding the pigs, milking and grazing the cow, fetching wood for the stove. He did get his own pony—Tippy.

15   It was also a sort of reward to skip school for a while. Bullies there teased him about his unusual name. Shy and serious, Philo didn't fight back.

16   He found it far more appealing to practice reading with his grandmother's Sears, Roebuck catalog. It had toys . . . as well as cameras, alarm clocks, and machines that used a new, invisible source of power. Electricity, it was called.

17   In his spare time, Philo raised lambs and sold them. When he had enough money saved up, he visited his grandmother to pick a bicycle out of her catalog.

captivated   If you are captivated by someone or something, you find that person or thing fascinating.

appealing   Something that is appealing has qualities that people find pleasing and attractive.

18   But somehow, she talked him into ordering a violin instead. Philo did love the sound of music, its orderly rhythms. And even at age ten, he dreamed of fame. Maybe he could find it by creating music like what he heard on the neighbor's phonograph.

19   Soon he was performing in dance bands, making five dollars every Friday night.

20   Playing the violin was one more thing for the bullies to tease him about. Then one day Philo fought back, and the teasing ended.

21   Trying for a better life, the Farnsworths moved from Utah to an Idaho farm with fields of beets and potatoes. Eleven-year-old Philo drove one of their covered wagons, carrying a crate of piglets, a cage of hens, his violin, and their new prize possession—a phonograph.

22   Arriving in the Snake River Valley, he noticed something up in the air—power lines. Their new home was wired for electricity! A generator ran the lights and water heater, the hay stacker and grain elevator, and other farm equipment.

23   And up in the attic was another welcome surprise. A shelf of old popular-science magazines, with thrilling articles about magnetism, electricity, and those new "magic boxes"—radios. Philo promptly claimed this as his bedroom. His chores began before dawn, but he trained himself to wake up an hour early so he could switch on the light and read in bed. Any spare money he had went to buy more magazines.

24   That's when he saw the word "television" for the first time. It meant a machine that was something like a radio, only it sent pictures instead of sounds.

25   It didn't actually exist yet, but scientists were racing to invent one.

26   The electric generator broke down a lot, and repairs were costly. Each time the repairman came, Philo bombarded him with questions.

orderly   When something is done in an orderly manner, it is done in an organized and controlled way.

bombarded   If you bombard someone with questions, you keep asking them a lot of questions.

27   After yet another breakdown, Philo set out to fix the machine himself. He took it apart, cleaned it, put it back together, and pressed the "on" button. It worked.

28   Philo's father was enormously proud of him. From then on, he was the Farnsworths' electrical engineer.

29   Philo tinkered with broken motors, reels of wire, old tools. He devised gadgets to hook up to the generator—anything to make his chores easier, like installing lights in the barn.

30   His least favorite thing was washing clothes—hours of standing while pushing and pulling the lever that swished the water around the washtub. So he attached a motor with pulleys to the lever to make it churn on its own, leaving him extra time to read.

31   When he was thirteen, Philo entered a contest sponsored by *Science and Invention* magazine. Using what he'd learned about magnets, he pictured an ignition lock that would make the new Model T Fords harder to steal.

32   When he won the contest, Philo spent the prize money on his first pair of proper long pants. Wearing boyish short pants at the Friday dances was just plain embarrassing.

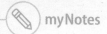

33 Philo went on investigating television. An article called "Pictures that Fly Through the Air" stimulated him. Scientists were having no luck—so far their ideas resulted in crude mechanical devices that used whirling disks and mirrors.

34 Philo doubted any disk could whirl fast enough to work. Much better to do the job electronically. To harness electrons, those mysterious, invisible particles that traveled at the speed of light . . .

35 One bright, sunny day, fourteen-year-old Philo plowed the potato fields. It was the best chore for thinking—out in the open country by himself. Back and forth, back and forth . . . the plow created rows of overturned earth. He looked behind him at the lines he was carving—perfectly parallel.

36 Then he almost fell off the plow seat. All his thoughts fused together. Instead of seeing rows of dirt, he saw a way to create television: breaking down images into parallel lines of light, capturing them and transmitting them as electrons, then reassembling them for a viewer. If it was done quickly enough, people's eyes could be tricked into seeing a complete picture instead of lines. "Capturing light in a bottle" was how he thought of it—using electricity, not a machine with moving parts inside.

37 Philo's grin was wide. He told the idea to his father, who tried to understand but couldn't keep up with his son.

38 In the autumn Philo started high school, riding horseback four miles each way.

39 Mr. Tolman, the senior chemistry teacher, noticed that this freshman devoured books the way other students ate popcorn. He started tutoring Philo, coming in early and leaving late.

stimulated If something stimulated you, it made you feel full of ideas and enthusiasm.
crude If you describe something as crude, it means it is not exact or detailed but may be useful in a rough, general way.

40   One day Mr. Tolman passed by a study hall and heard loud talking. Philo's latest hero was Albert Einstein, with his controversial new theory of relativity. Now Philo stood at the front of the room, enthusiastically explaining it to his classmates, step by step.

41   Usually Philo spoke little, with a halting voice. But when he could share his knowledge of science, he was a different boy.

42   Philo had been aching to discuss the idea he'd gotten in the potato field with someone who might understand. One day he finally told Mr. Tolman. All over the blackboard, he drew diagrams of his television.

43   His teacher was boggled. Philo ripped a page out of the notebook he always kept in his shirt pocket. He scribbled a diagram of an all-electric camera, the kind of converter he envisioned. An Image Dissector, he called it.

44   Mr. Tolman pointed out that it would take a lot of money to build such a thing. The only way he could think of helping was to encourage Philo to go on to college. But Philo was forced to quit college at eighteen, after his father died. By then the family had moved back to Utah, to the town of Provo, and Philo supported them by working at all sorts of jobs in nearby Salt Lake City.

45   His favorite one was repairing radios. Though commercial radio broadcasts had started four years earlier, Philo couldn't believe, in 1924, how many people still hadn't heard one. On weekends he organized "radio parties" so his friends could gather around one of the bulky wooden cabinets and listen to the new stations.

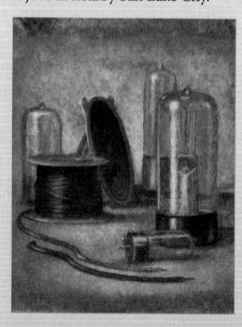

46   Pem Gardner, the girl next door, was interested in radio—and also in Philo.

47   Wasn't it funny, Philo remarked to Pem, how they liked to watch the radio even though there was nothing to see? Radio was such a fine way to bring folks together. And television, he sensed, would be even better. Thanks to his obsession with television, Philo had already lost one girlfriend, who called him too much of a dreamer. But Pem cheered him on. Now what he needed was money. He grew a mustache to look older, bought a new blue suit, and started to call himself Phil.

48   He met two California businessmen, and over dinner one night, he took them through a step-by-step explanation of his Image Dissector: a camera tube that would dissect an image into a stream of electrons, converting them into pulses of electrical current. A receiver would capture the current, then convert it back into points of light—the original image.

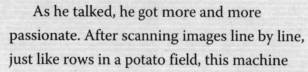

49   As he talked, he got more and more passionate. After scanning images line by line, just like rows in a potato field, this machine would beam them into homes. That was the best thing about television, he said—it would let families and whole communities share the same stories. By making people less ignorant of one another, he went on, it would teach and inspire. Maybe even lead to world peace.

50   The two businessmen exchanged looks, then agreed to put up $6,000 so Philo could build the first model. They gave him a year to make it work.

51   Philo hit upon a way to work twenty-four hours a day: he set himself problems to solve while sleeping.

52   He filed for several government patents that would protect his ideas for the next seventeen years. It was important to him to keep control, to get credit.

53   On their wedding night, he turned to Pem. "I have to tell you, there is another woman in my life—and her name is Television."

54   Pem helped out. Their first lab was their dining room table in Hollywood. Pem learned to use a precision welder to make tube elements—everything had to be built from scratch. When they needed a break, they went to one of the new talking movies.

> **dissect**   If you dissect something, you carefully cut it up to examine it scientifically.
>
> **precision**   When you do something with precision, you do it exactly the way it should be done.

55 Finally they got the lights, wires, and tubes to work in unison. But at the first demonstration, Philo forgot one item. He failed to take the power surge into account. The entire Image Dissector exploded. Pem, who took notes about everything, labeled this experiment "Bang! Pop! Sizzle!"

56 Still, Philo was able to find new investors, who gave him another year.

57   At his new lab in San Francisco, Philo met the deadline. In 1927, a small group of people watched as the first image in history flickered on a TV.

58   He said, "That's it, folks. We've done it— there you have electronic television."

59   That first image was not fancy. It was a straight line, blurry and bluish. Later he was able to show a dollar sign, and then the motion of cigarette smoke.

60   The first person to be televised was his true love, Pem, who didn't know she was on camera and had her eyes closed.

61   The following year, in front of a crowd of reporters, twenty-two-year-old Philo Farnsworth announced the invention of television.

62   That night he was behind the wheel of a borrowed car. He and Pem were heading home after catching a movie with another couple. They stopped to buy the *San Francisco Chronicle* from a newsboy. And there was a photo of Philo holding his invention. The article praised a "young genius" for creating a "revolutionary light machine."

63   Pem and his friends read it aloud, bouncing up and down, yelling. Philo was silent, but a big smile crossed his face.

64   He was a real inventor, like his heroes—someone who connected people, a shaper of the world to come. Thanks to him, the future would include **TV**.

> **revolutionary**   Revolutionary ideas involve great changes in the way that something is done or made.

Collaborative Discussion

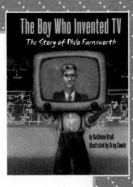

Look back at what you wrote on page 150. Tell a partner two things you learned from this text. Then work with a group to discuss the questions below. Refer to details and examples in *The Boy Who Invented TV* to explain your answers. Take notes for your responses. When you speak, use your notes.

1 Reread page 152. Many inventions mentioned in the reading are still used today, such as the radio and the telephone. How would your life be different if they didn't exist? Use details from the text to explain.

Listening Tip

Give your full attention to everyone in your group. Show you are listening by looking at the person speaking.

2 Reread pages 152–160. Why was Philo's life in Idaho better than his life in Utah? What was one important difference? Use examples from the reading.

Speaking Tip

Make sure to look at the other people in your group when you speak. Does anyone look confused? Invite that person to ask a question.

3 What characteristics did Philo have that helped him create the television? Use evidence from the text to support your response.

Write a List

In *The Boy Who Invented TV*, you read about the many things Philo Farnsworth did to become an inventor. How did he get his ideas? What individual behaviors, or habits, do you think helped him? Most inventors need money to get started on their work. Where did Philo get money for his invention?

Based on what you read in this selection, make a list of the five most important things an inventor can do to be successful.

Make a list of Philo's achievements, big and small. Then jot down a few reasons why each achievement happened. There may be information in the illustrations as well as the text.

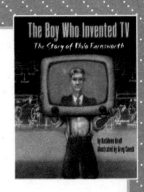

WRITE

Now write your list about the most important things an inventor can do to be successful, based on *The Boy Who Invented TV.*

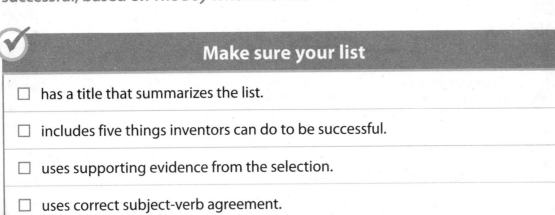

Make sure your list

☐ has a title that summarizes the list.
☐ includes five things inventors can do to be successful.
☐ uses supporting evidence from the selection.
☐ uses correct subject-verb agreement.

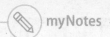
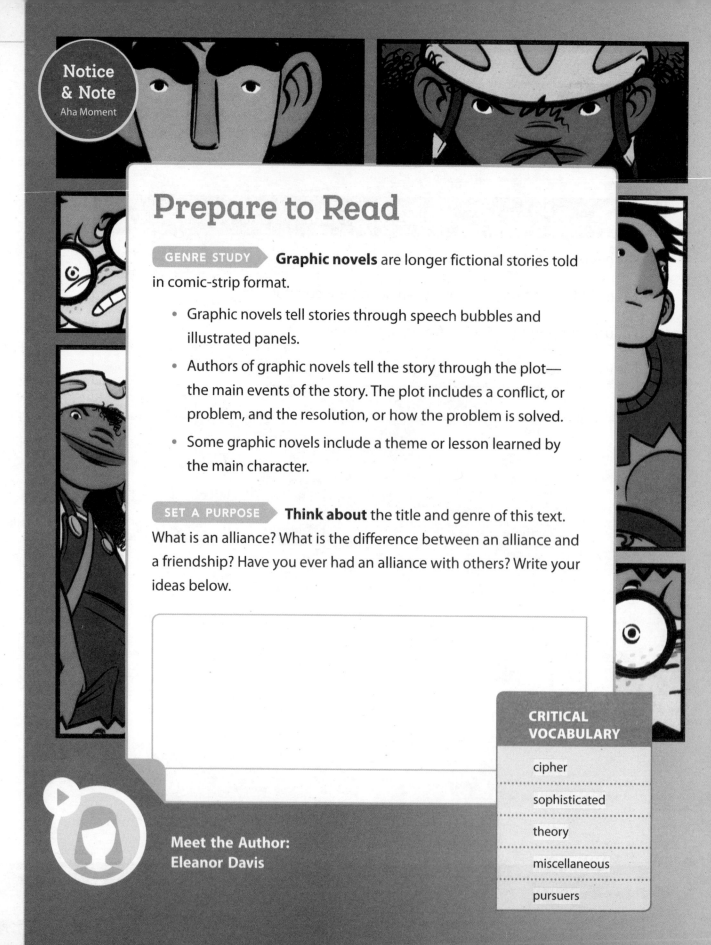

Notice & Note
Aha Moment

Prepare to Read

GENRE STUDY **Graphic novels** are longer fictional stories told in comic-strip format.

- Graphic novels tell stories through speech bubbles and illustrated panels.

- Authors of graphic novels tell the story through the plot—the main events of the story. The plot includes a conflict, or problem, and the resolution, or how the problem is solved.

- Some graphic novels include a theme or lesson learned by the main character.

SET A PURPOSE **Think about** the title and genre of this text. What is an alliance? What is the difference between an alliance and a friendship? Have you ever had an alliance with others? Write your ideas below.

Meet the Author:
Eleanor Davis

CRITICAL VOCABULARY

cipher

sophisticated

theory

miscellaneous

pursuers

Sixth-grader Julian Calendar has faced a lot of teasing because of his love for science and invention. So when Julian's family moves to a new city, he's excited to start over at a middle school where the other students don't know him as a nerd. Determined to fit in, Julian decides to keep his true interests a secret. But it's not long before a mysterious coded message leads Julian to a local diner, where he is soon outed as a science nerd. Worse yet, the classmates who discover Julian's secret are none other than basketball captain Ben Garza and his pal Greta Hughes—the scariest girl in school.

cipher   A cipher is a secret system of writing that you use to send messages.

sophisticated   A sophisticated machine or method is more complex than others.

theory The theory of a subject is the set of rules that form the basis of it. "String theory" is a theory in physics.

1) JULIAN 2) GRETA 3) ELEVATOR ACTIVATED BY GARAGE DOOR OPENERS 4) SHELVES RAISED AND LOWERED ON PULLEYS 5) MACHINING BENCH 6) CHOP SAW 7) DRILL PRESS 8) PULL-DOWN MAP OF THE CITY

9) LOFT WITH QUILT AND PILLOWS FOR RELAXING 10) WORK TABLE RAISED AND LOWERED ON PULLEYS 11) SPEAKING TUBE 12) STUFFED CROCODILE 13) COMPUTER 14) CHEMISTRY AREA 15) MINI FRIDGE 16) OXYACETYLENE RIG

17) BOXES OF MISCELLANEOUS PARTS   18) FISH TANK WITH JELLYFISH
19) CHALKBOARD   20) MICROSCOPE   21) ELECTRICAL CORD

22) TOOLS   23) VARIOUS ELECTRONICS TO SCAVENGE FOR PARTS
24) SCIENCE TEXTS AND COMICS   25) PERISCOPE TO SEE WHAT'S
ABOVE GROUND   26) CHAIR THAT CAN BE RAISED AND LOWERED
TO GET TO PERISCOPE   27) GLOBE   28) PINBALL MACHINE
29) PET TURTLES   30) BATHROOM

miscellaneous   A miscellaneous group is made up
of different types of things that are difficult to put into
one category.

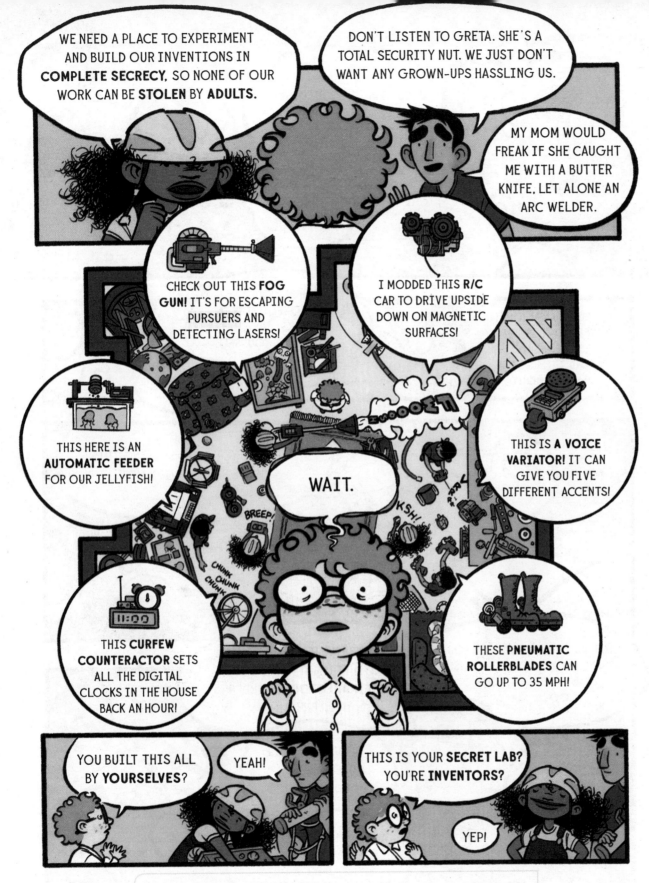

pursuers The people who are chasing or searching for you are your pursuers.

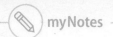

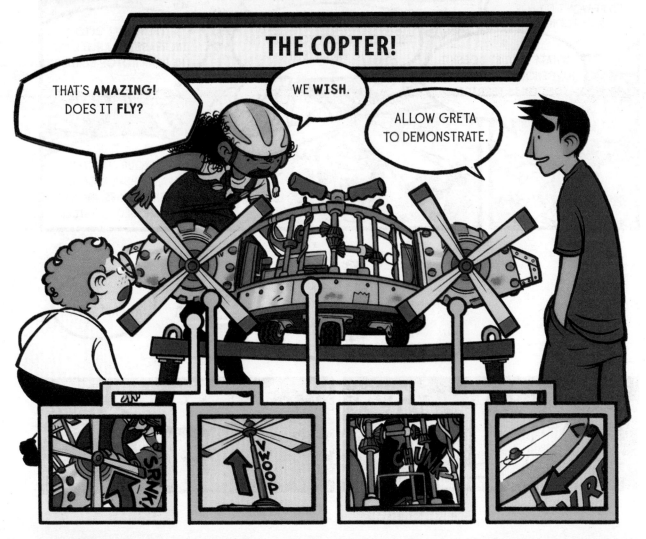

Collaborative Discussion

Look back at what you wrote on page 168. Tell a partner two things you learned from this text. Then work with a group to discuss the questions below. Refer to details and examples in *The Secret Science Alliance and the Copycat Crook* to explain your answers. Take notes for your responses. When you speak, use your notes.

1 In addition to the characters' facial expressions, body language, and dialogue, what helped you understand the story?

Listening Tip

Listen for specific details when the speaker is talking. What details or examples can you add?

2 Look at pages 176–177. Why did the author use numbers to label each item in the laboratory? How did this help you understand more about the laboratory?

Speaking Tip

Do you agree or disagree with what the speaker has said? Say so, and add your own ideas and opinions.

3 Why is Julian so surprised to learn that Greta and Ben are "secret scientists"? Does his opinion of them change?

Write a Letter

Imagine you go to school with Greta, Ben, and Julian from *The Secret Science Alliance and the Copycat Crook*. You like science and you want to join their Secret Science Alliance.

Write a short letter that explains why you want to join their Alliance and how your skills line up with what they need in a Secret Science Alliance member.

PLAN

Make notes about what qualities Greta and Ben admire in others and what skills they might need to help them invent things.

WRITE

Now write your letter about becoming a member of the Secret Science Alliance from *The Secret Science Alliance and the Copycat Crook.*

Make sure your letter
☐ includes a date and an opening that begins with *Dear*.
☐ states the purpose of the letter in the opening sentence.
☐ identifies skills that would make you a good member of the Secret Science Alliance.
☐ concludes by thanking the Alliance for its consideration of you as a new member.
☐ includes a closing, such as *Sincerely*, and your name.

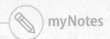

Prepare to Read and View

GENRE STUDY **Magazine articles** give information about a topic related to the publication's issue.

- Authors of magazine articles may organize their ideas by stating a problem and explaining its solution.

Lion Lights

Video Interviews present the point of view of real people on an event or topic.

- The people being interviewed can share their thoughts in a first-person voice.

SET A PURPOSE **Think about** the title and genre of this text and video. What do you think they will be about? How do you think the text and the video will differ? Write your ideas below.

Meet the Author:
Andrew Howley

CRITICAL VOCABULARY

households

livestock

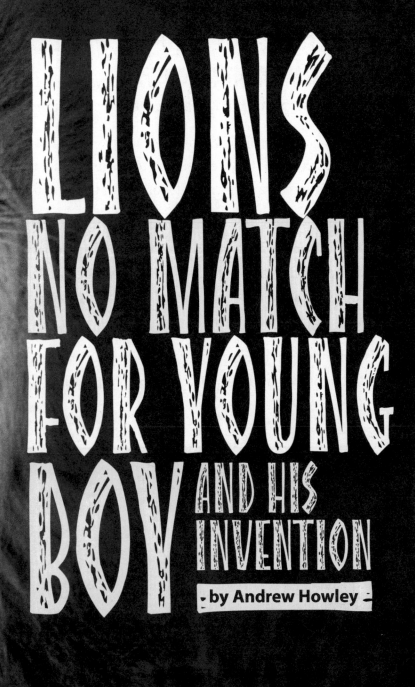

LIONS NO MATCH FOR YOUNG BOY AND HIS INVENTION

- by Andrew Howley -

1 **"AT THE AGE OF 6 TO 9, I WAS RESPONSIBLE FOR MY FATHER'S COWS,"** says Richard Turere. "And these lions were very annoying, because they were killing my father's cows."

2 Taking his responsibility seriously, Richard set out to find a solution. First, he tried fires, but the fires seemed to make it easier for the lions. Next he tried setting up a scarecrow. It worked for the first night, he said, "but lions are very clever."

3 Luckily, aside from learning the countless traditional whistle commands a Maasai herder can use to control his cows, Richard Turere also had a hobby of taking apart electronics (such as his mother's new radio), so he still had a few tricks to try.

4 Noticing the lions would stay away when he walked around with a flashlight, he had a new idea: moving lights. With a few simple wires and

Not only does Richard's invention protect his father's cattle from lions, it is now used across Kenya to protect livestock from lions, hyenas, and other predators — and to scare elephants away from cropland.

bulbs, he rigged up a series of flashing lights, and went to bed. Soon there were 7 households in his community using his "lion lights."

5 Now households across Kenya use lion lights and protect their livestock from predators and their crops from elephants.

6 As for the future, he says, "One year ago I was just a boy herding my father's cows. Now I want to be an engineer and pilot."

7 I asked him if he's worried the lions will figure out that moving lights do not necessarily mean someone is watching the cows.

8 "Maybe they'll figure out," he tells me. "But if they figure out, I'll get another way, because that's what I do."

> **household**   A household is all the people who live together in a house.
> **livestock**   Livestock are animals, such as cattle and sheep, which are kept on a farm.

191

Lion Lights

As you watch *Lion Lights*, notice the images as the narrator states some startling facts about lion populations. How do the images support or contrast with the narration? Write your ideas below.

In the video, you saw Richard's invention with a sign saying "100% effective" posted above the battery. What evidence did Richard give in this video to support that claim?

Collaborative Discussion

Lion Lights

Look back at what you wrote on page 188. Tell a partner two things you learned from this text and video. Then work with a group to discuss the questions below. Refer to details and examples in the text *Lions No Match for Young Boy and His Invention* and the video *Lion Lights* to explain your answers. Take notes for your responses. When you speak, use your notes.

1 What personal qualities help Richard succeed in creating his lion invention? Give examples from the article and the video.

Listening Tip

If you can't hear someone in your group easily, ask that person to speak a little louder.

2 How does the video appeal to viewers' emotions? Use details from the video to support your idea.

Speaking Tip

Make eye contact with group members as you speak to help you tell whether they understand your ideas.

3 The article and the video both conclude that it is important to preserve lion populations and prevent lion attacks on livestock. Do you agree with this conclusion? Why or why not?

Write an Advertisement

PROMPT

In *Lions No Match for Young Boy and His Invention* and *Lion Lights,* you learned that many communities in Kenya have lion problems. Lions kill farmers' livestock and then farmers kill lions to prevent the attacks.

Imagine you work for an online newspaper. Richard Turere wants to advertise his lion lights invention to other communities. Write an online advertisement that identifies the benefits of Richard's invention and persuades people to buy it.

PLAN

Make notes on the benefits of the lion lights invention. Identify details from the article and video that show how the invention helps both the lion population and the farmers.

Lion Lights

Now write your advertisement for the lion lights invention from *Lions No Match for Young Boy and His Invention* and *Lion Lights*.

Make sure your advertisement

- ☐ has a catchy sentence to get readers' attention.
- ☐ explains how the invention works.
- ☐ includes a visual that represents the invention.
- ☐ identifies how the invention benefits farmers and lion populations.
- ☐ uses persuasive language that encourages people to buy the invention.

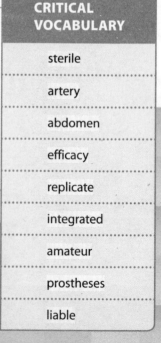

Prepare to Read

GENRE STUDY ▶ **Informational texts** give facts and examples about a topic.

- Authors of informational texts may organize their ideas using headings and subheadings. The headings and subheadings tell readers what the next section of text will be about.

- Informational texts include visuals, such as charts, diagrams, graphs, timelines, and maps. This article includes an infographic that helps readers understand how something is created on a 3D printer.

SET A PURPOSE ▶ **Think about** the title and genre of this text. What do you know about 3D printers? What can people make using 3D printers? Write your ideas below.

Build Background:
Computer-Aided Design

CRITICAL VOCABULARY
sterile
artery
abdomen
efficacy
replicate
integrated
amateur
prostheses
liable

3D Printing:
Imagination in Technology

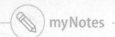

1 In a sterile operating room in a hospital at Sichuan University, in China, a rhesus monkey lay on a table. Around the animal, surgeons prepared for one of the most exciting operations of their lives.

2 With studied precision, the surgeons replaced a 2-centimeter segment of a damaged artery in the monkey's abdomen with a new blood vessel. The procedure was then repeated on a total of 30 monkeys. One month later, the monkeys were not only healthy, they were thriving.

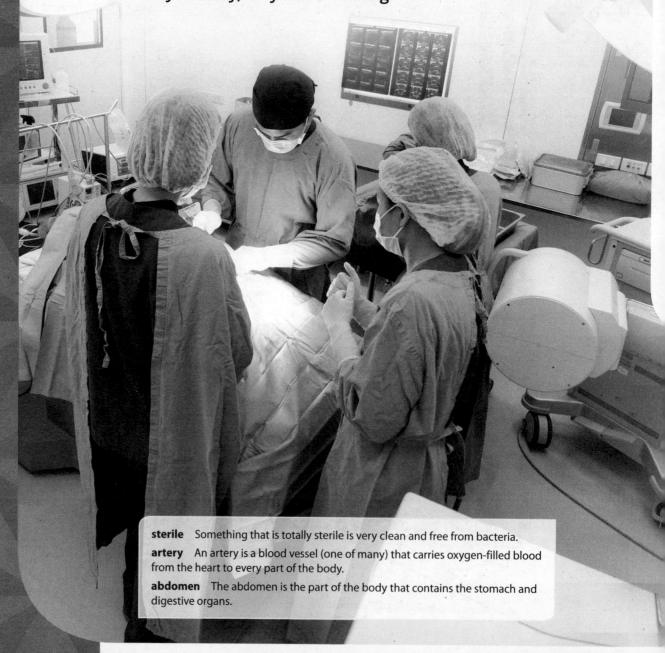

sterile Something that is totally sterile is very clean and free from bacteria.

artery An artery is a blood vessel (one of many) that carries oxygen-filled blood from the heart to every part of the body.

abdomen The abdomen is the part of the body that contains the stomach and digestive organs.

Life-Saving Technology

3 The operation was for research, to prove the efficacy of a new invention—blood vessels made on a 3D printer. The operation proved that this new invention worked just as well as natural arteries. Heart disease in humans is a major killer. If new blood vessels could be easily and cheaply printed, hospitals would not have to rely on hard-to-get and expensive live transplants.

4 Creating body parts with machines has long been a human fantasy. Today, thanks to 3D printing, researchers are working on ways to replicate blood vessels, skin, and other body parts that could revolutionize our ability to perform transplants and save lives.

5 Dr. Y. James Kang, the head researcher on this project at Sichuan University, presented his research on the monkeys to a packed house at a press conference. Dr. Kang and his group had launched the world's first 3D blood vessel bio-printer in 2015, and this was their first major success.

6 Dr. Kang explained how, once implanted, the 3D-printed blood vessels were integrated into the monkeys' bodies. After a month, no one could detect the difference between the parts of the vessel that were "original" and the part that was implanted.

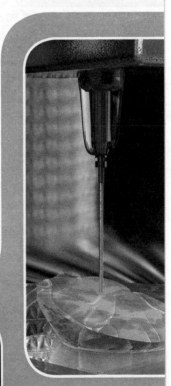

An artificial organ being printed by a 3D printer

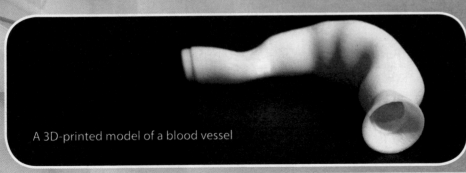

A 3D-printed model of a blood vessel

efficacy   The efficacy of something is its effectiveness and ability to do what it should.

replicate   If you replicate something, you do or make it in the exact same way as the original.

integrated   If you have integrated one thing with another, the two have been closely linked or form part of the same system.

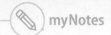
The Eureka Moment for 3D Printing

7 In 1983, on the night that 3D printing was invented, Chuck Hull called his wife at home from the lab where he was working. She changed out of her pajamas and came racing down to the lab.

8 Hull was excited because he had had a "eureka moment." He had been working for a small company in Germany that worked with ultraviolet light. In a lab, he was able to turn a liquid—made of acrylic—into a solid by using ultraviolet light. With careful planning, Hall was able to use this technique to create simple objects. He was the first person ever to make a 3D-printed object. Hull got a patent for his invention—at the time, called "stereolithography apparatus," or SLA.

9 Hull formed a company called 3D Systems in 1986, and was able to sell the first 3D printers starting in 1988. Other companies began to produce 3D printers as well, and scientists and engineers began to experiment with this new tool for creating objects.

This small plastic toy was created using a 3D printer.

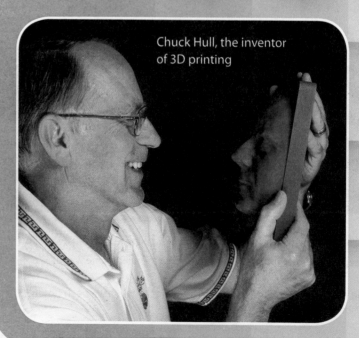

Chuck Hull, the inventor of 3D printing

The 3D Printing Industry

10 Since then, 3D printing has become a major industry. By 2020, analysts say that the companies making and selling 3D printer technology could earn up to $21 billion! This growth is driven by the increasing value in the use of 3D printing. Manufacturers of cars and medical equipment, for example, can now use a computer program and a 3D printer to cheaply print replacement parts for their machines. These parts, in the past, would have been made by complex, specially designed machines only available in a factory.

11 With a starting price for a 3D printer of only a few hundred dollars, many hobbyists, amateur inventors, and others are buying them for their own use.

Students make 3D-printed objects in a computer technology class.

amateur An amateur does something as a hobby and not as a job.

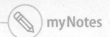

How 3D Printing Works

12 To print a three-dimensional object, the work starts on a computer. Three-dimensional computer-aided design programs, or CAD programs, have been used by engineers and architects since the 1970s. By the 1990s, three-dimensional CAD programs were available on desktop computers.

Plastic filament, below, is used for 3D printing.

13 There are several software programs that are available for free, and you can use models to tweak and combine shapes to create the object you want to make. For example, perhaps you want to create a model of an animal to use as part of a diorama for a science project. You design this model on the computer, then you send the design file to the printer. Check out the process at right to see how it works.

14 Most home-based 3D printers use a process called Molten Polymer Deposition (MPD). This means that plastic is melted (becoming "molten polymer"), pushed through a print head that looks somewhat like a needle, and then deposited on what's called a print bed in thin layers that are then built up to become an object.

15 In commercial 3D printing labs used by scientists and engineers, 3D printers can also use material like metal, plaster, ceramic, and even edible materials like pizza dough or chocolate.

A medical designer uses a CAD program to design orthopedics printed by a 3D printer (in the foreground).

3D Printing at Home in Three Steps

First, an object is designed using Computer-Aided Design (CAD) software.

1

2

Plastic filament (a spool of plastic "thread") is heated and pushed through the print head, or extruder, building up the shape of an object on the print bed.

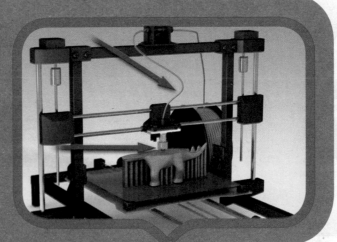

3

Within a short period of time, the printed object is complete. Home-based 3D printers can produce items made out of plastic that are the same quality as plastic building bricks.

3D Food

16 3D-printed food may sound a little odd—why would anyone want to make food on a 3D printer when we can grow food in the ground and cook it in our kitchens quite easily?

17 There are several reasons to make food with printers. NASA is constantly researching how we can use technology to help make astronauts' lives in space more efficient and pleasant. Food printed in space could help.

18 Also, even down here on Earth, some extremely fancy and complicated creations are actually easier to make with a machine than by hand.

A bowl of 3D-printed candy made from sugar and a single added flavor

The 3D Printing Pizza Maker

19   NASA contracted with a company in Austin, Texas, called BeeHex to invent a 3D printer that could make pizza. The printer uses a CAD file, like any other 3D printer, but instead of printing a plastic or metal object, the printer prints a custom-designed pizza. You can select the size, dough type, sauce, and toppings. After the printer prepares the pizza, it must be baked in a conventional oven.

20   One amazing feature of this pizza-making printer is that it can print the pizza in any shape that can be uploaded as a jpg file—a map of the U.S., a silhouette of your head—your imagination is the only limitation.

21   In 2032 when NASA plans to start the Mars mission, the pizza-making machine may join the astronauts on their journey to make the experience just a little more appealing.

A chocolate maker can make a 3D-printed chocolate that looks just like a customer—on demand!

Chocolate Printing

22   A company called Choc Edge Limited designs and manufactures 3D printers that can make objects out of—you guessed it—chocolate. High-end bakeries and restaurants buy these printers and create objects that amaze their customers. Chocolate spiders, flowers, words in 3D, and even portraits are possible with these amazing inventions.

3D-printed chocolate

Manufacturing Vehicles with 3D Printing Technology

23 In 1913, inventor Henry Ford installed a moving assembly line in his car factory. On the assembly line, each worker was responsible for making one unique part of each car. As the car frame moved down the line, workers added their pieces until the car was complete. This assembly-line method is still the way most cars are made today. Some car makers are trying to revolutionize car production with 3D printing.

A 3D-Printed Car

24 Local Motors, a company based in Phoenix, Arizona, designs and builds drones, vans, and 3D-printed cars. The Strati is the world's first 3D-printed vehicle, a small electric car built for a driver and one passenger.

25 The Strati is made entirely out of plastic. Besides being a relatively cheap material, plastic can be designed to be both strong and lightweight. It took about 40 hours to print the Strati, and materials for the entire vehicle cost a fraction of the cost of most traditionally produced cars.

The wheels of a 3D-printed car: the Strati

A 3D-printed car, the Strati, on display at the North American International Auto Show in Detroit, Michigan

A 3D-Printed Bicycle

26 A group of Dutch students, along with an Amsterdam-based company called MX3D, created a 3D-printed bicycle frame in 2016. MX3D's special printers have several arms that can eject metal and resin, a plastic substance, at the same time—in midair—which means that large objects—like a bike—are possible to make. Most 3D printers are only capable of making small items, which may then be fastened together. But this bike frame was made as one solid piece.

27 Upon completion, the students took the bike for a ride—it glided through the streets with ease. While this project was seen mostly as a way to demonstrate the MX3D printing process, the idea of being able to produce a custom bike is exciting for both athletes and anyone who depends on a bike for transportation, exercise, or leisure.

This Light Rider bicycle was printed using a 3D technique.

3D-Printed Prosthetics

28   Prosthetics are tools used by people who have lost—or have never had—a part of their body, such as an arm, a leg, or a hand. Using a prosthetic limb can help someone participate in activities that most people take for granted—walking, picking things up, drawing, or even playing sports.

29   It used to take weeks or even months to design prosthetics, and they have traditionally been very expensive, costing tens of thousands of dollars. For kids who need prosthetics, that's especially tough because they outgrow them every year, and active kids may accidently break their prosthetic. For people who live in countries without adequate medical care—they often have to go without.

30   3D printing technology has already begun to remove these barriers. The organization Enabling the Future connects universities and medical researchers who specialize in 3D printing technology with people around the world who need prosthetics. The prosthetic hands that they design—with fingers that can pinch and grab—cost less than a pair of shoes!

31   Beyond limbs, some people need prosthetic noses or ears. Because our faces are such an important part of our self-image, 3D imaging and printing professionals have worked extra hard to make facial prosthetics look as realistic as possible. Designers use 3D scanners to make sure they match the person's skin color, freckles, and wrinkles as closely as possible.

Noses and eyes can be printed with medical-grade silicone.

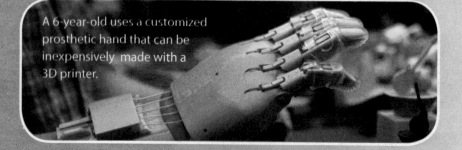

A 6-year-old uses a customized prosthetic hand that can be inexpensively made with a 3D printer.

prosthetics   Prosthetics are parts of the body that are artificial and are used to replace natural ones.

3D Printing's Ethical Issues

32 3D printing has so many exciting applications in all aspects of our lives, but there are a few drawbacks.

33 **Energy.** While the print-on-demand technology of 3D printers can be cheaper and more accessible, traditional manufacturing has the benefit of mass-production, which uses less energy per item.

34 **Copyright protection.** If a new toy cost $200, but you could design a knockoff on a home computer and print it yourself, would you? The way 3D printing could change manufacturing is similar to how music sharing on the Internet has changed the music industry. Piracy—using intellectual property without permission or payment—is a problem.

35 **Safety.** Who is responsible when someone is injured by a 3D-printed toy? Companies that sell toys are responsible for the safety of their products. But if you make the product yourself, you might be liable for any injuries that are caused by it.

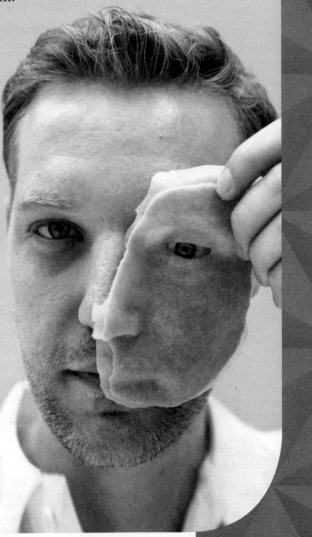

A 3D printing executive shows off a soft tissue prosthetic that someone with skin damage might use.

liable If you are liable for something, you are responsible or accountable for it.

The Future of 3D Printing

36   What's next? As 3D printing technology expands, we can expect to see more varied materials being used by printers. Besides plastics, metals, and food, scientists and engineers are beginning to experiment with medicines—mixed precisely and printed with a 3D printer.

37   What they will make depends on the creativity and skills of the engineers. Jennifer Lewis, a researcher at Harvard University, believes that 3D printing could ultimately save the lives of more than 220,000 people currently waiting for transplants through organ or kidney donations. However, developing any new technology or invention can take years of dedicated effort to ensure that the products are as safe and useful as possible. People depend on scientists to put in the work so that humanity can be rewarded, if not in one generation, then in the next.

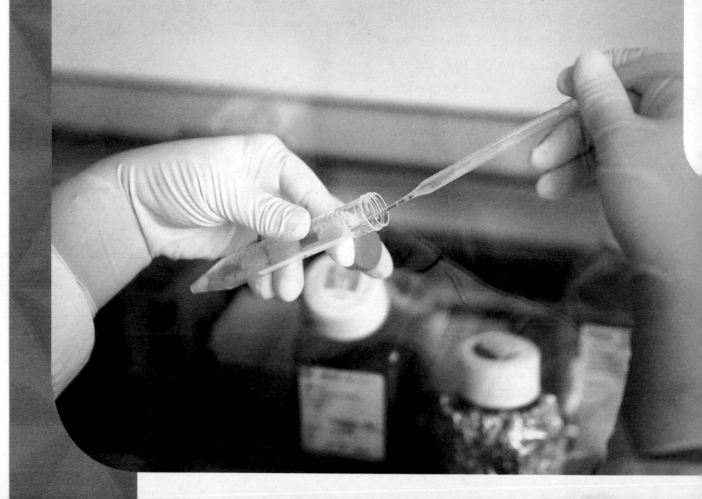

3D Printing: Imagination in Technology

Collaborative Discussion

Look back at what you wrote on page 196. Tell a partner two things you learned from this text. Then work with a group to discuss the questions below. Refer to details and examples in *3D Printing: Imagination in Technology* to explain your answers. Take notes for your responses. When you speak, use your notes.

1 Review page 199. The press conference was crowded when Dr. Kang presented the results of his research on the monkeys. Why were so many people interested in his work? Use text evidence in your response.

Listening Tip

Listen closely when the speaker is talking. Notice the information and details the speaker shares.

2 Look at the infographic on page 203. Why do you think this is included in the article?

Speaking Tip

When you share your ideas, make sure to speak clearly and at a pace that isn't too fast or slow.

3 What are the downsides to 3D printer technology? Use examples from the text.

Write a Project Proposal

PROMPT ....

In *3D Printing: Imagination in Technology* you read about how 3D printers are making everything from pizza to prosthetics.

Think of an everyday object you would like to print at home. Explain why having the object printed cheaply by a 3D printer would make your life better or more interesting.

PLAN ....

Think of an object that you would like to print. Then make a list of three to five ways that it would improve your life. Make notes about the advantages of using a 3D printer as described in the text.

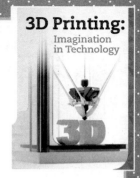

3D Printing:
Imagination
in Technology

Now write your project proposal about making a 3D-printed object, inspired by the article *3D Printing: Imagination in Technology*.

Make sure your project proposal

☐ opens with a proposal statement.
☐ gives facts and details about the object you want and how you will make it.
☐ explains the advantages of making the object with a 3D printer.
☐ uses transition words to connect your ideas.
☐ concludes with a summary of your proposal.

Essential Question

What inspires the most amazing inventions?

Write a News Report

PROMPT Think about what you learned about designing for the future in this module.

Imagine you are a television news reporter. Write a news report about how inventions change people's lives. Use evidence from the texts and video in this module to identify two or more inventions that affect the lives of people today. Be sure your news report includes what inspired the inventors to create their inventions.

I will write about _____.

✓ Make sure your news report
☐ provides an introduction that has an interesting hook and briefly explains the topic.
☐ identifies two or more inventions and explains how each affects people's lives.
☐ includes evidence about the inventions and what inspired their inventors to create them from the texts and videos.
☐ uses an appropriate tone for a spoken news report and includes transition words to connect ideas.
☐ concludes with a short statement or interesting question about the invention.

PLAN ········ **Gather information.**

What inventions will you write about? Look back at your notes, and revisit the texts and video as necessary.

In the top row of the chart below, write the names of two or more inventions that have changed people's lives. In the space below each invention, use evidence from the texts and video to write how each invention affects people's lives and what inspired the inventors.

My Topic: ______________________________

Invention	Evidence

DRAFT .... Write your news report.

Write an introduction that captures your audience's attention and clearly states the topic of the news report.

```



```

↓

For each **body paragraph,** use evidence from the texts and video to explain an invention that changed people's lives and what inspired the inventor to create it.

```



```

↓

For your **conclusion,** briefly summarize how these inventions are important to people's lives today.

```



```

REVISE AND EDIT .... Review your draft.

The revision and editing steps give you a chance to look carefully at your writing and make changes. Work with a partner to determine whether you have explained your ideas clearly to readers. Use these questions to help you evaluate and improve your article.

PURPOSE/ FOCUS	ORGANIZATION	EVIDENCE	LANGUAGE/ VOCABULARY	CONVENTIONS
☐ Does my news report explain how inventions affect people's lives? ☐ Did I provide information about two or more inventions?	☐ Will my introduction get a listener's attention? ☐ Does my conclusion summarize the importance of the inventions in people's lives?	☐ Did I use text evidence to explain how each invention affects people's lives and what inspired the inventors?	☐ Did I define scientific words in context?	☐ Have I used the correct spelling for *their, there,* and *they're*? ☐ Have I made sure that words with multiple meanings are used correctly?

PUBLISH .... Share your work.

Create a Finished Copy Make a final copy of your news report. You may wish to include an illustration or a chart. Consider these options to share your news report.

1. Publish your news report on your blog or social media.

2. Present your news report to your class like a television news reporter.

3. Submit your article to the school newspaper or a local paper.

On a Journey

"To get through the hardest journey
we need take only one step at a time,
but we must keep on stepping."

—Chinese Proverb

? Essential Question

How can a journey be more important than the destination?

Get Curious
Video

Words About Journeys

The words in the chart will help you talk and write about the selections in this module. Which words about journeys have you seen before? Which words are new to you?

Add to the Vocabulary Network on page 221 by writing synonyms, antonyms, and related words and phrases for each word about journeys.

After you read each selection in this module, come back to the Vocabulary Network and keep building it. Add more boxes if you need to.

WORD	MEANING	CONTEXT SENTENCE
passage (noun)	A passage is a journey by ship.	We booked a passage on a cruise to northern Europe.
craft (noun)	You can refer to a boat as a craft.	The sleek craft sails smoothly through the waves.
metropolitan (adjective)	If you describe a place as metropolitan, you mean that the place has the characteristics of a large city.	The streets of the metropolitan community were filled with people and towering skyscrapers.
destination (noun)	The destination is the place where you are going or are being sent.	Last year, we visited the twin Wailua waterfalls on Kauai, Hawaii, which is a popular tourist destination.

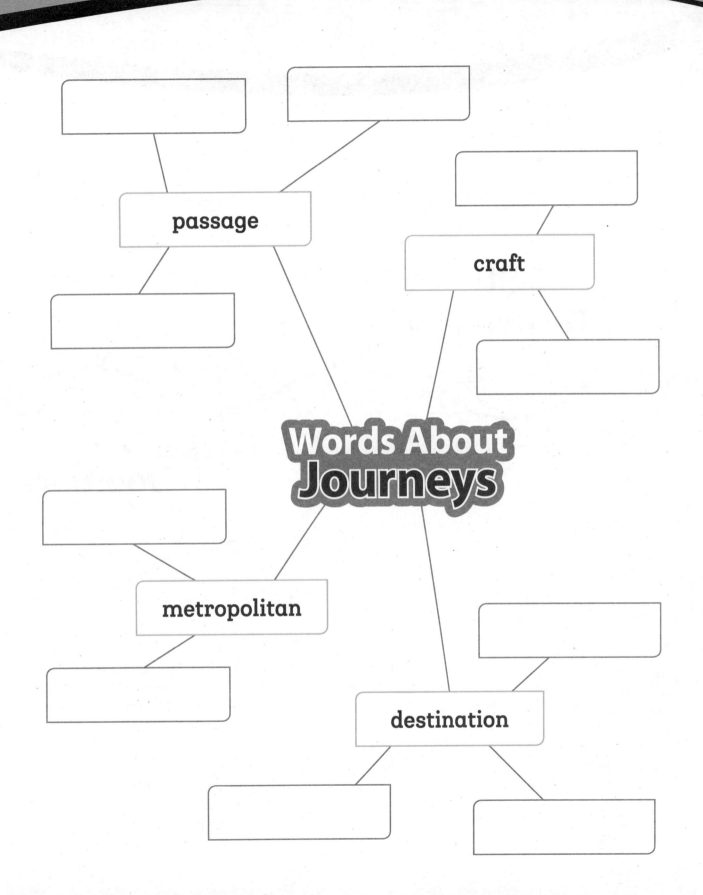

passage

craft

metropolitan

destination

Words About Journeys

Self-
Discovery

Journeys

Discoveries About the World

Travelers' Tales

The world of literature is filled with exciting journeys, and as a reader you get to travel along. This travel guide will acquaint you with the four amazing journeys you will read about in this module. Perhaps one day, you'll take an amazing journey, too!

The Wanderer
by Sharon Creech, page 227

Atlantic Ocean crossing from Connecticut to the coast of Ireland

Miles: 3,005

Flying Time: about 7 hours

Sailing Time: about one week by ocean liner

Crosshaven, Ireland

ATLANTIC OCEAN

Mystic Seaport, Connecticut

Most modern travelers fly across the Atlantic Ocean, but if you'd prefer, you can book passage on an ocean liner. If you're really adventurous, you can even captain your own small craft, like the characters in *The Wanderer*.

START Mystic Seaport, Connecticut
END Crosshaven, Ireland

Sacajawea
by Joseph Bruchac, page 263

Expedition from present-day North Dakota to Pacific Ocean, on foot

Miles: about 1,400

Flying Time: about 3 hours

Driving Time: about 21 hours

Walking Time: about 55 days, walking 8 hours per day

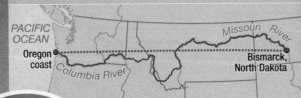

Shoshone guide Sacajawea lived in a small Native American village in present-day North Dakota when she joined American explorers Meriwether Lewis and William Clark in 1805 on their quest to find a waterway to the Pacific Ocean. Today, that village is part of a small metropolitan area near Bismarck, the capital city of North Dakota.

START present-day Bismarck, North Dakota
END The Oregon coast

Paul Revere's Ride
by Henry Wadsworth Longfellow, page 279

Urgent mission from Boston to Lexington, Massachusetts, on horseback

Miles: 18

Driving Time: about 30 minutes

Riding Time on Horseback: about 90 minutes

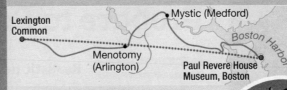

American patriot Paul Revere's famous 1775 ride from Boston's North End to Lexington was not long, but his mission—to warn his fellow patriots that the British were coming—was important.

START Boston's Paul Revere House museum
END Lexington Common

Jason and the Golden Fleece
Greek myth, page 245

Sea quest from Pelion, Thessaly, Greece to Colchis in Eurasia

Miles: about 1,300

Flying Time: about 2.5 hours

Sailing Time: about 6 days by yacht

Mythical hero Jason and his band of Argonauts embark on a quest to find the legendary Golden Fleece. To the ancient Greeks, the land of Colchis—Jason's destination—lay beyond the edge of the known world. Today, Colchis is the country of Georgia, where Europe and Asia meet.

START Mount Pelion, Greece
END present-day Georgia, in Eurasia

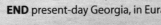

Notice & Note
Words of the Wiser

Prepare to Read

GENRE STUDY ▶ **Realistic fiction** tells a story about characters and events that are like those in real life.

- The events in realistic fiction build on each other to keep the plot moving forward.
- Realistic fiction includes characters who act, think, and speak like real people.
- Authors of realistic fiction may use sensory details and figurative language to develop the setting and the characters.

SET A PURPOSE ▶ **Think about** the title and genre of this text. How would you define the word *wanderer*? How do you think the word *wanderer* will be important to this story?

CRITICAL VOCABULARY

impulsive

motley

frets

slew

extensive

trial

scraggly

coordination

warping

**Meet the Author:
Sharon Creech**

THE WANDERER

by Sharon Creech
illustrated by Pepe Botella

1   So the story of *The Wanderer* is that the main character, Sophie, was in a boating accident with her parents as a young kid. They died; she survived and was eventually (at age 10) adopted. Now she's going on a trip across the Atlantic with her three (adoptive) uncles and two cousins. The cousins know she's adopted, but Sophie is weirdly in denial about it and talks about her adoptive parents and grandfather Bompie as though she's known them her whole life. This puzzles her cousins. What really happened is sort of a mystery that unfolds over the course of the novel.

THREE SIDES

SOPHIE

2 **I** am not always such a dreamy girl, listening to the sea calling me. My father calls me Three-sided Sophie: one side is dreamy and romantic; one is logical and down-to-earth; and the third side is hardheaded and impulsive. He says I am either in dreamland or earthland or mule-land, and if I ever get the three together, I'll be all set, though I wonder where I will be then. If I'm not in dreamland or earthland or mule-land, where will I be?

3 My father says my logical side is most like him, and the dreamy side most like my mother, which isn't entirely fair, I don't think. My father likes to think of himself as a logical man, but he is the one who pores over pictures of exotic lands and says things like "We should go on a safari!" and "We should zip through the air in a hot-air balloon!"

4 And although my mother is a weaver and spins silky cloths and wears flowing dresses, she is the one who gives me sailing textbooks and makes me study water safety and weather prediction and says things like "Yes, Sophie, I taught you to sail, but that doesn't mean I like the idea of you being out there alone on the water. I want you to stay home. Here. With me. Safe."

5 My father says he doesn't know who my hardheaded mule side resembles. He says mules don't run in the family.

6 I am thirteen, and I am going to sail across the ocean. Although I would like to go alone—*alone! alone! flying over the water!*—I'm not.

---

impulsive Someone who is impulsive does things without thinking about them carefully first.

My mule-self begged a place aboard a forty-five-foot sailboat with a motley crew: three uncles and two cousins. The uncles—Stew, Mo, and Dock—are my mother's brothers, and she told them, "If the slightest harm comes to my Sophie, I'll string you all up by your toes."

7   She isn't worried (although maybe she should be) about the influence of my cousin Brian—quiet, studious, serious Brian—but she frets over the bad habits I might learn from my other cousin, Cody. Cody is loud, impulsive, and charming in a way my mother does not trust. "He's *too* charming," she says, "in a dangerous sort of way."

8   My mother isn't the only person who is not thrilled for me to take this trip. My uncles Stew and Mo tried their best to talk me out of it. "It's going to be a bunch of us guys, doing guy things, and it wouldn't be a very pleasant place for a girl," and "Wouldn't you rather stay home, Sophie, where you could have a shower every day?" and "It's a lot of hard work," and yakkety-yak they went. But I was determined to go, and my mule-self kicked in, spouting a slew of sailing and weather terms, battering them over the head with all the things I'd learned in my sailing books, and with some things I'd made up, for good measure.

9   Uncle Dock—the good uncle, I call him, because he's the one who doesn't see any harm in my coming—said, "Heck, she knows more about boats than Brian and Cody put together," and so they caved in.

10   There are two other reasons my mother has not tied me to my bed and refused to let me go. The first is that Uncle Dock gave her an extensive list of the safety provisions aboard the boat, which include a satellite navigator, the Global Positioning System. The second reason, not a very logical one, but one that somehow comforts my mother, is that Bompie is on the other side of the ocean. We will end up in Bompie's arms, and she wishes she could join us just for that moment.

---

motley   A motley group seems strange because its members are all very different from one another.

frets   Someone who frets about something worries about it.

slew   A slew is a lot of something.

extensive   Something that is extensive is far reaching or covers a wide range of details.

11   Bompie is my grandfather—my mother's father, and also Uncle Dock, Stew, and Mo's father—and he lived with my parents for many years. He is like a third parent and I love him because he is so like me. He is a man of three sides, like me, and he knows what I am thinking without my having to say it. He is a sweet man with a honey tongue and he is a teller of tales.

12   At the age of seventy-two, Bompie decided to go home. I thought he was already in his home, but what he meant by home was the place where he was born, and that place was "the rolling green hills of England."

13   My father was wrong about mules not running in the family. When Bompie decided to return to England, nothing was going to stop him. He made up his mind and that was that, and off he went.

14   Bye-bye, Bompie.

AFLOAT

SOPHIE

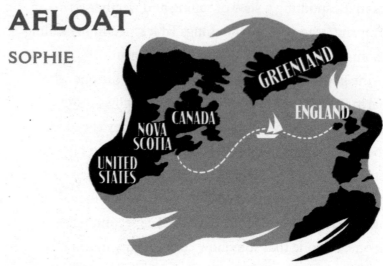

15   We have begun!

16   Last night, when we sailed by the stars along the Connecticut coastline on a trial run, I thought my heart would leap out into the sky. Overhead, all was velvety blue-black pierced with pearly stars and blending into shimmery black ocean. The smell of the sea, the feel of the wind on your face and your arms, the flapping of the sails—oh, it was magic!

> **trial**   When you take a trial run, you test or practice something before you actually do it.

17   We are really on the way! The sea is calling, calling, *Sail on, sail on!* and the gentle rocking of *The Wanderer* makes me think of Bompie— was it Bompie?—holding me on his lap when I was young, whispering stories into the air.

18   The first leg of our journey will take us through Long Island Sound to Block Island, and then a short hop on to Martha's Vineyard, a loop around Cape Cod and up the northern coast, and then on to Nova Scotia, and finally the long stretch to Ireland and to England, land of Bompie! Uncle Dock estimates that it will take us three to four weeks, depending on how long we stop when we spy land.

19   Cody is keeping a journal, too, only he calls it a *dog.* When I first heard him say that, I said, "You mean a *log*?"

20   He said, "No, a dog. A dog-log." He said he is keeping this dog-log because he has to, for a summer project. "It was either that or read five books," he said. "I figure it'll be a lot easier keeping a dog-log than reading all those words somebody else wrote."

21   Uncle Dock maintains the official captain's log, and in the front of it are neat maps that chart our journey. Uncle Stew and Brian said they'd be too busy "to record the highlights," and when I asked Uncle Mo if he was going to keep any sort of record of the trip, he yawned. "Oh," he said, tapping his head. "I'll keep it all in here. And maybe I'll sketch a few things."

22   "You mean draw? You can draw?"

23   "Don't sound so surprised," he said.

24   I *was* surprised, because it doesn't seem like he has the energy to do much of anything.

25   We all have daily chores (from Brian's list) and duty watches, and Uncle Stew came up with the idea that each of us has to teach something along the way.

26   "Like what?" Cody asked.

27   "Anything—navigating by instruments, by stars—"

28   "Right," Cody said. "Easy for you, but what if we don't know any of that stuff?"

29   "You must know something you could teach us," Uncle Stew said with a little smirk.

30   "How about juggling?" Cody said. "I could teach you all how to juggle."

31   "Juggle?" Brian said.

32   "Doofus," Cody's father said.

33   "I'd like to learn how to juggle," I said. "I bet it's not as easy as it looks."

34   "What's juggling got to do with anything?" Brian asked.

35   "Well, if you think it'd be too hard for you—" Cody said.

36   "Who said anything about hard? I could juggle. It just seems a stupid thing to learn on a boat."

37   I'm not sure yet what I could teach, but I'll think of something. We have to decide by tonight.

38   The weather is perfect today—sunny and warm—the current is with us, and the wind has been gently nudging us toward the hazy cliffs of Block Island. I've been to Block Island before, once, but I don't remember who it was with. My parents and grandfather? I remember walking on top of a big hill with lush purple and yellow flowers and scraggly brush growing around the rocks. And I remember the old blue pickup truck with lawn chairs in the back and riding along narrow lanes, staring out at the ocean and singing: "Oh, here we are on the Island of Block, in a big blue pickup truuuuuuck—"

39   My grandfather bought me a captain's cap, which I wore every day. We went clamming at night, and I scouted airplanes in the cottage loft. And every summer after that, I longed to return to Block Island, but we never did. There wasn't time.

40   I've thought of something I could teach my boat family: the stories that Bompie taught me.

41   Dock and Cody have just caught two bluefish. Success! But I didn't like watching Cody club and gut them. We're all going to have to do this, though. It's one of the rules. It's my turn next, and I don't want to do it.

42   But the bluffs of Block Island are in sight, and the bluefish is filleted for lunch, and I am hungry. . . .

---

scraggly   Something that is scraggly is messy or raggedy looking.

SLUGS AND BANANAS

CODY

43 **M**y father is driving me bananas. He lies around like a slug and doesn't help with anything and barks orders right and left. Sophie is lucky; she doesn't have any parents to bug her.

44 Uncle Stew said the only reason she's on this trip is because Uncle Dock took pity on the orphan. That's what Uncle Stew calls Sophie: the orphan. I want to slug him when he calls her that.

45 Sophie talks about my aunt and uncle as if they are her real parents, even though they are only her adopted parents and she's only been with them three years. Brian says Sophie lives in a dream world, but I think it's kind of neat that she does that. At least she isn't sitting around moping about being an orphan.

46 Sometimes I wish I were an orphan, because my father is a big crab and my mother is afraid of him and always hiding in the corner looking pitiful.

47 But I guess I'm not supposed to write about stuff like that in this dog-log. I guess I'm supposed to write about the journey and all that.

48 We started it. The journey, I mean. Amazing. I thought we were going to be stuck on land forever, what with Brian coming up with new lists every day. That boy sure likes to make lists. So does his father. They're a real list-making team.

49 Nothing is happening except that the boat is actually sailing and not leaking too much or tipping over. Yet.

JUGGLING

SOPHIE

50   **L**ater, we got our first juggling lesson from Cody. I thought he was a really good teacher, because he started out very simply, with just one thing to toss in the air. We were practicing with packets of pretzels.

51   "This is stupid," Brian said.

52   Uncle Mo was on watch, but he turned around to mutter, "Juggling. Geez."

53   Then Cody had us toss two pretzel packets in the air, one from each hand. That was easy, too. But when we added the third pretzel packet, we were all fumbling and clumsy. Pretzels went zinging over the side of the boat.

54   "It's all in the motion of your hands," Cody said. "Just get in a rhythm."

55   "This is really stupid," Brian said.

56   "It might help your coordination," Cody said.

57   "What's wrong with my coordination?"

58   It got ugly after that, so we stopped the juggling lesson.

59   Brian and Uncle Dock are going over the charts and trying to catch the weather forecast on the radio. Tomorrow we leave for Nova Scotia, a straight ocean sail that should take three or four days, with no sight of land. *No land!* I can't imagine it; I can't think what it will be like to see nothing but ocean, ocean all around.

60   "This will be our first big shakedown, yep," Uncle Dock said.

coordination   If you have good coordination, you are able to move smoothly and efficiently.

61   Uncle Stew tapped his fingers on the table. "Weather forecast doesn't sound too good."

62   "Aw, what's a little weather?" Uncle Mo said.

BLAH-BLAH-BLAH

CODY

63   Stupid day.

64   Stupid Brian was blah-blah-blahing about points of sail, as if he knows everything there is to know about everything.

65   He doesn't know how to juggle, that's for sure.

66   This morning, Brian said to me, "You like Sophie better than me, don't you?"

67   I said, "Yep."

68   Well. It's the truth.

69   Tomorrow Sophie is going to tell the first of Bompie's stories. Now, *that* ought to be interesting.

SHAKEDOWN

SOPHIE

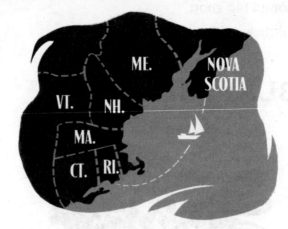

70   I'm not really sure what day it is anymore. These duty watches are warping my sense of time.

71   For the first couple days, there were two of us on a watch (I was paired with Uncle Dock), and we were on for four hours at a time, off for eight, then on for four more. Four hours is a lot, especially when it's dark, and every muscle in your body is tensed, listening, watching. Everyone else is asleep then and you know it's only the two of you keeping them safe.

72   Out here, there isn't day and night and then a new day. Instead, there are degrees of light and dark, merging and changing. It's like one long stream of time unfolding in front of you, all around you. There isn't really a *yesterday* or *day before*, which is weird, because then what is *tomorrow*? And what is *last week* or *last year*? And if there is no yesterday or last year—or ten years ago—then it must be all now, one huge big present thing.

73   This makes me feel very strange, as if I could say, "Now I am four," and by saying so, I could be four again. But that can't be. Not really. Can it?

74   We've been sailing up through the Gulf of Maine, toward Grand Manan Island in the Bay of Fundy, just west of Nova Scotia. Uncle Dock calls the wind "a capricious lady" because it comes in fits and starts. Yesterday (I still have to use words like *yesterday*, because I don't

---

warping   If something is warping something, it is distorting it or twisting it out of shape.

know how else to talk about things that happened *before*), when we had a spell of fog, Uncle Dock recited a poem about fog creeping along on little cat feet, and as soon as he said that, that's what I saw when I looked out into the gray mist: hundreds of little cat feet tiptoeing along. Later, when the fog rolled along in deeper, darker clumps, I imagined great big tiger feet loping toward us—soft, furry, graceful tiger feet.

75   I had a mournful lonely spell when I was on watch, peering through all that gray, and suddenly I didn't want to leave the shores of North America, to set off across the ocean, to be so far from land. But I didn't have long to be mournful, because the wind came up strong from the north, which meant we had to do a lot of tacking and heeling. The waves were huge—six to eight feet—or at least I thought they were huge, but Uncle Stew called them baby waves.

76   "You getting scared, Sophie?" Uncle Stew said, and it seemed as if he hoped I *was* scared, so I said, "No, I'm not a bit scared. Not the least bit." I *was* scared, but I didn't want him to know it.

77   Below deck, it was chaos. It was Cody's and my turn to cook lunch, and we had food sloshed all over the place.

78   "Mind the mizzen pot! Hoist the flibber-gibbet!" Cody shouted, as the pot's hot contents went sloshing over the side.

79   "Cody, are you *ever* serious?" I said.

80   He tossed a clamshell right in the soup. "Oh brother," he said, "sooner or later, everybody asks me that."

81   I guess it's a touchy subject.

82   *The Wanderer* has had a few problems on her shakedown: leaks in the aft cabin and water in the sump. We spend a lot of time crawling around looking for trouble and then trying to fix whatever's wrong. So far we've been able to plug all the leaks. You don't feel too worried when you know you can get to land within an hour or two if you have to, or where there is enough boat traffic so that you can hail help easily, but once we set off from Nova Scotia, what will we do if we spring a major leak?

83   I don't want to think about that. I'd rather think about the good omens: dolphins have visited us three times! They come in groups of four or five and swim alongside the boat. They usually come when we're sailing fast, whipping along. It's as if they're racing us. They play up in front of the bow, darting back and forth right below the water, only inches from the hull.

84   They're the most graceful creatures I've ever seen, gliding through the water without any apparent effort, and then arching at the surface and raising their fins and backs out of the water.

85   Cody calls them *darlings*. "Here, dolphin darlings! Over here!"

86   I always feel a little sad when they finally swim away and Cody calls, "Bye-bye, dolphin darlings! Bye-bye!"

87   We've changed the shifts around in order to have three people on watch through the fog (Cody's on with us now). Right now I'm bundled up in my foul-weather gear, watching the sun rise in front of us and the moon set at our stern. I'm tired and damp and desperately need a shower, but I am in heaven.

88   I'm learning so much every day, and the more I learn, the more I realize how much more there is to know about sailing and water and navigation and weather. Today Uncle Stew gave us a lesson in sextant readings. It's harder than I expected, and Uncle Stew and Brian keep scolding me and Cody, telling us we're not pulling our weight unless we learn how to do all this, because their lives might depend on the two of us.

89   "You'd better *hope* your lives don't depend on me and Sophie," Cody joked.

90   Uncle Stew got mad. "Not everything is funny, Cody, and when you're in the middle of that ocean, you'll be praying that if anything happens, everybody on board this boat will be capable of saving your hide. You could at least do the same for us."

91   "Yeah, yeah, yeah, I hear ya," Cody said, as he went below deck.

92   Even Uncle Dock seemed annoyed at Cody this time. "I sure hope that boy gets serious about something," he said.

93   I had a dream last night (or was it in the afternoon? or the morning? or the day before?) about being adrift in the ocean with no food, and we were all languishing on deck with no energy to do anything, and the boat was tossing and heaving around, and then a seagull flew overhead and landed on the boom and Brian said, "Kill it! Kill it!"

94   It's now about two in the afternoon, and the sun has broken through the clouds, and we're about thirty-six miles from Grand Manan. We're hoping to get there before dark. It's my watch now, so I'd better get busy.

BOMPIE AND THE CAR

CODY

95   Got yelled at for not understanding all the navigation gobbledygook. Got yelled at for joking around too much. Got yelled at for breathing. Well, almost.

96   Sophie told her first Bompie story today. It went something like this:

97   When Bompie was a young man, he lived on a farm, and his family was very poor. They didn't even have a car or a truck. But one day they traded two mules for a car. The only thing was, no one knew how to drive it. Bompie had ridden in cars, though, and he didn't think it could be all that hard to drive one. So Bompie volunteered to go to town to pick up the car and drive it home.

98   It was raining, raining, raining. You should hear Sophie tell a story. She really gets into it. You can almost feel the rain on your head when she tells it. You can feel it, you can smell it. It's really something.

99   Anyway, Bompie goes to pick up the car and it's raining, raining, raining. He's driving home and he gets to the place where he has to cross the creek. There's no bridge or anything. When they'd walked that way, or ridden the mules, they'd always just waded across it.

100   So Bompie drives the car into the creek, but the water is rushing, rushing so fast, it's like a big wall of water coming down at him, and Bompie is yelling, "Hey! *Giddy-up!*" but the car won't *giddy-up*, and that wall of water turns the car over, and Bompie scrambles out and watches the new car float down the stream.

101   When Bompie finally got home, he got a scolding from his father and an apple pie from his mother.

102   "Why'd she give him an apple pie?" Brian asked Sophie.

103   "Because she was grateful that he was alive, that's why," Sophie said.

104   "So how do you know this story anyway?" Brian said.

105   "Hush up, Brian," Uncle Dock said.

106   But Sophie said, "Because Bompie *told* it to me, that's how I know it."

107   You could tell Brian wanted to say something else, but he didn't. No one did.

108   I was sitting there thinking about Bompie getting out of that car and his mother giving him an apple pie.

109   Today Sophie and Uncle Dock each juggled three pretzel packets for a couple minutes! They were so excited. I felt pretty good myself. I'm a teacher!

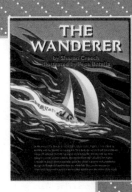

Collaborative Discussion

Look back at what you wrote on page 226. Tell a partner two things about the characters or events in the story that surprised you. Then work with a group to discuss the questions below. Refer to details and examples in *The Wanderer* to explain your answers. Take notes for your responses. When you speak, use your notes.

1 On page 237, how does Sophie's Uncle Dock describe the foggy weather? How does this description reflect on the events in the story?

2 On pages 239–240, we hear the first Bompie story through Cody's perspective, although Sophie is the one who tells it. How does this text structure help us learn about both Cody and Sophie?

3 On page 228, we learn about "Three-sided Sophie." So far in the story, do you think Sophie has been in dreamland, earthland, or mule-land, and why? Use examples from the text to support your answer.

Listening Tip

When a group member speaks, listen to the specific details that are said. Then think of other details you can add to the discussion.

Speaking Tip

When it is your turn to speak, build on what other speakers have said before you. If you agree with a previous speaker's ideas, say so.

Write a Postcard

PROMPT ....

After Sophie and her family set out on their journey, Sophie is enjoying the trip so much that she says, "I thought my heart would leap out into the sky."

Imagine that Sophie is able to send a postcard to Bompie. Write a short message for the postcard explaining what she has experienced, enjoyed, and learned about on the trip so far.

PLAN ....

List three things that Sophie has enjoyed seeing, doing, or learning on the journey so far. Refer to *The Wanderer* as you decide which details to include in your postcard.

WRITE

Now write your postcard from Sophie from *The Wanderer*.

✓	Make sure your postcard
☐	begins with a greeting to Bompie.
☐	includes descriptive details about what Sophie has enjoyed and learned on the trip so far.
☐	is written in the first person using pronouns such as *I, me,* and *we*.
☐	ends with a closing and Sophie's signature.

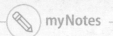

Notice & Note
Aha Moment

Prepare to Read

GENRE STUDY   A **play** is a story that can be performed for an audience.

- Plays begin with a cast of characters. The cast of characters lists each character and may include a brief description of the character's role.

- Authors of plays tell the story through the plot—the main events of the story. The plot includes a conflict, or problem, and the resolution, or how the problem is solved.

- The events in a play build on each other to keep the plot moving forward.

SET A PURPOSE   **Think about** the title and genre of this text. What do you think the Golden Fleece is? What can you predict about the characters and the plot of the play?

Meet the Author: Apollonius of Rhodes

CRITICAL VOCABULARY

usurped

banished

vanquished

disposal

mystifies

JASON
AND THE
GOLDEN
FLEECE

based on the ancient Greek epic poem
The Argonautica

BY APOLLONIUS OF RHODES

illustrated by Javier Olivares

ANTAEUS

KING PELIAS

KING AEETES

MEDEA

JASON

HERACLES

ATALANTA

CHARACTERS

STORYTELLER, the narrator

JASON, the leader of the Argonauts

KING PELIAS [PEEL•ee•us], Jason's uncle, who stole the throne from Jason's father

GUEST 1

GUEST 2

ATALANTA [at•uh•LAN•tuh], an Argonaut and a huntress

HERACLES [HAIR•uh•kleez], an Argonaut and a man of great strength and courage

ANTAEUS [an•TAY•us], an Argonaut and a half giant

KING AEETES [ee•YEE•teez], King of Colchis, owner of the Golden Fleece

MEDEA [muh•DEE•uh], daughter of King Aeetes and an enchantress

PROLOGUE

1   **Storyteller:** Long ago in Greece, there was a man named Aeson /**EE**•son/. He was the king of the city of Iolcus /ee•**UHL**•koose/. Unfortunately, his brother, Pelias, also wanted to be king, so he usurped the throne from Aeson. Fortunately, Aeson's wife, Alcimede /al•suh•**MEE**•dee/, was thinking ahead, and she sent away their son, Jason, so that King Pelias wouldn't get any ideas about killing the heir to the throne. (Well, Pelias probably *still* had ideas but at least this way he couldn't do anything about them.) Even though Pelias got what he wanted, he remained unsatisfied. Our tale starts when King Pelias is hosting a banquet, and when Jason arrives most unexpectedly, everything comes to a screeching halt.

SCENE 1

2   *A magnificent hall, laden with the finest food and drink.*

3   **Jason:** King Pelias! I demand your attention!

4   *Hundreds of people turn to look at the man who has interrupted the festivities.*

5   **Jason:** It is I, Jason, son of your brother, Aeson. Perhaps you remember him? He's the man from whom you stole the throne, thus depriving him and his wife—my mother—of *me*, their son. I have returned to claim the throne, sir, for it is rightly mine.

6   *King Pelias throws his head back and laughs, his drink sloshing out of his cup and onto his garments.*

7   **King Pelias:** Is that how you see things? I must say, I disagree, young man! Though I can tell you are who you say you are—I would recognize the face of my brother anywhere, especially on his son—I have been king of Iolcus for many years, and as you can imagine, I don't take kindly to a man arriving and laying claim to my throne. Since you fancy yourself fit to rule, tell me—what would you do if our positions were reversed?

8   *Jason thinks for a moment as the king's guests continue to stare. He hears their whispers and doubt begins to creep into his very soul . . .*

---

usurped   If someone usurped a job or position, he or she took it illegally or by force.

9   **GUEST 1:** Why should *he* be our king?

10   **GUEST 2:** What makes *him* worthy?

11   *But then Jason gets an idea, and doubt is* banished *as courage fills his heart.*

12   **JASON:** I would tell the man that he must perform an act of heroism, an act that requires courage and strength the likes of which the world has never seen. I would send him across the ocean to take the Golden Fleece from ruthless King Aeetes in Colchis, and demand that he bring it to me. A man who succeeds in such a quest is surely worthy to rule Iolcus.

13   **STORYTELLER:** I will interrupt here only to say that the Golden Fleece of which Jason speaks once belonged to a magical ram who rescued a man named Phrixus [**FRIK•**sis]—an ancestor of Jason's. King Aeetes killed the ram and hung its golden fleece in a grove guarded by a dragon. He believed he would lose his kingdom if he lost the fleece . . . but that is a story for another time. Back to King Pelias and Jason.

14   **KING PELIAS:** Any man who succeeds in acquiring the Golden Fleece from King Aeetes would indeed deserve the glory of a throne, Jason. So? Go, then. Bring it to me.

15   **JASON:** I shall, Uncle. And when I return—

16   **KING PELIAS:** Don't you mean "if"?

17   *King Pelias laughs, and his guests laugh along with him. As he lifts his glass to toast Jason, Jason opens his mouth to speak, then thinks better of it, and turns and leaves. The laughter of King Pelias trails after him. Jason is more determined than ever.*

SCENE 2

18   **STORYTELLER:** With the help of the famous shipbuilder Argus, and a touch of divine intervention from the goddess Athena, Jason builds a huge boat with 50 oars. Then he sends out a call throughout Greece for heroes to accompany him on his quest. Ancient Greece is full of heroes, and Jason

---

banished   If something is banished, it is chased away.

has his pick. Among many others, he chooses Heracles, an extremely strong man wielding a club (whom you may know as Hercules); Antaeus, a giant of a man carrying a huge axe; and Atalanta, an extremely fast runner and a famous huntress with a bow and arrow.

19 **JASON:** I thank you all for coming on this quest with me. It is time to take the throne from my traitorous uncle and restore it to me, its rightful heir.

20 *Atalanta raises her voice to be heard over the cheers of the heroes.*

21 **ATALANTA:** We are honored to be chosen for this noble endeavor, Jason!

22 **HERACLES:** Plus, some of us can't resist an impossible quest!

23 **ANTAEUS:** The more dangerous, the better!

24 **JASON:** Well, in that case, you're in luck. The object of our quest is the Golden Fleece, which sits atop a beautiful oak tree in a faraway land at the edge of the world, guarded by a fire-breathing dragon who never bothers to sleep. They say this dragon can reduce men to ash before they have time to scream in terror.

25 **HERACLES:** *(chuckling)* Who screams in terror over a dragon? *(Then:)* How strong is it?

26 **ATALANTA:** How fast can it move?

27 **ANTAEUS:** How big is it?

28 **JASON:** I don't know how strong, fast, or big the dragon is. But I warn you, friends. We are going to the edge of the world, beyond what is known. You may never see your beloved Greece or your families again. Our chances of survival are slim.

29 **ATALANTA:** "Slim" is not none. We are made for quests such as this!

30 *Jason laughs, and the heroes cheer again.*

31 **JASON:** Then let me introduce you to the magnificent vessel I have built.

32 **HERACLES:** She *is* a beautiful ship. The *Argo* is her name? I suppose that makes us Argonauts.

33 **ANTAEUS:** "Argonauts." Well said. When we succeed in our quest, we shall be known as the Argonauts throughout history!

34 *The Argonauts cheer again as they make their way onto the* Argo.

SCENE 3

35 **STORYTELLER:** It is a wild journey that takes the Argonauts across the Black Sea to Colchis. Along the way, they narrowly escape being crushed between the Symplegades /sim•PLEG•uh•deez/, two huge rocks rising up out of the ocean that delight in crushing ships that pass between them. After many days at sea, Jason and his Argonauts finally arrive at Colchis, the kingdom at the edge of the world. It is ruled by King Aeetes, who despises strangers. (Probably because they are always trying to take his Golden Fleece. Which is, of course, exactly what Jason and the Argonauts are trying to do.)

36 *Jason rises and stands at the front of the* Argo, *addressing the heroes.*

37 **JASON:** Argonauts! Colchis lies ahead!

38 **ATALANTA:** Let us now see what fate has in store for all of us.

39 **ANTAEUS:** Well we know one thing that's in store—a sleepless, fire-breathing dragon.

40 **ATALANTA:** If I didn't know you better, Antaeus, I'd think you were . . . concerned.

41 **HERACLES:** We were handpicked for this quest. If we can't secure the Golden Fleece, no one can.

42 **JASON:** We now embark on the most perilous part of our quest. If we succeed, we return to Iolcus where I shall be king—

43 **ATALANTA** *(quietly)*: If King Pelias is true to his word.

44 **JASON:** —and will handsomely reward you for your loyalty.

45 **HERACLES:** Return to Greece with the Golden Fleece, or perish with honor!

SCENE 4

46 *The* Argo *rests on the shores of Colchis as Jason and Heracles stand in front of the beautiful palace of King Aeetes, covered in vines and blooms, surrounded by fountains.*

47 **HERACLES:** *(in awe of the beauty)* Is that a fountain . . . of nectar?

48 **JASON:** I believe it is. And one of milk, and one of oil. This doesn't look like the palace of a ruthless king—perhaps this will not be the difficult task I originally thought.

49   **HERACLES:** Let us not be fooled by fountains and flowers, Jason. Not only is Aeetes ruthless, but so are his Colchians.

50   *Jason and Heracles enter the palace to see King Aeetes, an old man with a white beard and menace in his eyes. Next to him stands his daughter, Medea. As Medea looks at Jason, she is oddly overwhelmed.*

51   **MEDEA:** *(to herself)* That man . . . have I seen him before? There is something about him. I cannot tear my eyes away! I feel strange, and faint. Is this . . . love? That cannot be! I am not some foolish girl who falls for the first handsome stranger!

52   **STORYTELLER:** Medea is not wrong—she *is* a fierce, strong enchantress. But she has been enchanted herself. The gods have intervened to help Jason defeat King Aeetes by asking the goddess of love—Aphrodite—to make Medea fall in love with Jason on sight. For Medea, as you will soon see, has her own special talents, and will make a perfect ally for Jason.

53   **KING AEETES:** Who are *you*? What do you want? No, don't tell me. Let me guess. You are yet another stranger come to Colchis to steal what belongs to me.

54   **JASON:** King Aeetes. I am Jason, rightful king of Iolcus. My warriors—the Argonauts—are on your shores. And yes, I have come for the fleece, for procuring it is the only way I can claim my throne.

55   **KING AEETES:** You expect me to hand over my prized possession simply because you *want* it?

56   **JASON:** I am a descendant of Phrixus, King Aeetes. That fleece belongs in Greece.

57   *King Aeetes slowly approaches Jason. Heracles takes a step toward the menacing king to protect Jason, but Jason holds up a hand to stop him. Jason stands his ground as best he can. The king gets close—too close—and whispers:*

58   **KING AEETES:** Would you like to know, Descendant of Phrixus, what I do to men who arrive in my kingdom demanding my Golden Fleece?

59   *Medea steps forward, stepping between her father and Jason.*

60   **MEDEA:** Father, perhaps we might show these men some hospitality, or at least kindness? They have clearly traveled a long way.

61   *Medea turns her eyes to Jason, struggling not to feel faint at the very sight of him.*

62 **MEDEA:** Am I right, good sir?

63 **JASON:** You are. We *have* traveled a long way. And I am not demanding you give me anything, King Aeetes. Simply tell me what we can do to earn the Golden Fleece. Is there a land you'd like conquered? A people you'd like vanquished? My warriors and I are at your disposal.

64 *A hush falls over the court as the king stares at Jason with cold, calculating eyes. Medea tears her gaze away from Jason to take her father's hand.*

65 **MEDEA:** Surely there is something this man can do, some way to prove he is worthy of your greatest treasure.

66 **KING AEETES:** Perhaps there is. I have a trial in mind—it is something I myself do for sport. I have two bulls with bronze feet and breath of flame in my fields. I yoke the dangerous beasts and plow the field, planting not seeds but dragon's teeth from which grows an army in bronze armor with all manner of weapons. Then I fight and defeat them—all of them. If you can match me in bravery, I will hand over the fleece and you shall have your throne. If you cannot, Descendant of Phrixus, you and your men are mine to do with as I please.

67 *Medea's face grows pale at her father's pronouncement. She turns to Jason, who stares at the king, stunned.*

68 **MEDEA:** What do you say to this, Future King of Iolcus?

69 **JASON:** *(taking a deep breath)* I accept this trial.

70 **KING AEETES:** Go to your ship and rest. The trial is at dawn.

71 *Medea watches Jason go, her heart nearly breaking with the agony of what will surely be the man's death. She startles as her father declares:*

72 **KING AEETES:** Never will that man have what is mine. Never.

SCENE 5

73 *That night, Medea dreams, tossing and turning in the grip of a nightmare.*

74 **MEDEA:** No . . . Jason, do not attempt it, you will *die* . . . it is a task devised by my father to bring about your death! I will do it for you, and then we must flee Colchis!

75 *Medea bolts upright in bed in a cold sweat, wide awake.*

---

vanquished Vanquished means defeated.

disposal If you have something at your disposal, you can use it however and whenever you want.

76 **MEDEA:** Is this to be my fate? Am I to betray my family for this man I seem to love? I can think of nothing but how to help him, which goes against my father's wishes. And yet, I cannot seem to stop myself. I . . . I must protect him!

77 *Medea wraps herself in a hooded robe and goes to her door.*

SCENE 6

78 *On the* Argo, *Jason recounts the details of the trial to come. The Argonauts are not pleased.*

79 **ANTAEUS:** It is more of a death sentence than a trial.

80 **HERACLES:** Not with us by his side!

81 **ATALANTA:** Did King Aeetes not say that Jason must do this alone?

82 **JASON:** He did, and Heracles knows as much, though I appreciate the offer of help.

83 **HERACLES:** Then we must kill King Aeetes before the trial—

84 **ANTAEUS:** —and take the fleece ourselves.

85 **JASON:** No. I must do this with honor, and accomplish what he asks. But do not fear, Argonauts, for I believe we have the gods on our side.

86 *No sooner have the words left his mouth than a messenger in a hooded robe arrives on the ship. The Argonauts leap to their feet.*

87 **HERACLES:** Announce yourself!

88 *The messenger throws back the hood of her robe— it's Medea.*

89 **MEDEA:** I am here as a friend. May I speak with you, Jason? Alone?

90 **JASON:** Of course. I am eager to hear what you have to say, daughter of King Aeetes.

91 *Jason and Medea move away from the Argonauts. Medea takes a deep breath, trying to calm her nerves, for she is about to betray her blood.*

92 **MEDEA:** I must tell you that there is a prophecy regarding my father and his kingdom. If he loses the Golden Fleece, he loses Colchis. Therefore, he has given you a task designed to bring about your death, for he is a man who will stop at nothing to keep his power.

253

93 **JASON:** I am honored that you would bring me this information, especially since it means defying your father. You have a true heart.

94 *Jason smiles at her, and Medea nearly melts.*

95 **MEDEA:** The strength of my desire to help you overwhelms and mystifies me, Jason. But nonetheless, I have brought something to protect you in your trial. You must put this oil on your body as well as your sword and shield. Not only will you be protected from fire and hooves of bronze, but you will feel you could take on the very gods themselves. And when the bronze army rises from the ground, all you need to do is toss a boulder amongst them and the rest will take care of itself.

96 **JASON:** Medea, I hardly know how to thank you. Know that when we are back in Iolcus, you will be revered by all who reside there. For it will be thanks to you that the Argonauts and the Golden Fleece have safely returned home.

97 *Medea clasps Jason's hands, then pulls her hood up.*

98 **MEDEA:** I must return before I am discovered. Sleep well in the knowledge that you will be well protected tomorrow.

99 *Jason watches as Medea hurries off the* Argo *and disappears into the mist.*

SCENE 7

100 **STORYTELLER:** The next morning, an excited crowd of Colchians gathers to watch Jason's trial. King Aeetes, dressed in his finest armor, is accompanied by Medea. As she stands next to her father, she is wracked with guilt over the fact that she betrayed him. And yet even now, she is overwhelmed by love for the handsome stranger. As Medea is lost in her torment, Jason covers himself and his weapons with the oil she gave him.

101 **ATALANTA:** *(to Jason)* How do you feel? Is the oil working?

102 *Jason stands tall as the oil seeps into his skin. He begins to feel strength and courage rushing through his veins.*

103 **JASON:** It is indeed. I feel I could take on an entire army by myself and come out the victor!

104 **HERACLES:** I am glad of that, for that is exactly what you are about to do.

---

mystifies   If something mystifies you, you find it impossible to explain or understand.

105 *Across the field, King Aeetes turns to his daughter, unable to contain the wicked glee he feels.*

106 **KING AEETES:** Jason will be incinerated before the trial has even begun!

107 *At that instant, Jason cannot stop himself—with the battle cry of a great warrior, he rushes onto the field toward the bulls. They stamp and snort, fire shooting from their nostrils, bronze hooves kicking, horns aimed toward his heart. Jason easily withstands their attack, fending them off with his shield. The Argonauts leap to their feet to cheer.*

108 **ATALANTA/HERACLES/ANTAEUS:** For the throne of Iolcus!!!

109 *Jason grabs the bulls by their horns and brings them to their knees, quickly yoking them together. Then he guides the raging bulls across the field, forcing them to plow it for him.*

110 **KING AEETES:** How can this be?! **MEDEA:** I cannot say, Father. He is clearly . . . extraordinary.

111 **KING AEETES:** *(furious)* It is *luck*, not skill. And it will never hold. He can't possibly survive what comes next.

112 *As Jason drops the dragon's teeth into the plowed earth, an army begins to spring up from the ground and lunge forward to attack Jason.*

113 **KING AEETES:** Destroy him!

114 **MEDEA:** *(whispering to herself)* Jason, I beg you, do not forget what I told you—

115 *As if he could hear her, Jason picks up a boulder and throws it into the fray. The boulder crashes into the army, causing momentary confusion. Jason takes the opportunity to rush in and put an end to the bronze-covered enemy. A roar of anger rises from the Colchians, but it is no match for the cheers of the Argonauts. They run to Jason, pick him up, and carry him across the field on their shoulders. King Aeetes seethes.*

116 **KING AEETES:** This is not possible! This cannot be!

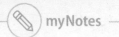

117 **MEDEA:** He has accomplished what you asked, Father. Now you must honor the terms of the trial and give him the Fleece.

118 *King Aeetes turns to his daughter, but she is not looking at him—she is staring at Jason. Suddenly everything becomes clear. Rage turns his eyes to fire as he grabs his daughter by the chin and forces her to look at him.*

119 **KING AEETES:** Though this was all quite entertaining, I think I will enact a new plan. I will keep my Golden Fleece, and kill Jason and every last one of his Argonauts. And perhaps, dearest daughter, you will perish along with them, for I scarcely doubt Jason could have accomplished this task without your help.

120 *With that, King Aeetes departs the field, leaving Medea breathless with terror over what will happen next. Her eyes turn back to Jason, and she knows what she must do.*

SCENE 8

121 *As the Argonauts celebrate, Medea approaches, trying to stay as calm as she possibly can.*

122 **MEDEA:** May I congratulate you on a victory well earned, Jason.

123 **JASON:** Thank you, Medea. And thank you for your help—without you, it would not have been possible.

124 *Jason notices that she is trembling.*

125 **JASON:** Are you all right? It seems perhaps you are not well.

126 **MEDEA:** I fear you may need my help yet again. It seems my father has no intention of honoring the agreement he made with you.

127 **HERACLES:** And this man calls himself a *king*?!

128 **ATALANTA:** He would not be the first ruler to have made promises he never intended to keep.

129 **MEDEA:** You must get the Fleece and leave before he kills you. *All* of you, and—

130 *The Argonauts grab their weapons, ready to hunt down and kill King Aeetes immediately.*

131 **JASON:** Hold! Let us hear what else Medea has to say!

132 *Medea prepares herself to say what she must say, torn between sorrow over the betrayal of her father and love for the man who stands before her.*

133 **MEDEA:** I can help you get the Fleece, but you must understand that my father now knows I have helped you, and I will have to flee Colchis or he will kill me, too. Will you take me with you to Iolcus, Jason?

134 *Jason takes Medea's trembling hands in front of the Argonauts.*

135 **JASON:** Medea, as thanks for all you have done for the kingdom of Iolcus, you shall be my queen, by my side as I take the throne. And even that will not be enough thanks for what you have done for my people!

136 *Tears of joy and sorrow stream down Medea's face.*

137 **MEDEA:** Then let us go now. There is no time to waste.

SCENE 9

138 **STORYTELLER:** Jason and Medea arrive at the sacred grove of oak trees where the Golden Fleece lies atop the tallest tree, glowing as if it were the sun itself. But no sooner does Jason lay eyes on it than the famed sleepless dragon unfurls itself from under the tree, spitting flame and emitting a roar that can be heard for miles. Terror strikes Jason's heart as the dragon snaps at him with massive jaws, wanting nothing more than to devour him whole. Jason claps his hands over his ears, sweat rolling down his face as flames shoot from the dragon's mouth.

139 **JASON:** Medea! How can we possibly tame this beast?!

140 **MEDEA:** I will show you! But stay back—move no closer!

141 *Medea falls to her knees and begins to sing a beautiful song. Slowly, the dragon's eyes close. It tries to fight the power of her song, its mouth opening and closing more and more slowly until it finally crashes to the ground in a deep sleep.*

142 **MEDEA:** Now, Jason! Now!

143 *Jason rushes to the magnificent oak tree, climbs it in a flash and grabs the Fleece. It glows in his hands, mesmerizing him before he shakes himself out of his reverie and drapes the long, heavy fleece over his shoulder. He takes Medea by the hand and dashes out of the grove, leading her to the Argo as fast as his feet will carry him.*

SCENE 10

144 *As Jason and Medea approach, the Argonauts cheer and shout, surrounding them, in awe of the gleaming fleece.*

145 **ATALANTA:** It is more luminous than I ever could have imagined!

146 **ANTAEUS:** Bright as the lightning of Zeus!

147 **HERACLES:** You've done it, Jason! The throne will be yours!

148 *The thunderous sound of an approaching army reaches their ears, and Jason looks back at the shore to see King Aeetes and his Colchians with torches and raised spears.*

149 **JASON:** Argonauts, the Colchians approach! Make haste!

150 **KING AEETES:** I have come for my Fleece, you thieves! And for my daughter!

151 *But the Colchians are no match for the speed of the Argonauts, who take to their oars and row like they have never rowed before. The Argo easily escapes the Colchians' spears, and Jason and the Argonauts are finally on their way back to Iolcus with their prize, and a new queen.*

EPILOGUE

152 **STORYTELLER:** You would think, wouldn't you, that the tale of *Jason and the Golden Fleece* has a happy ending? Alas, it does not. Although Jason—thanks entirely to Medea—succeeds in bringing the Golden Fleece back to Iolcus, King Pelias is as true to his word as King Aeetes was to his, and Jason's uncle has to be tricked into giving up his throne. But that is a tale for another time, my friends . . .

Collaborative Discussion

Look back at what you wrote on page 244. Tell a partner two things you learned from this play. Then work with a group to discuss the questions below. Refer to details and examples in *Jason and the Golden Fleece* to explain your answers. Take notes for your responses. When you speak, use your notes.

1 Once he becomes king, how do you think Jason will be similar to and different from King Aeetes? Use details from the play to support your opinion.

2 The gods cause Medea to fall in love with Jason and help him defeat King Aeetes. Do you think Medea's actions are helping or hurting her? Explain using evidence.

3 Where can you find foreshadowing, or hints at what will happen, in the play? How does this foreshadowing affect how you read the play?

Listening Tip

If you cannot hear a group member, politely ask that member to speak louder.

Speaking Tip

Be sure to speak clearly, at a comfortable pace, and loud enough for the entire group to hear you.

Write a Diary Entry

At the end of *Jason and the Golden Fleece*, King Aeetes has lost both the Golden Fleece and his daughter Medea. The prophecy that he will lose his kingdom without the Fleece is surely on his mind.

Imagine that the king keeps a diary. What might he write in his diary after he watches the *Argo* sail toward the horizon? Use details from the text to write a short diary entry for King Aeetes that describes his thoughts and feelings.

PLAN

Write down three details that are likely affecting King Aeetes' thoughts and feelings at the end of the play.

WRITE

Now write your diary entry for King Aeetes from *Jason and the Golden Fleece.*

Make sure your diary entry
☐   is written in the first person from the perspective of King Aeetes.
☐   includes details about events that have just happened.
☐   uses descriptive language to describe the king's thoughts and feelings.
☐   uses transition words to connect the king's ideas.

Prepare to Read

GENRE STUDY **Historical fiction** is a story that is set in a real time and place in the past.

- Authors of historical fiction tell the story in chronological order, or the order in which the events happened.
- Authors of historical fiction may use sensory details to develop the setting and the characters.
- Authors of historical fiction might tell the story through first-person point of view. In first-person point of view, a character in the story is the narrator. First-person pronouns include *I, me, my, mine*, and *we*.

SET A PURPOSE **Think about** the title and genre of this text. What do you know about Sacajawea? How do you think this text might blend fact and fiction?

Meet the Author:
Joseph Bruchac

CRITICAL VOCABULARY

descend

practicable

undertaking

expedition

civilized

Sacajawea

By Joseph Bruchac

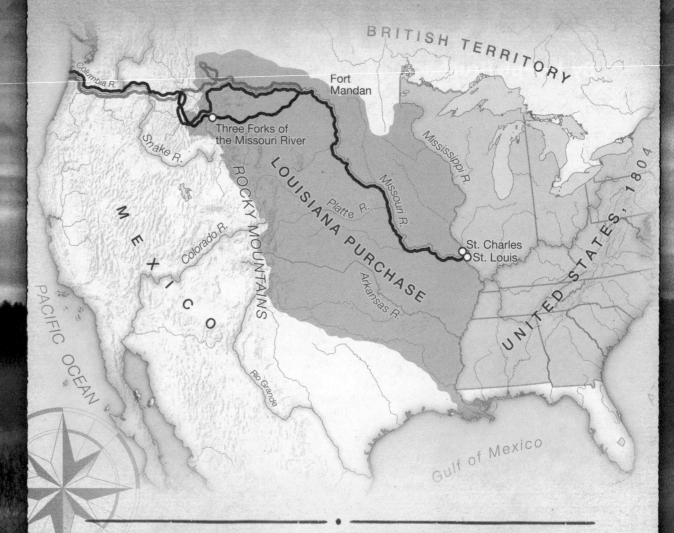

The Voyage of Lewis and Clark

BRITISH TERRITORY

UNITED STATES, 1804

Columbia R.

Fort Mandan

Snake R.

Three Forks of
the Missouri River

ROCKY MOUNTAINS

LOUISIANA PURCHASE

Mississippi R.

Missouri R.

Platte R.

St. Charles
St. Louis

MEXICO

Colorado R.

Arkansas R.

PACIFIC OCEAN

Rio Grande

Gulf of Mexico

MAP LEGEND

—— Lewis and Clark's Journey West

—— Lewis and Clark's Journey Home

—— Lewis's Return Route

—— Clark's Return Route

○ **Three Forks of the Missouri River—** *Sacajawea is captured, 1799.*

○ **St. Louis, MO—***Preparation for the expedition, 1803–1804.*

○ **St. Charles, MO—***Beginning of actual journey, May 21, 1804.*

○ **Fort Mandan, ND—***Lewis and Clark meet Charbonneau and Sacajawea, 1804. Jean Baptiste Charbonneau is born, February 11, 1805.*

Jean Baptiste Charbonneau

GREEN RIVER TRADERS' RENDEZVOUS, 1833

1   **M**y friends, as we gather around this fire, let me tell you a story. It is the story of how the worlds of the white men and the Indians came together. There is no one better to tell the story than I, Jean Baptiste, for I am of both worlds. I was there on that great journey. Now I am a man who has seen twenty-eight winters, but then I was a child.

2   It is a story of hard travels and many wonders, a story of bravery and kind deeds, of treachery and great danger, of strange men and even stranger places, of high mountains and rivers. It is a story of suffering and triumph.

3   I have been far since then. I have been to the schools of the white men, I have traveled to Europe, and I have made friends with kings and princes, guiding them to hunt the buffalo on the plains. I have ridden, too, by the side of war chiefs and shared the lodges of many Indian nations. Yet no kings or princes, no warriors or chiefs were ever better men than those who took me on that journey with them. Of all those who were part of that great adventure, there is one who was the bravest and best of them all. A great-hearted woman. Though she was little more than a child when it all began, she was the finest person I ever knew. That woman was my mother, Sacajawea.

4   But I cannot tell the whole of the story, for I was only a baby during those years. It is the custom of my mother's people, the Shoshones, that one can tell only what they have seen. When the Shoshones come to something they do not know, one who was there must tell the tale.

5   Those two voices who told that tale to me, my mother's and my uncle's, will now tell it to you. It is the shared telling of this story that is the beginning of my life. Now, brought back to life and breath are those voices, as I remember them in my heart. Here is my mother, Sacajawea. Here is my adopted uncle, Captain William Clark.

6   Listen. Here is our story.

William Clark
The Corps of Discovery

7   The first time we met your mother was November of 1804. At Fort Mandan, on the north bank of the Missouri River, just across from the lower Mandan village led by Big White and Little Raven.

8   Why were we there? I will tell you the tale, a bit of it at least, today. Maybe more tomorrow. It is the tale of the best group of men and the finest captain I have ever known, God rest my dear friend's soul. It is the story of the Corps of Discovery, and your mother's story, too. Her life was as much changed by our journey as our lives were changed, for the better, by knowing her.

9   For me it began when a letter written on June 19, 1803, came.

10   Who was it from? Right, indeed, lad. It was from Meriwether Lewis. Captain Lewis, by then. When I first met him, in 1795, he was an ensign on the Ohio frontier and under my command.

11   He served only six months in my Chosen Rifle Company, but in that time the two of us became as close friends as any two can ever be. When we parted company he clasped my hand with just as much warmth as I did his.

12   "Billy," he said, "one day we two shall do great things together."

13   Now, if another man said that, you might have laughed. But not when it was said by Meriwether Lewis. So I just nodded back to him, not knowing how true those words of his would prove to be. Then, almost eight years later, that letter arrived. It asked me to take part with him in an adventure. These words I know by heart:

14   "My plan," Captain Lewis wrote, "is to descend the Ohio River in a keeled boat, thence up the mouth of the Mississippi to the mouth of the Missouri, and up that river . . . to its source, and if practicable, pass over to the waters of the Columbia or Oregon River and by descending it reach the Western Ocean."

15   That plan, of course, came from Thomas Jefferson. Everyone knew that our new president longed to have the western part of the continent explored.

---

descend   To descend means to move from a higher point to a lower point.
practicable   A practicable plan is possible to carry out.

Captain Lewis had been taken on as the personal secretary to Jefferson several years before, so that Meri could be trained to lead just such an undertaking. Jefferson also had an abiding curiosity about all things scientific and human. So we were to make maps, observe latitude and longitude, and collect specimens and information wherever we went. Making contact with the various Indian nations was to be one of our primary objectives, as was the arranging of peace treaties among Indian nations.

16   Think of that, the boldness of it. We would cross the continent and be the first Americans to do it. That in itself was enough to make me as eager as a starved trout is to bite on a baited hook.

17   The best of the letter was at the end. Though this would be an enterprise with its share of fatigue, dangers, and honors, if there was anything that might induce me to participate, he said, "There is no man on earth with whom I should feel equal pleasure in sharing them as with yourself."

18   Not only that, we would share the command. Two captains together, striking out across the continent. I lost no time in writing back to my dear old companion.

19   "My friend," I told him, "I join you with hand and heart."

Sacajawea

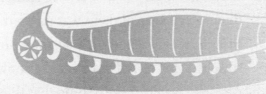

20   When did I first see the captains? I remember the first day we saw them. It was the Moon when the Leaves Fall from the Cottonwoods. Word had spread that their great boat filled with good things was still coming up the river. Word about their travels had spread like a fire across the dry autumn grass of the prairie.

21   Then, that day, a group of boys came running into Mitutanka, the lower village of the Mandans. We were there that day, my friend Otter Woman and I, along with your father, Charbonneau. He had brought us along to carry the things he was trading for.

undertaking   An undertaking is a large or difficult task or job.

22   "They are almost here," the boys shouted. "The boat with many guns is almost here."

23   All other things were forgotten. Everyone rushed to the river. Men and women, children and elders, even former captives such as myself and Otter Woman.

24   "Hurry up," Otter Woman said to me as we ran. "Are you too fat now to run?"

25   It was true. You were with me, Firstborn Son. Do you remember how I always talked to you, while you were growing and waiting till the day when you would take your first breath? I did so then.

26   People were lined up all along the river. They were shouting and waving at the men on the boats. The big boat was not as huge as some had said. Some had made it sound as if it was as big as a whole village, so large its sides would scrape the riverbanks on both sides. But it was still very big.

27   While some of the men pushed with big poles and others paddled, still more men stood holding rifles in their arms. Their faces were serious.

28   Even from the place on the bluff where we stood, we thought we could see who the most important ones were. There were three men who stood out from all the others because of their height and the way they carried themselves. One of them was painted black, or so we thought then, to show that he was their greatest warrior. The other two had hair that was a strange color, as red as paint. We could see by their hand gestures and the way they watched everything that they were the ones all the others listened to. Clearly, those two were the leaders.

29   Otter Woman and I raised our arms and called out to them, making those high ululating cries that our women make to call attention or give honor.

30   One of those two leaders did not look up. His face was serious, and he looked worried. Yes, that one was Captain Lewis. But the other man seemed to find it harder to be serious. His head lifted up and he saw us and his face opened into a smile that seemed to have as much light in it as the rising sun.

31   Do you remember what I said to you then, Firstborn Son? I spoke it in a low voice so that Otter Woman could not hear. "That is the one," I said to you. "That laughing man with the sun in his hair is the one we will follow."

William Clark
Making Peace

32   Let me continue with my tale of how we came to the Mandans. Suddenly, after no Indians at all, they were everywhere, on both sides of the river. Men and women alike, they shouted at us from the riverbanks, watched us from the high bluffs. They waved for us to come in. But we were careful. We did not know yet what these Mandans intended.

33   Soon the winter would be upon us and the waters would freeze. We could travel no farther. This was where we had planned to stay. But we needed to be safe while we lived there. One of our first thoughts was to build a strong fort so that we would be secure through the winter.

34   A French trader named Jessaume told us that another of the Frenchmen there had a wife who came from the Snake nation, far up the river. Those were the very people from whom we hoped to get horses. We were eager to make the acquaintance of that man, Charbonneau, and his wife. Such a woman who knew the land and the people would be of great use. Perhaps we could persuade her and her husband to accompany us when we resumed our journey.

35   *EDITOR'S NOTE: Lewis and Clark planned to travel westward. The Snake nation, also known as the Shoshone people, were Sacajawea's family. Sacajawea also knew the Minnetaree tribe, which captured her as a child and kept her as a slave until Charbonneau bought her and married her. Because of her expertise with those languages and the areas in which those tribes lived, her skills would be valuable to Lewis and Clark on their expedition.*

expedition   An expedition is a journey organized for a particular purpose, such as exploration.

William Clark

36   The day we chose to depart was Monday, April 7. At 4:00 P.M. we sent the keelboat back down the river. Your father and mother—and you, a baby held in your mother's arms—would be the only new additions to our Corps of Discovery.

37   Were we fearful before we set out up the river? Perhaps we might have been. The unknown lay ahead of us. All contact with the civilized world would now be left far behind. Should disaster overtake us, we might vanish into that great unmapped wilderness without a trace. Yet all we felt was excitement. There was perfect harmony and good understanding among us. Such harmony and understanding I have never seen again in any group like our small party of adventurers. My dear friend Meri felt just as I did. We were about to voyage into the unknown.

38   He grasped me by the shoulder as we stood watching our men ready the boats for our departure. We looked at our little fleet of six small canoes and the two large pirogues.

39   "Billy," he said with a smile, "behold our little fleet."

40   "Not quite as respectable as Columbus," said I.

41   "Nor Captain Cook," Meri replied with a laugh. "Think of it. We are about to penetrate into a country two thousand miles wide, on which the foot of civilized man has never trodden. All the good or evil it has in store for us is for experiment yet to determine. Those little vessels of ours contain every article by which we are to expect to subsist or defend ourselves. Yet I do believe we shall succeed."

42   "And I believe the same," I said, my smile as broad as his.

43   We took an early supper. That night we chose to sleep in a tent made in the Indian style, of the dressed skins of buffalo. Setting up the tent was your mother's responsibility, and she made it seem an easy one.

civilized   Something that is civilized is considered advanced in its development and customs.

I saw her do it many times in the months to come. The twelve poles raised and attached at the top in almost no time, other poles leaned in, the leather covering thrown over to make a cone. Inside that buffalo-skin lodge, your uncle Captain Lewis, George Drouillard, and I slept toward the front. At the back of the lodge, across the fire from us, were you, your father, and your mother. We were a little family within that lodge, and no man in our party ever showed anything less than perfect respect to your mother, though she was the only woman with us. Those sleeping arrangements were exactly as they would be for almost every night from then on until we reached the ocean.

44   The next day we set out very early. I was onboard the white pirogue, which carried our most precious things. In that white boat were our astronomical instruments, our best trade goods, our portable desks for writing, our medicines, much of our gunpowder, and all our journals and field notes. Six paddlers propelled us up the river. Yes, you and your father and your mother rode with me in that very boat. Captain Lewis was so restless to be on the way that he felt the need for exercise and walked along the shore that first day—as he would in many of the days to come. He reached our first destination well ahead of us.

45   We reached the point of land where he awaited us by noon. It had not been easy, for the wind had been hard against us. One of the small canoes had filled with water, ruining a quantity of biscuit and some thirty pounds of powder. This was a serious thing, though it proved our wisdom in packing the rest of our powder in tins that were watertight. Though there had been some difficulty, all in all that first day was a good one. We were on our way toward the undiscovered country.

Sacajawea
To Be of Use

46 Did I show them the way to go as we went up the Great Muddy River? No, Firstborn Son, how could I? Though I remembered well being stolen from my people at the Three Forks, those Minnetarees who took me did not come back to their village by boat. We came overland on horses. So after we passed the creek where your father had trapped beaver the year before, everything along the river was new to me.

47 But I was quick to show them how I could be of use to them, even before the time came for me to help them speak with our people. Their canoes and the two big boats were filled with wonderful things of all sorts. They carried with them provisions of different kinds, including salted meat and food that had been dried in preparation for a long journey. But they did not have enough food with them to feed more than twenty hungry mouths. They needed to hunt to survive.

48 The two captains were fine hunters. In those first days of travel their talk was often of the animals they had been told about but had not yet seen.

49 They talked especially about the One Who Walks Like a Man. That is how our people always speak of the great bear, my son. If you do not show respect to the bear, he will not respect you. So it was that I worried when I heard the captains talk with excitement about hunting the grizzly bear. I hoped they would remember to respect him. They had many guns and they were great hunters, but even great hunters find it hard to kill the Old One.

50   In the meantime, they brought in elk and buffalo, deer and beaver. It seemed a plentiful hunt, even though some of the animals were still skinny and tough from the long winter. I knew, though, that the time would come when hunting would not be enough. High in the mountains, where our people live, animals would not be as numerous as they were in the lands we passed through at first. One day we would leave behind the great herds of buffalo. There would come a time when any animal would be hard to find. That was why, every fall, our people would leave the safety of the mountains and go out on the plains to hunt the buffalo. Even though our enemies, the Blackfeet, might attack us there with their guns, we needed to hunt the buffalo and bring its meat back to our winter lodges. Without the buffalo hunt, we would not have had enough meat to survive until the spring run of salmon up the streams. Also, we women had learned long ago how to find food other than the animals the men hunt.

51   I kept my eyes open. There is always the chance of attack by enemies when you travel out of your own land. Though the captains never seemed fearful of such dangers, I was. I had your safety to think about as well as my own. Yet good fortune stayed by our sides. Day after day passed without even a single sign of an enemy.

52   I was watchful also for other things. On the second evening after we left the Mandan villages, I saw one of those things I had been looking for along the shore. There was a great pile of driftwood in a place where the earth seemed to be piled up on the bank of the river. I chose a strong driftwood stick of just the right size and began thrusting it into the soft earth.

53   Where were you then? Do you not remember? You were right there with me in your cradleboard.

54   Soon I broke through the roof of one of the granaries made by the harvester mice. It was stuffed with a great mound of the round white roots that are the size of a man's finger. Those roots have a sweet taste and the mice gather them in great numbers.

55   By then Captain Lewis was watching me with such care that I was certain he would make markings that night about what I had done. I had never seen men spend so much of their time making those markings in the little bundles of white leaves sewed together, which I later learned were called journals. Those journals, your good uncle explained to me, were as important to them as their own lives. Like the drawings on a winter count robe, the markings would help them and other men remember what they had seen and learned. It was strange to me, for I could see the pictures on a winter count robe clearly—the shapes of men and buffalo, of horses and lances. But all that I could see in the lines the two captains drew were shapes that made no sense to me. Yes, my wise son, I know that you are able to write such talking lines and understand what the talking lines made by others say to you. This is why your good uncle wishes you to stay with him. He wants you to know such powerful things as well as any white man.

56   I thanked the little harvester mice and gave them a present from my pouch. Then I filled the basket, making sure to leave some for the mice themselves, so that their own little ones would not starve. The captains and all the men were very pleased when they tasted those roots. Your father was as proud as if he had garnered those roots himself. He kept looking over at me and nodding. They ate all I had gathered and urged me to find more whenever I could. Then everyone sat around the fire, talking of that day's travel, and I sat with them. Captain Lewis's great dog, the one as large as a buffalo calf, came up and lay down beside me and then placed its head in my lap. I was happy that evening as I spread out our buffalo robe inside the tipi.

Collaborative Discussion

Look back at what you wrote on page 262. Tell a partner two things you learned about Sacajawea from this text. Then work with a group to discuss the questions below. Refer to details and examples in *Sacajawea* to explain your answers. Take notes for your responses. When you speak, use your notes.

1 Sacajawea and William Clark are real people who traveled together in the 1800s. How does this excerpt of *Sacajawea* show the features of historical fiction—instead of a biography?

Listening Tip

When group members speak, notice their facial expressions and gestures. This will help you understand their ideas better.

2 What does the text about Sacajawea and the mice's root harvest say about Sacajawea's character? What does it tell you about what might happen later in the story?

Speaking Tip

When you speak, notice your group members' facial expressions. If anyone looks confused, invite that person to ask a question.

3 Sacajawea and Clark are both narrators in *Sacajawea*. How do their two perspectives help you learn about the people and events involved with the expedition? Use examples from the text in your answer.

Write a Résumé

PROMPT

In *Sacajawea*, you learned about Sacajawea from the narrator, William Clark, and from Sacajawea herself. She has a strong character and many skills.

A résumé is a list describing a person's accomplishments, positive skills, and qualities. It can be used when applying for a job. Write a résumé for Sacajawea. What can she do? What are her personal qualities? Help others understand Sacajawea's many strengths.

PLAN

List five qualities and skills of Sacajawea. Support each quality or skill with evidence from the text.

WRITE

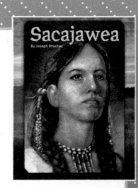

Now write a résumé for Sacajawea from *Sacajawea*.

Make sure your résumé
☐ includes a bullet point for each quality or skill.
☐ supports each quality or skill with text evidence.
☐ contains sentences that are specific and brief.
☐ lists information in a logical order.
☐ is written using a formal, professional tone.

Notice & Note
Again and Again

Prepare to Read and Listen

GENRE STUDY **Narrative poetry** tells a story in a poetic structure.

- Narrative poetry contains the elements of a story and uses poetic elements to help tell it. For example, rhythm might be used to build suspense, and stanzas might separate scenes.

Paul Revere's Ride

An **audio recording of a poem** is the recorded reading of a poem that can add drama and emotion to the poem through changes in tone and emphasized words.

SET A PURPOSE **Think about** the title and genre of this text and recording. Look at the illustration on the next page. Why might a midnight horseback ride inspire a poet? Write your ideas below.

Meet the Author:
Henry Wadsworth Longfellow

CRITICAL VOCABULARY
belfry
muster
rafters
tread
fleet
tranquil
skirt
peril

Paul Revere's Ride

by Henry Wadsworth Longfellow
illustrated by Martin Bustemante

1   Listen my children and you shall hear
    Of the midnight ride of Paul Revere,
    On the eighteenth of April, in Seventy-five;
    Hardly a man is now alive
    Who remembers that famous day and year.

2   He said to his friend, "If the British march
    By land or sea from the town to-night,
    Hang a lantern aloft in the belfry arch
    Of the North Church tower as a signal light,--
    One if by land, and two if by sea;
    And I on the opposite shore will be,
    Ready to ride and spread the alarm
    Through every Middlesex village and farm,
    For the country folk to be up and to arm."

3   Then he said "Good-night!" and with muffled oar
    Silently rowed to the Charlestown shore,
    Just as the moon rose over the bay,
    Where swinging wide at her moorings lay
    The Somerset, British man-of-war;
    A phantom ship, with each mast and spar
    Across the moon like a prison bar,
    And a huge black hulk, that was magnified
    By its own reflection in the tide.

4   Meanwhile, his friend through alley and street
    Wanders and watches, with eager ears,
    Till in the silence around him he hears
    The muster of men at the barrack door,
    The sound of arms, and the tramp of feet,
    And the measured tread of the grenadiers,
    Marching down to their boats on the shore.

> **belfry** A belfry is a bell tower, sometimes part of a church,
> where bells are housed.
>
> **muster** A muster is a formal gathering of soldiers, especially
> for inspection or exercise.

5   Then he climbed the tower of the Old North Church,
    By the wooden stairs, with stealthy tread,
    To the belfry chamber overhead,
    And startled the pigeons from their perch
    On the sombre rafters, that round him made
    Masses and moving shapes of shade,--
    By the trembling ladder, steep and tall,
    To the highest window in the wall,
    Where he paused to listen and look down
    A moment on the roofs of the town
    And the moonlight flowing over all.

6   Beneath, in the churchyard, lay the dead,
    In their night encampment on the hill,
    Wrapped in silence so deep and still
    That he could hear, like a sentinel's tread,
    The watchful night-wind, as it went
    Creeping along from tent to tent,
    And seeming to whisper, "All is well!"
    A moment only he feels the spell
    Of the place and the hour, and the secret dread
    Of the lonely belfry and the dead;
    For suddenly all his thoughts are bent
    On a shadowy something far away,
    Where the river widens to meet the bay,--
    A line of black that bends and floats
    On the rising tide like a bridge of boats.

7   Meanwhile, impatient to mount and ride,
    Booted and spurred, with a heavy stride
    On the opposite shore walked Paul Revere.
    Now he patted his horse's side,
    Now he gazed at the landscape far and near,
    Then, impetuous, stamped the earth,
    And turned and tightened his saddle girth;

rafters Rafters are the sloping pieces of wood that support a roof.
tread A tread is the sound of a person's footsteps.

But mostly he watched with eager search
The belfry tower of the Old North Church,
As it rose above the graves on the hill,
Lonely and spectral and sombre and still.
And lo! as he looks, on the belfry's height
A glimmer, and then a gleam of light!
He springs to the saddle, the bridle he turns,
But lingers and gazes, till full on his sight
A second lamp in the belfry burns.

8 A hurry of hoofs in a village street,
A shape in the moonlight, a bulk in the dark,
And beneath, from the pebbles, in passing, a spark
Struck out by a steed flying fearless and fleet;
That was all! And yet, through the gloom and the light,
The fate of a nation was riding that night;
And the spark struck out by that steed, in his flight,
Kindled the land into flame with its heat.
He has left the village and mounted the steep,
And beneath him, tranquil and broad and deep,
Is the Mystic, meeting the ocean tides;
And under the alders that skirt its edge,
Now soft on the sand, now loud on the ledge,
Is heard the tramp of his steed as he rides.

9 It was twelve by the village clock
When he crossed the bridge into Medford town.
He heard the crowing of the cock,
And the barking of the farmer's dog,
And felt the damp of the river fog,
That rises after the sun goes down.

10 It was one by the village clock,
When he galloped into Lexington.
He saw the gilded weathercock
Swim in the moonlight as he passed,

fleet When something is fleet, it is fast and nimble.
tranquil Something that is tranquil is calm and peaceful.
skirt Things that skirt an area form its border or edge.

282

And the meeting-house windows, black and bare,
Gaze at him with a spectral glare,
As if they already stood aghast
At the bloody work they would look upon.

11 It was two by the village clock,
When he came to the bridge in Concord town.
He heard the bleating of the flock,
And the twitter of birds among the trees,
And felt the breath of the morning breeze
Blowing over the meadow brown.
And one was safe and asleep in his bed
Who at the bridge would be first to fall,
Who that day would be lying dead,
Pierced by a British musket ball.

12 You know the rest. In the books you have read
How the British Regulars fired and fled,--
How the farmers gave them ball for ball,
From behind each fence and farmyard wall,
Chasing the redcoats down the lane,
Then crossing the fields to emerge again
Under the trees at the turn of the road,
And only pausing to fire and load.

13 So through the night rode Paul Revere;
And so through the night went his cry of alarm
To every Middlesex village and farm,--
A cry of defiance, and not of fear,
A voice in the darkness, a knock at the door,
And a word that shall echo for evermore!
For, borne on the night-wind of the Past,
Through all our history, to the last,
In the hour of darkness and peril and need,
The people will waken and listen to hear
The hurrying hoof-beats of that steed,
And the midnight message of Paul Revere.

> **peril** Peril is a state of risk or danger.

THE TRUE STORY OF

Revere's Ride

14 In the spring of 1775, Paul Revere was employed as an express rider to carry information from Boston to as far away as New York and Philadelphia.

15 On the evening of April 18, 1775, Paul Revere was given the task of riding to Lexington, Massachusetts, with the news that British troops were about to march into the countryside northwest of Boston. Supposedly, these troops planned to arrest patriots Samuel Adams and John Hancock, who were staying at a house in Lexington. The troops would probably continue on to Concord to capture or destroy military stores—

gunpowder, ammunition, and cannons—that had been stockpiled there. (In fact, the British troops had no orders to arrest anyone. Intelligence on this point was faulty.) Revere contacted a friend and instructed him to shine two lanterns in the tower of the Old North Church as a signal in case Revere was unable to leave town. The two lanterns meant that the British troops—called Regulars—planned to row "by sea" across the Charles River to Cambridge, rather than march "by land" out to Boston Neck.

16 Revere then stopped by his own house to pick up his boots and overcoat. He proceeded the short distance to Boston's North End waterfront where two friends waited to row him across the river to Charlestown. Slipping past a British warship in the darkness, Revere landed safely. He informed local Sons of Liberty about recent events in Boston and verified that they had seen his signals in the North Church tower. Then, Revere borrowed a horse from a Charlestown merchant. While the horse was being made ready, Revere was warned that there were British officers in the area who might try to intercept him. About eleven o'clock, Revere set off. After narrowly avoiding capture just outside of Charlestown, Revere changed his planned route. He rode

Paul Revere

through Medford, where he alarmed the captain of the local militia. He then alarmed almost all the houses from Medford through Menotomy (today's Arlington). He carefully avoided the Royall Mansion, because the owner was a well-known Loyalist—a colonist loyal to Great Britain. Revere arrived in Lexington sometime after midnight.

17   There, as Revere approached the house where Adams and Hancock were staying, a guard outside the house requested that he not make so much noise. "Noise!" cried Revere, "You'll have noise enough before long. The Regulars are coming out!" At this point, Revere still had difficulty gaining entry until, according to tradition, John Hancock, who was still awake, heard his voice and said, "Come in, Revere! We're not afraid of you." Revere was then allowed to enter the house and deliver his message.

18   About half past twelve, another messenger arrived in Lexington carrying the same message as Revere. After both men had "refreshed themselves" (gotten something to eat and drink), they decided to continue on to Concord, Massachusetts, to verify that the military stores had been properly dispersed and hidden away. A short distance outside of Lexington, they were overtaken by a fellow "high Son of Liberty." A short time later, a British patrol intercepted all three men. The two other men escaped; Revere was held for some time, questioned, and let go. Before he was released, however, his horse was confiscated to replace the tired mount of a British sergeant. Left alone on the road, Revere returned to Lexington on foot in time to witness the latter part of the battle on Lexington Green.

Paul Revere's Ride

As you listen to "Paul Revere's Ride," notice how the speaker's voice adds emotion and suspense to the poem. How does the speaker increase suspense? What do the special effects, like footsteps, add? How does listening to the recording help you understand the poem? Write your ideas below.

If you had to choose how to present this poem to younger students, would you have students read the poem or listen to the recording of the poem? Explain your thinking.

Collaborative Discussion

Look back at what you wrote on page 278. Describe to a partner two details of the poem that you found interesting. Then work with a group to discuss the questions below. Refer to details and examples in *Paul Revere's Ride* to explain your answers. Take notes for your responses. When you speak, use your notes.

1 The seventh stanza describes Paul Revere waiting for the signal and the moment when the signal appears. How does the poet create suspense and drama in those 16 lines?

 Listening Tip

Listen to the information a speaker chooses to share with the group. Do not volunteer your ideas until the speaker is finished.

2 The poet uses the phrase "It was ___ by the village clock" several times. What effect does this repetition have?

 Speaking Tip

When your group leader says it is your turn to speak, be sure to speak clearly and make eye contact with all your group members.

3 What did you learn about Paul Revere and his friend by the end of the poem? Use evidence from the poem to support your response.

Write a Super Short Story

In *Paul Revere's Ride*, Henry Wadsworth Longfellow describes the night Paul Revere warned people that British troops were coming. Longfellow uses poetic elements, such as rhyme, rhythm, imagery, and stanzas, to shape his narrative.

Imagine that you have just 30 seconds to retell these same events. Which details would you include? How would you maintain suspense? Write a super short story of Paul Revere's ride, and then time yourself reading it. Make sure you can finish within half a minute!

PLAN

Write down five details about Paul Revere's ride that you would like to include in your short story.

WRITE

Now write your short story based on *Paul Revere's Ride*.

Paul Revere's Ride

Make sure your short story:

☐ has a beginning, middle, and end.

☐ includes the characters of Paul Revere and his friend.

☐ tells the setting (where and when the events occur).

☐ has drama and suspense.

☐ places events in chronological order.

(?) **Essential Question**

How can a journey be more important than the destination?

Write a Narrative

PROMPT Think about what you learned about journeys in this module.

Help! The president's dog is lost! During a trip to South America, the dog ran away into the jungle. The president chooses two characters from two different texts in this module to find the dog and return it to Washington, DC.

Write a short narrative that identifies the characters, describes the skills each has, and tells the story of what happens when they first meet and make a plan for finding the dog. Draw on details from the texts as you decide how the characters will speak and interact with each other.

I will write a narrative about _____.

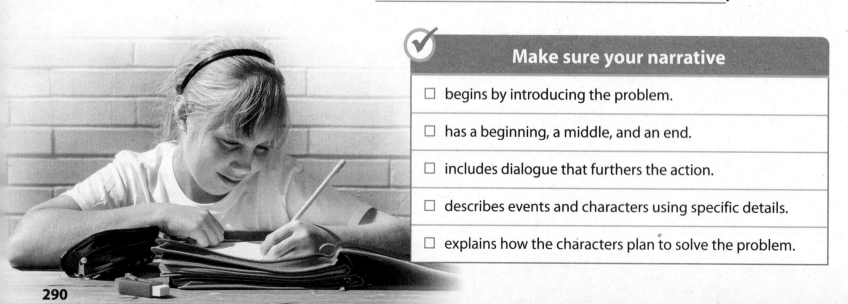

Make sure your narrative

☐ begins by introducing the problem.

☐ has a beginning, a middle, and an end.

☐ includes dialogue that furthers the action.

☐ describes events and characters using specific details.

☐ explains how the characters plan to solve the problem.

How will the characters behave in your narrative? Revisit the texts as you think about the characters' strengths and weaknesses, as well as how the characters will use their personal skills and experiences to find the missing dog.

In the story map below, outline the main parts of your narrative. Identify traits of the characters from two different texts and give details about how they plan to solve the problem. Record where and when these characters will first meet. Then write what will happen in the beginning, middle, and end of the narrative. Use Critical Vocabulary words where appropriate.

My narrative title: _____

Characters	
Problem	**Setting**
Beginning	
Middle	
End	

DRAFT ·· Write your narrative.

Write the **beginning** of your narrative. Introduce the president's problem and how the characters meet.

For the **middle** of your narrative, have the characters interact. Bring out their unique personalities as they get acquainted and form opinions of each other, as well as plan their dog rescue.

Write the **end** of your narrative. Show the characters setting out on their journey. You might also hint at the conflict or challenges to come!

REVISE AND EDIT · Review your draft.

The revision and editing steps give you a chance to look carefully at your writing and make changes. Work with a partner to determine whether you have explained your ideas clearly to readers. Use these questions to help you evaluate and improve your narrative.

✓ PURPOSE/ FOCUS	ORGANIZATION	EVIDENCE	LANGUAGE/ VOCABULARY	CONVENTIONS
☐ Does my narrative tell how the characters plan to solve a problem? ☐ Does my narrative include descriptive details about the characters' skills and traits?	☐ Does my narrative have a beginning, a middle, and an end? ☐ Are the events of my narrative told in chronological order?	☐ Did I use details from the texts to describe and develop my two main characters? ☐ Do my characters think and act like they did in their original texts?	☐ Did I use Critical Vocabulary words where appropriate? ☐ Did I use details to help the narrative's events come alive?	☐ Have I used proper spelling? ☐ Have I used quotation marks for dialogue?

PUBLISH · Share your work.

Create a Finished Copy Make a final copy of your narrative. You may wish to include an illustration. Consider these options to share your narrative.

1 Gather the narratives your class has written into an anthology, and place it in your classroom library.

2 Read your narrative aloud to students in a younger grade.

3 Publish your narrative on a class blog.

Good Times, Bad Times

"To some generations much is given.
Of other generations much is expected."

—Franklin Delano Roosevelt

Essential Question

What in our American spirit helps us survive tough times?

Get Curious
Video

Words About the Great Depression

The words in the chart will help you talk and write about the selections in this module. Which words about the Great Depression or U.S. history have you seen before? Which words are new to you?

Add to the Vocabulary Network on page 297 by writing synonyms, antonyms, and related words and phrases for each word about the Great Depression.

After you read each selection in this module, come back to the Vocabulary Network and keep building it. Add more boxes if you need to.

WORD	MEANING	CONTEXT SENTENCE
persisted (verb)	If something persists, it continues to exist.	We moved our picnic blanket, but the ants persisted in crawling toward our food.
industry (noun)	Industry is the work involved in the processing of raw materials and then making them into products in factories.	Almost everyone growing up in our small town had a job in the coal industry.
stocks (noun)	If you own stocks in a company, you are entitled to a share in the company's profits.	Dad checks the newspaper every day to see if the price of his stocks is increasing.
investors (noun)	Investors are people or organizations that buy stocks or shares to receive a profit.	In the 1980s, investors were excited to buy stocks in the new computer company that offered popular gaming systems.

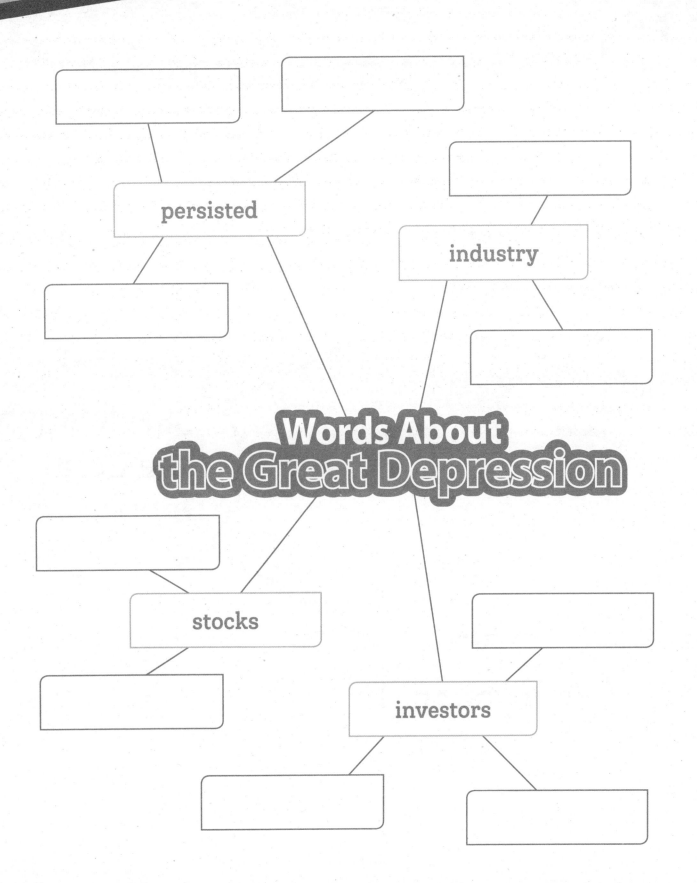

Words About the Great Depression

persisted

industry

stocks

investors

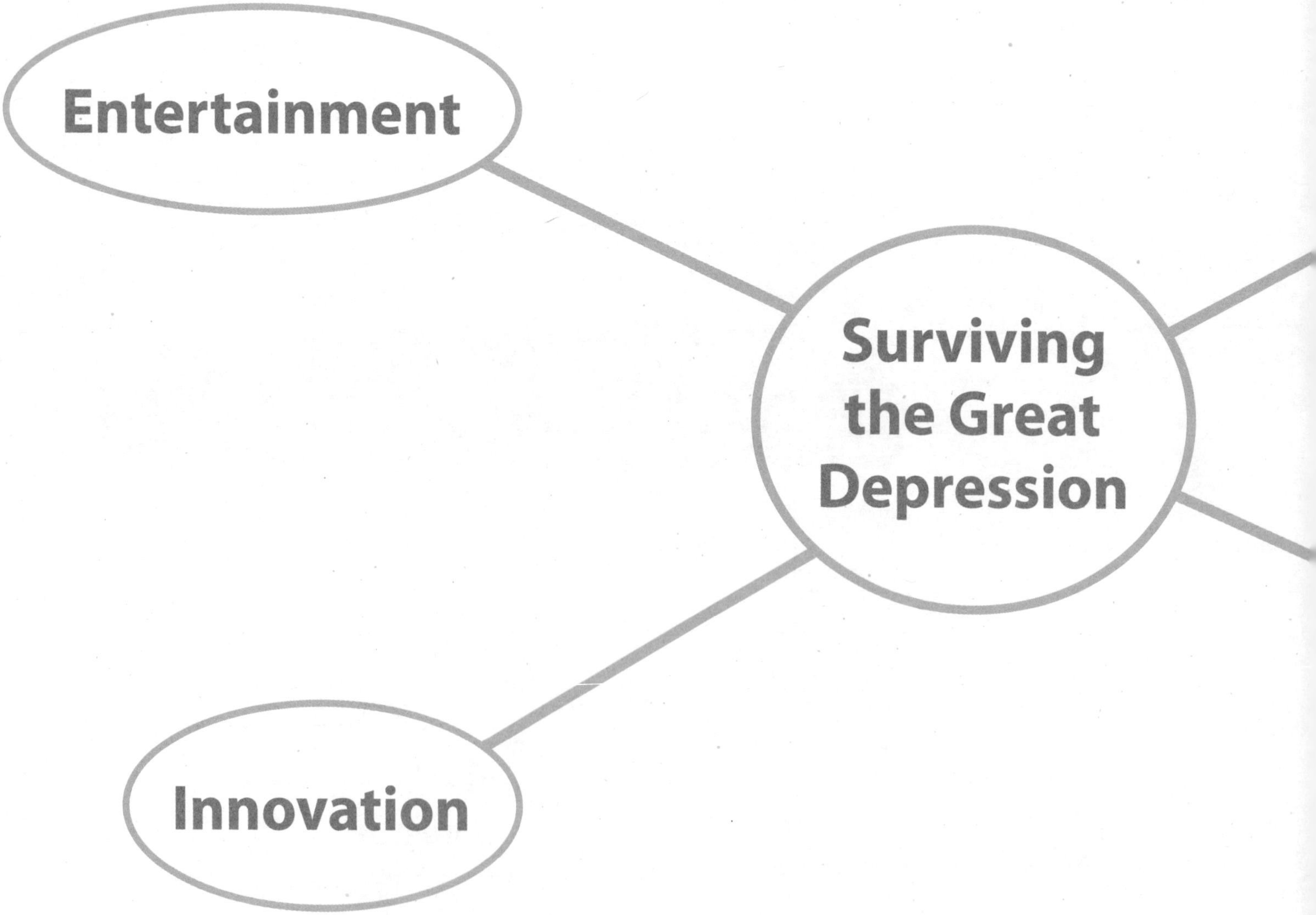

Entertainment

Surviving the Great Depression

Innovation

Work

Community

Short Read

A Crisis in History

The stock market crash of 1929 shocked the nation.

THE GREAT DEPRESSION
WAS THE WORST ECONOMIC CRISIS IN UNITED STATES HISTORY. IT BEGAN IN 1929 AND PERSISTED THROUGHOUT THE 1930s.

1 **Black Tuesday** The 1920s was an era of invention and industry in the United States. Millions of Americans invested in stocks—small ownership shares—in exciting new businesses. By 1929, the investment craze had driven stock prices much higher than their actual value. Then, on Tuesday, October 29, 1929, prices suddenly plummeted. They continued to drop as panicked investors raced to sell their stock. At its lowest point, the stock market lost 90 percent of its value. That was in 1932. A share of U.S. Steel once sold for $262. Now it sold for $22. Millions of investors lost everything they owned.

2 **A Perfect Storm** The Crash of 1929 was just one of several factors that combined to create the Great Depression. Others included the following:

3 **OVERPRODUCTION:** In the years before the crash, farms and factories had been producing more goods than people could buy. When the crash came, prices collapsed. Many farms and businesses failed, putting Americans out of work.

4 **BANK FAILURES:** In the wake of the crash, fearful customers lined up to withdraw their money from banks. (Many banks had invested in the stock market). Banks were unable to hand over so much money at once. About 11,000—more than half of all U.S. banks—failed nationwide. Millions of customers lost a total of one billion dollars in savings.

5 **DECREASED SPENDING:** As broke and wary consumers spent less money, businesses continued to fail.

6 **DROUGHT:** In addition to falling crop prices, farmers in the Plains region were hit with a series of severe droughts. These droughts persisted throughout the 1930s. Combined with over-farming and poor soil management, they led to massive dust storms that destroyed 100 million acres of farmland in southeastern Colorado, southwest Kansas, and

Photojournalists captured the struggles and joys of families living through the Great Depression. Left, a photo by Dorothea Lange, right, a photo by Gordon Parks.

the Texas and Oklahoma panhandles. This area became known as the Dust Bowl.

7 **A Country in Crisis** The effects of the Depression were dramatic. About 300,000 businesses closed. Unemployment skyrocketed from three percent before the crash to a peak of 25 percent. Family incomes dropped by 40 percent on average and hundreds of thousands lost their homes.

8 Millions of Dust Bowl residents abandoned their ruined farms and migrated west to start over. Many unemployed men, and some women, rode the rails across the country, seeking work. They were joined by approximately 250,000 teenagers hoping to ease the burden on their families. In cities, millions lined up for free meals at "soup kitchens." The homeless built tent camps in city parks.

9 **A New Deal for America** In 1932, Franklin Delano Roosevelt was elected president. Assuring Americans that he would "wage war against the emergency," he pushed through fifteen major laws during his first 100 days in office. The New Deal— Roosevelt's program to address the economic crisis— created new government offices and 40 new agencies.

10 The New Deal created jobs, fed and housed people in need, and placed new safety regulations on banks and the stock market. Still, the Great Depression would not fully come to an end until World War II began in 1939, putting businesses and people back to work manufacturing supplies for the war effort.

President Roosevelt speaks to the nation.

Notice & Note
Memory Moment

Prepare to Read

GENRE STUDY **Historical fiction** is a story that is set in a real time and place in the past.

- Authors of historical fiction tell the story through the plot—the main events of the story. The plot includes a conflict, or problem, and the resolution, or how the problem is solved.

- Historical fiction includes characters who act, think, and speak like real people from the past.

- Historical fiction might tell the story in a real setting from the past.

SET A PURPOSE **Think about** the title and genre of this text. *Bud, Not Buddy* takes place during a very difficult and unhappy time for many people in U.S. history known as the Great Depression. Many people lost their jobs, their money, and their homes. What challenges do you think children faced during this time? Write your ideas below.

Meet the Author:
Christopher Paul Curtis

CRITICAL VOCABULARY
foster
mission
considerate
tragedy
wringer
stricken
matrimonial
gait

BUD, Not BUDDY

by Christopher Paul Curtis

illustrated by Lisa Fields

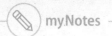

1   *It's 1936 in Flint, Michigan. Young Bud Caldwell has been alone in the world ever since his mother died. When Bud is sent to live with a foster family, his social worker assures him he should feel grateful. After all, there's a depression going on, and times are tough for everybody.*

2   *But Bud's new big "brother" is a nasty bully, so Bud strikes out on his own to find the father he's never met. As he pulls a blanket out of his suitcase and prepares to spend his first night "on the lam" hiding out under a pine tree, Bud decides his next stops will be a soup kitchen for free food, and the local library to consult with his favorite person in Flint—Miss Hill, the librarian. That's what Bud plans, but both stops get complicated . . .*

3   Right now I was too tired to think anymore so I closed my suitcase, put the proper knots back in the twine, crawled under the Christmas tree and wrapped myself in the blanket.

4   I'd have to wake up real early if I wanted to get to the mission in time for breakfast, if you were one minute late they wouldn't let you in for food.

5   Uh-oh. My eyes opened and I could see the sun behind the branch of a Christmas tree.

6   I jumped up, folded my blanket inside my suitcase, hid it and started running the six or seven blocks down to the mission.

> **foster**   Foster parents take a child into their family for a period of time.
> **mission**   A mission is an organization that helps people in need.

7   I turned the corner and said, "Whew!" There were still people lined up waiting. I started walking along the line. The end was a lot farther away than I thought. The line turned all the way around two corners, then crossed over one street before I saw the last person. Shucks. I walked up to get behind him.

8   He said, "Line's closed. These here folks are the last ones." He pointed at a man standing next to a woman who was carrying a baby.

9   I said, "But sir . . ."

10   He said, "But nothing. Line's closed. These here folks are the last ones."

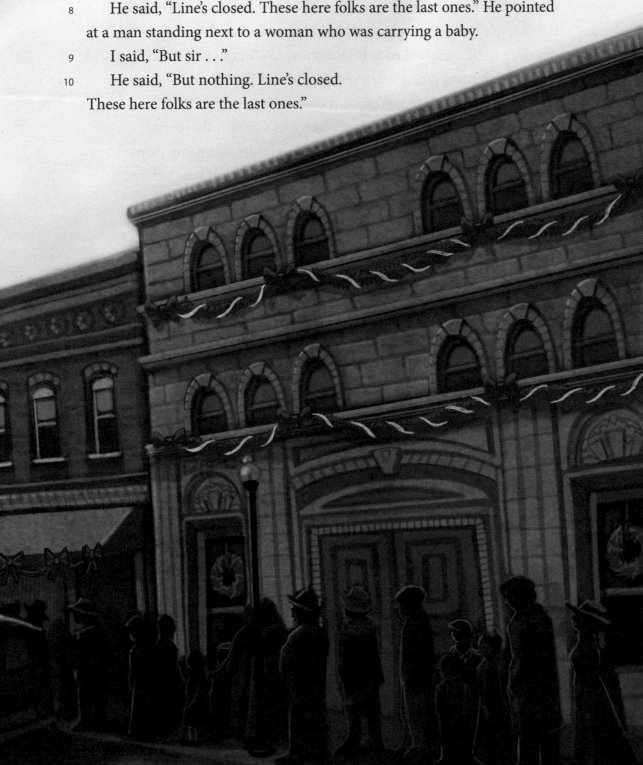

11   It was time to start lying. If I didn't get any food now I'd have to steal something out of someone's garbage or I wouldn't be able to eat until the mission opened for supper.

12   I said, "Sir, I—"

13   The man raised his hand and said, "Look, kid, everybody's got a story and everybody knows the rules. The line closes at seven o'clock. How's it fair to these people who been here since five o'clock that you can sleep until"—he looked at his wristwatch—"until seven-fifteen, then come busting down here expecting to eat? You think you got some kind of special privilege just 'cause you're skinny and raggedy? Look in the line, there's lots of folks look just like you, you ain't the worst.

14   "Supper starts at six P.M., but you see how things is, if you plan on getting fed you better be in line by four. Now get out of here before I get rough with you."

15   Shucks, being hungry for a whole day is about as bad as it can get. I said, "But . . ."

16   He reached in his pocket and pulled something out that looked like a heavy black strap and slapped it across his hand. Uh-oh, here we go again.

17   He said, "That's it, no more talk, you opened your mouth one time too many. You rotten kids today don't listen to no one, but I'ma show you something that'll improve your hearing." He slapped the strap on his hand and started walking toward me.

18   I was wrong when I said being hungry for a day is about as bad as it can get, being hungry plus having a big knot on your head from a black leather strap would be even worse.

19   I backed away but only got two steps before I felt a giant warm hand wrap around my neck from behind. I looked up to see whose doggone hand was so doggone big and why they'd put it around my neck.

20   A very tall, square-shaped man in old blue overalls looked down at me and said, "Clarence, what took you so long?"

21   I got ready to say, "My name's not Clarence and please don't choke me, sir, I'll leave," but as soon as I opened my mouth he gave my head a shake and said, "I told you to hurry back, now where you been?" He gave me a shove and said, "Get back in line with your momma."

22   I looked up and down the line to see who was supposed to be my momma when a woman pointed her finger at her feet and said, "Clarence, you get over here right now." There were two little kids hanging on to her skirt.

23   I walked over to where she was and she gave me a good hard smack on the head. Shucks, for someone who was just pretending to be my momma she sure did slap me a good one.

24   I said, "Ow!"

25   The big square man who'd grabbed my neck looked at the man with the strap and said, "Boy had to go use the toilet, told him not to waste time, but like you said, these kids today don't listen to nobody."

26   The strap man looked at the size of the man who called me Clarence and walked back to the end of the line.

27 When the overall man got back in line I said, "Thank you, sir, I really tried to get—" But *he* popped me in the back of the head, hard, and said, "Next time don't be gone so long."

28 The two little kids busted out laughing and said, "Nyah-nyah-nyah-nyah-nyah, Clarence got a lickin', Clarence got a lickin'."

29 I told them, "Shut up, and don't call me—" Then *both* my pretend poppa and my pretend momma smacked my head.

30 She looked at the people direct behind us and said, "Mercy, when they get to be this age . . ."

31 The people weren't too happy about me taking cuts in the line, but when they looked at how big my pretend daddy was and they saw how hard him and my pretend momma were going upside my head they decided they wouldn't say anything.

32 I was grateful to these people, but I wished they'd quit popping me in the head, and it seems like with all the names in the world they could've come up with a better one for me than Clarence.

33 I stood in line with my pretend family for a long, long time. Everybody was very quiet about standing in line, even my pretend brother and sister and all the other kids. When we finally got around the last corner and could see the door and folks going in, it seemed like a bubble busted and people started laughing and talking. The main thing people were talking about was the great big sign that was hanging over the building.

34 It showed a gigantic picture of a family of four rich white people sitting in a car driving somewhere. You could tell it was a family 'cause they all looked exactly alike. The only difference amongst them was that the daddy had a big head and a hat and the momma had the same head with a woman's hat and the girl had two big yellow pigtails coming out from above her ears. They all had big shiny teeth and big shiny eyes and big shiny cheeks and big shiny smiles. Shucks, you'd need to squint your eyes if that shiny family drove anywhere near you.

myNotes

35   You could tell they were rich 'cause the car looked like it had room for eight or nine more people in it and 'cause they had movie star clothes on. The woman was wearing a coat with a hunk of fur around the neck and the man was wearing a suit and a tie and the kids looked like they were wearing ten-dollar-apiece jackets.

36   Writ about their car in fancy letters it said, THERE'S NO PLACE LIKE AMERICA TODAY!

37   My pretend daddy read it and said, "Uh-uh-uh, well, you got to give them credit, you wouldn't expect that they'd have the nerve to come down here and tell the truth."

THERE'S NO PLACE LIKE AMERICA TODAY!

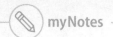
38   When we finally got into the building it was worth the wait. The first thing you noticed when you got inside was how big the place was, and how many people were in it and how quiet it was. The only sound you could hear was when someone scraped a spoon across the bottom of their bowl or pulled a chair in or put one back or when the people in front of you dragged their feet on the floor moving up to where they were spooning out the food.

39   After we'd picked up our spoons and bowls a lady dug a big mess of oatmeal out of a giant pot and swopped it down into our bowls. She smiled and said, "I hope you enjoy."

40   Me and my pretend family all said, "Thank you, ma'am." Then a man put two pieces of bread and a apple and a big glass of milk on your tray and said, "Please read the signs to your children. Thank you."

41   We all said, "Thank you, sir." Then we walked past some signs someone'd stuck up on the wall.

42   One said, PLEASE DO NOT SMOKE, another said, PLEASE EAT AS QUICKLY AND QUIETLY AS POSSIBLE, another one said, PLEASE BE CONSIDERATE AND PATIENT—CLEAN UP AFTER YOURSELF—YOUR NEIGHBORS WILL BE EATING AFTER YOU, and the last one said, WE ARE TERRIBLY SORRY BUT WE HAVE NO WORK AVAILABLE.

43   My pretend daddy read the signs to my pretend brother and sister and we all sat at a long table with strangers on both sides of us.

44   The oatmeal was delicious! I poured some of my milk into it so it wouldn't be so lumpy and mixed it all together.

45   My pretend mother opened her pocketbook and took out a little brown envelope. She reached inside of it and sprinkled something on my pretend brother's and sister's oatmeal, then said to them, "I know that's not as much as you normally get, but I wanted to ask you if you minded sharing some with Clarence."

46   They pouted and gave me a couple of dirty looks. My pretend mother said, "Good," and emptied the rest of the envelope over my oatmeal. Brown sugar!

considerate   To be considerate is to think of the feelings and needs of others.

47   Shucks, I didn't even mind them calling me Clarence anymore. I said "Thank you, Momma, ma'am."

48   She and my pretend daddy laughed and he said, "It took you long enough to catch on, Clarence." He acted like he was going to smack me again but he didn't.

49   After we'd finished all our food we put our bowls up and I thanked my pretend family again, I asked them, "Are you going to be coming back for supper?"

50   My pretend momma said, "No, dear, we only come here mornings. But you make sure you get here plenty early, you hear?"

51   I said, "Yes, Momma, I mean, ma'am."

52   I watched them walking away. My pretend brother looked back at me and stuck out his tongue, then reached up and took my pretend mother's hand. I couldn't really blame him, I don't think I'd be real happy about sharing my brown sugar and my folks with any strange kids either.

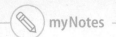

53 I pushed the heavy door open and walked into the library. The air in the library isn't like the air anywhere else, first it's always cooler than the air outside, it feels like you're walking into a cellar on a hot July day, even if you have to walk up a bunch of stairs to get into it.

54 The next thing about the air in the library is that no other place smells anything like it. If you close your eyes and try to pick out what it is that you're sniffing you're only going to get confused, because all the smells have blended together and turned themselves into a different one.

55 As soon as I got into the library I closed my eyes and took a deep breath. I got a whiff of the leather on all the old books, a smell that got real strong if you picked one of them up and stuck your nose real close to it when you turned the pages. Then there was the smell of the cloth that covered the brand-new books, the books that made a splitting sound when you opened them. Then I could sniff the paper, that soft, powdery, drowsy smell that comes off the pages in little puffs when you're reading something or looking at some pictures, a kind of hypnotizing smell.

56   I think it's that smell that makes so many folks fall asleep in the library. You'll see someone turn a page and you can imagine a puff of page powder coming up really slow and easy until it starts piling on the person's eyelashes, weighing their eyes down so much that they stay down a little longer after each blink and finally making them so heavy that they just don't come back up at all. Then their mouths come open and their heads start bouncing up and down like they're bobbing in a big tub of water for apples and before you know it, . . . woop, zoop, sloop . . . they're out cold and their face thunks down smack-dab on the book.

57   That's the part that gets the librarians the maddest, they get real upset if folks start drooling in the books and, page powder or not, they don't want to hear no excuses, you gotta get out. Drooling in the books is even worse than laughing out loud in the library, and even though it might seem kind of mean, you can't really blame the librarians for tossing drooly folks out 'cause there's nothing worse than opening a book and having the pages all stuck together from somebody's dried-up slobber.

58   I opened my eyes to start looking for Miss Hill. She wasn't at the lending desk so I left my suitcase with the white lady there. I knew it would be safe.

59   I walked between the stacks to see if Miss Hill was putting books up. Three doggone times I walked through the library, upstairs and down, and couldn't find her.

60   I went back up to the librarian at the lending desk. I waited until she looked up at me. She smiled and said, "Yes? Would you like to retrieve your suitcase?" She reached under the desk.

61   I said, "Not yet, ma'am, could I ask you a question?"

62   She said, "Of course, young man, how may I help you?"

63   "I'm looking for Miss Hill."

64   The librarian looked surprised. "Miss Hill? My goodness, hadn't you heard?"

65   Uh-oh! That's Number 16 of Bud Caldwell's Rules and Things for Having a Funner Life and Making a Better Liar Out of Yourself, that's one of the worst ones.

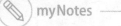

66

RULES AND THINGS NUMBER 16

If a Grown-up Ever Starts a Sentence by Saying "Haven't You Heard," Get Ready, 'Cause What's About to Come Out of Their Mouth Is Gonna Drop You Headfirst into a Boiling Tragedy.

67   It seems like the answer to "Haven't you heard" always has something to do with someone kicking the bucket. And not kicking the bucket in a calm, peaceful way like a heart attack at home in bed either, it usually is some kind of dying that will make your eyes buck out of your head when you hear about it, it's usually the kind of thing that will run you out of a room with your hands over your ears and your mouth wide open.

68   Something like hearing that your grandmother got her whole body pulled through the wringer on a washing machine, or something like hearing about a horse slipping on the ice and landing on some kid you went to school with.

69   I answered, "No, ma'am," and got my stomach ready to hear about Miss Hill biting the dust in some way that was going to give me nightmares.

70   The librarian said, "There's no need for you to look so stricken. It's not bad news, young man."

71   She laughed a quiet, librarian-type laugh and said, "Really, it's not bad news. Unless you had matrimonial plans concerning Miss Hill."

72   I pretended I knew what she was talking about, most times if you listen to how grown folks ask a question they let you know what it is they want to hear.

73   I said, "No, ma'am, I didn't plan that at all."

74   She laughed again and said, "Good, because I don't think her new husband would appreciate the competition. Charlemae . . . Miss Hill is currently living in Chicago, Illinois."

75   I said, "Husband? You mean she got married, ma'am?"

76   The librarian said, "Oh, yes, and I must tell you, she was radiating happiness."

> **tragedy** A tragedy is a very sad event.
> **wringer** A wringer is a device that squeezes water out of laundry.
> **stricken** To be stricken is to be deeply affected by something.
> **matrimonial** Matrimonial issues have to do with marriage.

77   I said, "And she moved all the way to Chicago?"

78   "That's right, but Chicago isn't that far. Here, I'll show you."

79   She reached under her desk and pulled out a thick leather book called *Atlas of the United States of America.*

80   She thumbed through a couple of pages and said, "Here we are." She turned the book to me, it was a big map of Michigan and a couple of the states that were next to it.

81   "We're here." She pointed to the spot that said Flint. "And Chicago is here in Illinois."

82   They looked pretty close, but I know how tricky maps can be, shucks, they can put the whole world on one page on a map, so I said, "How long would it take someone to walk that far?"

83   She said, "Oh, dear, quite a while, I'm afraid. Let's check the distance."

84   She reached under the desk and pulled out another thick book called *Standard Highway Mileage Guide* and turned to a page that had a million numbers and city names on it. She showed me how to find Chicago on the line that was running across the page and Flint on the line that was running down the page and then to look at the number that was writ where the two of them joined up. It said 270.

85   She pulled a pencil out and said, "OK, this is how one figures the amount of time required to walk to Chicago. Now—" She pulled a third book out.

86   Shucks, this is one of the bad things about talking to librarians, I asked one question and already she had us digging through three different books.

87   She thumbed through the book until she said, "Aha, it says here that the average male human gait is five miles an hour. OK, assuming that you could cover five miles an hour, all we have to do is divide two hundred seventy by five."

88   She did it and said, "Fifty-four hours! Much too long to be practical. No, I'm afraid you'll simply have to wait until Mrs. Rollins comes back to Flint for a visit."

89   Shucks. Chicago might as well be a million miles away from Flint and Miss Hill might as well be a squashed, crunched-up mess in a washing machine when it came down to helping me now.

90   I thanked the librarian for the bad news and went to sit at one of the big heavy tables so I could think what to do next.

91   Going back to the Home was out, it used to be that we'd get a new kid every once in a while, but lately it seems like there's a couple of new kids every day, mostly babies, and they're most always sick. It's not like it was when I first got there, shucks, half the folks that run it don't even tell you their name and don't remember yours unless you're in trouble all the time or getting ready to move out.

92   After awhile I got my suitcase and walked into the regular air and stinking smells of Flint.

93   That library door closing after I walked out was the exact kind of door Momma had told me about. I knew that since it had closed the next one was about to open.

94   I went back under my tree and before I knew it I was asleep.

> **gait**   A gait is a way of walking.

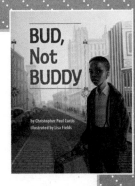

Collaborative Discussion

Look back at what you wrote on page 302. Tell a partner what you think is the greatest or most difficult problem Bud is experiencing and why. Then work with a group to discuss the questions below. Refer to details and examples in *Bud, Not Buddy* to explain your answers. Take notes for your responses. When you speak, use your notes.

1 Do you think the man in charge of the food line was right to turn Bud away from the mission breakfast? Why or why not?

> [blank response box]

Listening Tip

Listen closely when others are sharing their ideas. Be sure the speaker has finished before sharing your own ideas.

2 Why did the family in line pretend Bud was their son? Based on the text, how did Bud feel about being Clarence?

> [blank response box]

Speaking Tip

Speak clearly and make eye contact with each member of your group as you speak.

3 This story is told from Bud's point of view. How does this help you better understand Bud and the events in the story?

> [blank response box]

Write a Thank-You Note

PROMPT

In *Bud, Not Buddy*, you read about a boy living in Flint, Michigan, during the Great Depression. In the story, Bud arrives too late for a free breakfast. A family that is waiting in line takes pity on him and pretends to be his family so he can stay and eat.

Imagine that you are Bud and you want to thank this family for their kindness. Write a thank-you note to the family members that expresses your feelings about what they did for you. Use details from the text to write your note.

PLAN

Make notes about Bud, his pretend family, what the family did for Bud, and how he feels about the family.

WRITE

Now imagine you are Bud and write your thank-you note to your pretend family for helping you get breakfast at the mission.

✓	Make sure your thank-you note
☐	begins with a salutation to the family.
☐	includes details from the text and descriptive language telling how Bud feels about the family's help and generosity.
☐	uses at least two Critical Vocabulary words.
☐	uses correct capitalization for proper nouns.
☐	ends with a closing and Bud's signature.

Notice & Note
3 Big Questions

Prepare to Read

GENRE STUDY ▸ **Narrative nonfiction** gives factual information by telling a true story.

- Narrative nonfiction presents events in sequential, or chronological, order. This helps readers understand what happened and when.

- Texts about events that happened in the past include real people and may include how they felt about events.

- Social studies texts also include words that are specific to the topic. These are words that name things or ideas.

SET A PURPOSE ▸ **Think about** the title and genre of this text. This text was written about the Great Depression and putting unemployed people to work. What kind of jobs do you think *Men of the Woods* describes? Write your ideas below.

CRITICAL VOCABULARY

labor

erosion

mandatory

surveying

**Build Background:
The Civilian Conservation Corps**

Men of the Woods:
The Civilian Conservation Corps

Above, men from a Civilian
Conservation Corps work group stand
on a log. At right, the Civilian
Conservation Corps Emblem Patch.

Focus on the Youth

President Roosevelt visits a CCC camp in the Shenandoah Valley, Virginia.

Men enjoy mealtime at Camp Sanders, in Louisiana, 1937.

1   When President Franklin D. Roosevelt came into office in 1933, he put America back to work. He began with the Works Progress Administration, which hired people around the country to build roads, bridges, and buildings, and even to write poetry and songs.

2   The unemployed young people of America, however, were a special case. Many of these people— even at ages 22 or 23 —had never had the opportunity to work for a living. Many of them had few skills and no job prospects.

3   The president signed into effect the Civilian Conservation Corps (CCC), which was specifically created for young men between the ages of 18 and 25. Here's how the program worked: Work camps were set up in state and national parks and forests nationwide. Men lived in barracks and followed a strict, militaristic code of behavior. They had to do hard physical labor for work. Of their $30 per month pay, all but $5 was sent home to their families.

4   The young men who joined up were previously unemployed. They might have been riding the rails looking for work. Many were unskilled and aimless. When they came to camp, many of these young men were also hungry. Their weight upon entering the CCC was recorded by those overseeing the camps. The men gained an average of 11¼ pounds in the first three months. Some of the corpsmen were illiterate. About 57,000 men learned to read while serving in the Civilian Conservation Corps.

labor   Labor is work—especially hard, physical work.

5   The men built trails, cabins, and bridges in parks across the country. They learned to lay rock, pour cement, build lakes, operate bulldozers, and drive trucks. They worked with axes, rakes, and saws to create the trails, roads, and buildings that now exist throughout our nation's national and state parks and forests. These are some of their stories.

Far from Home

6   Some CCC workers ended up traveling for hundreds—or thousands—of miles to get to their worksite. One Alabama teen, Armond Allbritton, rode a train north with his group to Chicago, and then transferred to another train headed west. The train passed through scenery and mountains that Allbritton had never seen the likes of before, including crossing the Continental Divide near Butte, Montana. His group made it all the way to the Pacific Ocean, which he saw for the first time, and then to his camp in Warrenton, Oregon. Allbritton's work with the CCC involved planting grass on the beach to help control erosion, and he also worked in Fort Stevens State Park and at Fort Clatsop National Monument.

Men peel a log for a building, at Camp F-20 in the Olympic National Forest, Washington.

erosion   Erosion is the process of wearing away something by wind, water, or other natural agents.

A Strict Code

7   Ed Braun, who was working in a camp near Greenriver, Utah, remembers how tight the living quarters were and how strictly camp directors kept order. The men in his group lived in barracks that held 20 beds, with each man storing his possessions in a foot locker. Beds were made with military precision. It was mandatory for workers to clean their shoes—even the soles of their shoes—daily. In each barracks, there was one leader, one assistant leader, and 18 "grunts," or men who followed orders.

8   Braun also remembers the food fondly. He said that the food was actually much more nutritious than what the young men were getting at home during the height of the Great Depression. He remembers a sign that said, "Take all you want, but eat what you take." Even fifty years after serving in the corps, Braun remembers the pineapple fritters the mess sergeant (camp cook) made.

Dangerous Beauty

9   James Justin, another young man of the CCC, described working near Buffalo, New York, in the snowy winters. His job was surveying the land and creating maps and diagrams of the areas near his camp. He remembers not being able to walk without skis or snowshoes. One time, while cross-country skiing in a beautiful part of the woods, he dropped through soft snow into a creek bed and was buried up to his neck. Luckily, his comrades were there to pull him out.

Men of the CCC participate in a bunk inspection.

Men in a work group hew trees for their cabin fireplace and the kitchen stove.

mandatory   Something that is mandatory is required by rules or the law.

surveying   If you are surveying land, you are finding its shape, area, and boundaries by measuring.

10   Justin worked in two different camps, and in his second camp in Delaware, where during the day the men would work to drain swamps to control the mosquito population, the men spent their evenings putting together plays and even an opera. He remembered the CCC fondly his whole life. Once he had children, he would take his family on wilderness vacations to share the love of nature he developed in the CCC.

Separate Buses, Separate Camps

11   For African Americans, the segregation they faced in many elements of ordinary life was also the case in the CCC. Luther C. Wandall was an African American man from New York City. He enrolled in the CCC, and took a bus to New Jersey without knowing what would happen next.

12   Wandall ended up being separated with the other black men, and then after eight days, he took a train to a camp in the upper South. The officers who ran the camp were white, but the athletic director and vocational teacher were African American. All of the men in his camp were African American. The food was good, there was a nice recreation hall, and the work was healthy and outdoors. Although Wandall was not happy about the segregation, he left the CCC with a positive impression.

A CCC worker surfaces a road in Beltsville, Maryland.

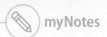

Lasting Impact

13 If you've ever been in a national or state park, you've likely enjoyed the results of the work of the CCC. The men planted more than 3 billion trees—which earned them the name of "Roosevelt's Tree Army." They built campgrounds, picnic shelters, swimming pools, restrooms, and more than 3,470 fire towers.

CCC workers construct a road.

14 The program ended in 1942, and over the years nearly three million men, and even about 8,500 women, participated in the program. Those who participated in the CCC gained valuable skills, which then made them more employable in the larger world outside the camps, especially once the American economy started to improve. And, when the U.S. entered World War II after the Japanese bombed Pearl Harbor, Hawaii, in 1941, these men had an excellent foundation of physical fitness, outdoor skills, and military discipline that America needed most of all at that time.

15 The CCC was a bold idea formed in a troubled time in American history, and it benefited the individuals who served in it, the parks and forests of our nation, and our nation as a whole.

CCC workers plant trees.

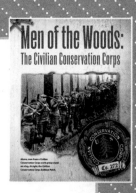

Men of the Woods:
The Civilian Conservation Corps

Collaborative Discussion

Look back at what you wrote on page 320. Tell a partner a question you have after reading this text. Then work with a group to discuss the questions below. Refer to details and examples in *Men of the Woods* to explain your answers. Take notes for your responses. When you speak, use your notes.

1   Why do you think President Roosevelt had the Civilian Conservation Corps recruit young men for the program? Use text evidence to support your answer.

 **Listening Tip**

Look at other group members as they speak. Notice their facial expressions or gestures they use to help explain their ideas.

2   What did you learn about the Civilian Conservation Corps from reading the stories of people who participated in the program?

Speaking Tip

As you speak, look at the others in your group. Does anyone look confused? Invite that person to ask you a question.

3   What is the author's opinion of the Civilian Conservation Corps? Explain how you know this.

Write a Personal Statement

PROMPT

In *Men of the Woods* you read about President Roosevelt's Civilian Conservation Corps (CCC). You learned why the president created the program, and you read the personal stories of young men who participated in the CCC.

Reread the personal stories in the selection. Choose one of the stories and imagine you are that person. Or, create a character that had some combination of their experiences. Write a paragraph in the first-person voice, telling your story to your grandchild. Try to use some of the Critical Vocabulary words in your writing.

PLAN

Write details about the person and his experience in the Civilian Conservation Corps.

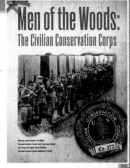
WRITE

Now write your personal statement in the first-person voice, telling your story of the Civilian Conservation Corps to your grandchild.

✓ Make sure your personal statement

- ☐ is told in the first-person voice.

- ☐ includes details from the selection.

- ☐ uses descriptive language, including sensory words that describe what you experienced and felt while serving in the Civilian Conservation Corps.

- ☐ includes at least one Critical Vocabulary word.

- ☐ uses proper punctuation, including commas in complex sentences and transitions.

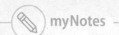

Prepare to View

GENRE STUDY **Video Interviews** present the point of view of real people on an event or topic.

- The people being interviewed can share their thoughts in a first-person voice.

- Participants may be giving oral histories, or stories from their past that help explain what it was like to live in a particular time and place.

SET A PURPOSE **Think about** the title and genre of this text. Who do you think will be in the video? What stories do you think they will tell about the Great Depression? Write your ideas below.

**Build Background:
The Great Depression**

CRITICAL VOCABULARY

deplorable

downturn

abundance

graces

adversity

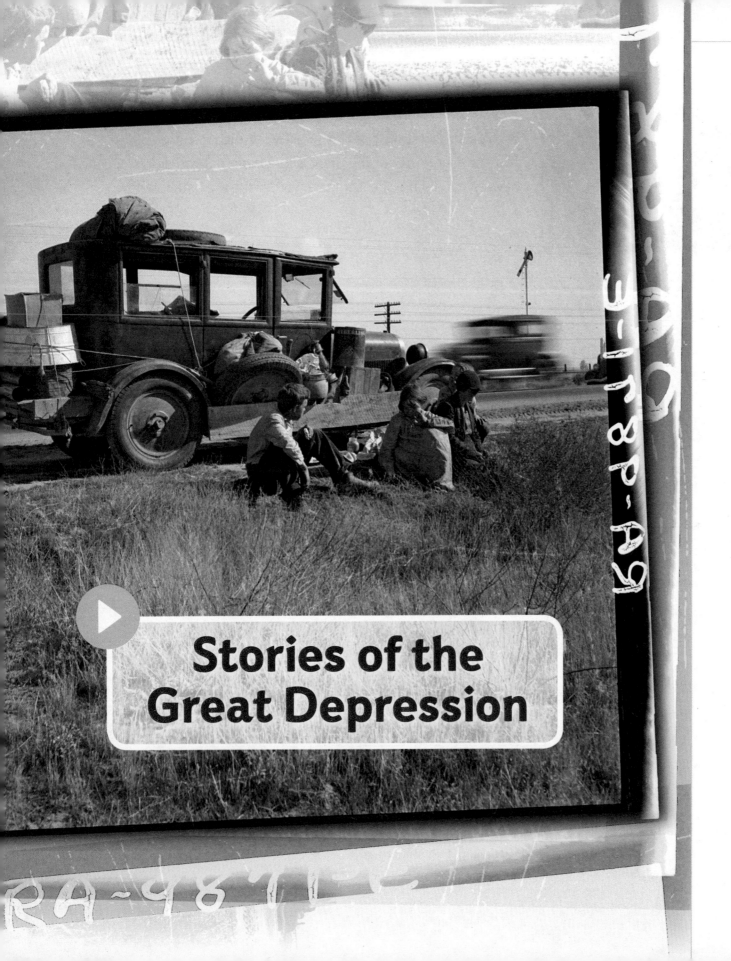

Stories of the
Great Depression

As you watch *Stories of the Great Depression,* listen carefully to each person's response to the questions. Which response gave you information about the Great Depression that you didn't have? What did the speaker teach you? Write the details below.

Listen for the Critical Vocabulary words *deplorable, downturn, abundance, graces,* and *adversity.* Pay attention to how each word is used to see if the speaker gives clues to the word's meaning. Take notes in the space below about how each word is used.

deplorable A deplorable situation is terrible and unacceptable.

downturn A downturn is a decline in the economy or a business.

abundance If you have an abundance of something, you have a lot of it.

graces The graces of neighbors is the kindness of neighbors.

adversity Adversity is a hardship or a difficult situation.

Collaborative Discussion

Stories of the Great Depression

Look back at what you wrote on page 330. Tell a partner something you learned from this video. Then work with a group to discuss the questions below. Refer to details and examples in *Stories of the Great Depression* to explain your answers. Take notes for your responses. When you speak, use your notes.

1 What sacrifices did families have to make during the Great Depression?

2 What characteristics helped people survive the Great Depression? Use evidence from the video to support your opinion.

3 What additional questions would you ask if you could interview someone who lived during the Great Depression?

Listening Tip

Listen closely to information each speaker shares. Be sure the speaker has finished before you share your ideas.

Speaking Tip

Say each word clearly and at a pace that isn't too fast or too slow.

Write a List

PROMPT

In *Stories from the Great Depression* you learned about this tragic time in U.S. history from everyday people who were children during that time. They gave many details about the good and the bad times they and their families experienced.

Write a list of five details you learned from this video about life during the Great Depression. Before you write each detail, start by naming the category of information each detail describes, for example: jobs, food, school. Then add the story or detail the person shared about that category.

PLAN

Write five categories of information from the video that you would like to write about. Then make notes about the details or story that fit into each of those categories.

WRITE

Stories of the Great Depression

Now write your list of details from *Stories of the Great Depression*.

Make sure your list

- ☐ includes five different categories of information.
- ☐ uses details from the video for each category.
- ☐ has each category beginning on a new line.
- ☐ includes some Critical Vocabulary words.
- ☐ uses proper capitalization and sentence structure.

Notice & Note
3 Big Questions

Prepare to Read

GENRE STUDY ▶ **Informational texts** give facts and examples about a topic.

- Authors of informational texts may organize their ideas using headings and subheadings. The headings and subheadings tell readers what the next section of text will be about.

- Authors of informational texts may organize their ideas by main ideas. Each main idea is supported by key details, including facts, definitions, examples, or quotations.

SET A PURPOSE ▶ **Think about** the title and genre of this text. Based on what you have learned, what do you think daily life was like for children living in cities and towns during the Great Depression? Write your ideas below.

Meet the Author:
Russell Freedman

CRITICAL VOCABULARY
lax
vocational
rigid
ease
insisted
crusade
administer
perennial
improvised

Children
OF THE GREAT DEPRESSION

By Russell Freedman

Children in a library tent for migratory farm workers

1   The hardships faced by Depression families placed heavy responsibilities on the shoulders of the young. Children had to grow up fast. They were called on to contribute to the meager family income by working full-time or part-time, assuming they could find a job.

2   "There are no advantages in staying in school for my children," one parent said, "for we could not keep them there long enough to [become] teachers or get enough education to do some other professional work, so it is better for them to get to work early."

3   "It's better to go to work and bring money home," agreed a mill worker's son, who had six brothers and sisters living at home. "Schools are only for the rich. Poor people must work for their living."

Kids at Work

4   Often it was the sixteen- and seventeen-year-olds who dropped out of school to find work. But it wasn't unusual to find much younger children laboring long hours for little pay. Fourteen-year-old boys worked in coal mines, twelve-year-old girls in knitting factories. Among migrant farm workers, children as young as five or six labored in the fields beside their parents, working from sunup to sundown.

5   Some states had enacted laws prohibiting or limiting child labor, but for the most part those laws were weak and enforcement was lax. At the beginning of the Depression, there was no national child-labor law that applied equally to all American children.

6   In 1930, according to the census, two and a quarter million boys and girls between the ages of ten and eighteen were working in factories, canneries, mines, and farms. Tens of thousands of other children *under* the age of ten, who were laboring on farms, as street peddlers, and in home workshops, were not counted by the census. Because kids could be hired for lower wages than grownups, they often replaced adults who had been laid off. A child's wages might make up the entire family income. "I don't expect I'll ever get back to school," said a thirteen-year-old girl who was working in the same cotton garment factory that had laid off her father.

7   A girl who started work when she was fourteen described her daily routine: "At 5:30 it is time for me to get up . . . I hurriedly eat my breakfast, and I am ready to go to work. It is a chilly winter morning, but I know it will be hot in the mill. I start on my three mile walk to the factory. As I walk, I see others hurrying to work. I look at the older people and wonder if they, too, feel the resentment every morning that I do, or if as the years go by their spirits are deadened.

lax   If something is lax, it has been done in a lazy way—rather than carefully.

A young girl works at a cranberry bog in Burlington County, New Jersey.

8   "I arrive at the factory. The sight that I dread to see meets my eyes: the line of unemployed people waiting for the boss to come and hoping for work."

9   Kids who were able to stay in school found a variety of part-time jobs. They were employed as newspaper carriers, babysitters, store clerks, and delivery boys. One boy from a hard-pressed Michigan home delivered newspapers in the afternoon, ushered at a theater in the evening, and worked at a gas station on weekends. He also helped his mother at home while his father was away searching for a job. A North Carolina girl went to school mornings and worked at the local cotton mill in the evenings "because I wanted to help my parents and not be a burden to them."

A young worker at a cotton mill in Taftville, Connecticut

"I wanted to help my parents and not be a burden to them."

10   Vincent Ferrara managed to stay in college by working in his family's New York City pizzeria. "If I wasn't there, I was in school or I was doing my homework," he recalled. "Saturday night was a busy night, so was Sunday. I saved my tip money, and I worked in the church hall for thirty-seven dollars a month, and all put together enabled me to pay for my tuition at Fordham. I went during the day, and at night I was in the store. I did my homework on the rear table."

11   Some teenagers found a novel, if dangerous, way to make money when a tree-sitting craze swept the country. A boy would climb to the highest branch of a tall tree and sit there for days on end, hoping to break a tree-sitting record and earn some cash from donations dropped into a coin box placed at the foot of the tree. Local merchants often paid tree-sitters to advertise their wares, and some boys made extra money by selling their autographs.

12   A teenage couple could get some money by entering a dance marathon. These events also became a 1930s craze. Spectators paid to watch young couples dance hour after hour until they dropped to the floor, exhausted. Those who stayed on their feet the longest earned a little prize money.

13   Young people who managed to save enough money to pay tuition often went to vocational schools, where they trained to become secretaries, bookkeepers, mechanics, beauticians, refrigeration technicians, and even commercial pilots. But no matter how impressive their skills, they had a hard time finding work. The depressed job market of the 1930s hit the young especially hard. In 1934–35, unemployment rates among sixteen- to twenty-four-year-olds hovered around 50 percent. In New York City, nearly 80 percent of sixteen-year-olds who were out of school and looking for work could not find jobs.

14   "Maybe you don't know what it's like to come home and have everyone looking at you," one teenager complained, "and you know they're thinking, even if they don't say it, 'He didn't find a job.' It gets terrible. You just don't want to come home."

Bootblacks in Market Square, Waco, Texas

vocational Vocational schools train students to do various jobs.

A delivery person in Caruthersville, Missouri

15   Among black youths, the unemployment situation was critical.
Although Northern blacks did not face the rigid segregation of the Deep
South, job discrimination was still the rule in Northern cities. Black
workers of any age were always "the last hired and the first fired," as the
saying goes. And jobs previously held by unskilled black workers were now
being grabbed by whites willing to work as waiters, garbage collectors, and
domestic servants.

16   At first, none of the massive government programs designed to ease the
pain of the Depression did much to meet the needs of an estimated three
million young people who were said to be "out of work, out of school, and
out of luck." The Civilian Conservation Corps (CCC), established in 1933,
hired unemployed young men between the ages of seventeen and twenty-
eight and put them to work in national forests and parks. They planted
trees, fought fires, and improved beaches and campgrounds. It was hailed
as a successful program, but it excluded young women and did nothing to
help students.

> **rigid**   Something that is rigid is unable to adapt and difficult to change.
> **ease**   When something eases, its impact decreases.

Eleanor Roosevelt at White Top Mountain, Virginia, August 1933. During her first year in the White House, she received more than 300,000 letters, many of them from children.

17   Eleanor Roosevelt insisted that the nation's youth deserved the government's help as much as any other group. Because she received an overwhelming volume of mail, she was unable to respond in the very personal ways the letter writers hoped. Instead, as First Lady, she used her considerable influence and popularity to crusade for expanded federal aid to poor children and teens. "I have moments of real terror when I think we might be losing this generation," she said. "We have got to bring these young people into the active life of the community."

18   Mrs. Roosevelt pressed government leaders to set up a special agency for young Americans who were still in school. Finally, she persuaded her husband, Franklin D. Roosevelt, to issue an executive order in 1935 creating the National Youth Administration (NYA). And she insisted that the new agency administer aid without discrimination, so that it reached blacks as well as whites, girls as well as boys.

19   The NYA provided grants to help Depression-squeezed young people stay in school. Under this program, high-school and college students were paid to work part-time in libraries and as research assistants. For many of these students, an NYA job meant the difference between staying in school and dropping out. Between 1936 and 1943, more than two million low-income students were able to continue their education through NYA work-study jobs. Another two and a half million youths were employed by the NYA in its after-school work-relief projects.

insisted   If you insisted that something should be done, you said so firmly and refused to give up.

crusade   If you crusade for something, you work hard to make sure it succeeds.

administer   When you administer something, you take responsibility for supervising or managing it.

20   The NYA had its critics. They charged that the program undermined the initiative and self-reliance of the nation's youth. Segregationists objected because black youths were included in NYA projects. Despite this opposition, the NYA became one of the most popular of all federal government programs. A teenager from Pittsburgh who had been hired by the program wrote: "Words cannot express my gratitude to our president, who had made this [employment] possible for me and thousands of others."

21   Years later, people who had grown up during the worst times of the Great Depression looked back with a certain pride. They had missed out on some of the carefree years that are the special gift of youth, but they had gained, they felt, a sense of heightened self-confidence and an understanding of the needs of others. Hard times had propelled them into the adult world much sooner than they might have wished, yet they had discovered within themselves strengths and skills that would last throughout their lives.

22   "It was an enormously hard life," author Margot Hentoff recalled. "But there was also a sense of great satisfaction in being a child with valuable work to do and being able to do it well, [able] to function in this world."

Student assistants at the Greenwood Negro Library, Leflore County, Mississippi, May 1936. NYA work grants helped students like these stay in school.

A young boy packing shingles at a Jefferson, Texas, lumber mill

Lining up for the movie matinee in Pittsburgh, Pennsylvania

The Lone Ranger and *Captain Midnight*

23 Kids who could afford to buy a ticket looked forward to Saturday afternoon at the movies. Admission to the Saturday matinee cost ten cents. That seemed like a lot of money during the Great Depression, but it bought a lot of entertainment.

24 For one thin dime a kid could see a double feature (two full-length movies), an animated cartoon, a short newsreel dealing with current events, a humorous short subject, and the latest episode of a serial—a continuing adventure story told one chapter a week. Along with all that, some theaters offered a bonus: a free ice cream or a frozen chocolate-covered banana.

25 The serial especially packed them in every Saturday. Each episode had a cliffhanger ending: The hero seemed hopelessly cornered by evildoers or trapped by an avalanche, a stampede, a tidal wave, or some other catastrophe. Suspense built up all during the week as every movie fan tried to guess how the hero could possibly escape.

26 Favorite serial heroes included Tarzan of the Apes, Flash Gordon of the distant planet Mongo, and Wild West figures such as the Lone Ranger, who also appeared in many full-length features. These films were so involving that some kids brought cap guns to the theater and fired noisily at the outlaws and cattle rustlers on the silver screen. Theater owners began to insist that young gunslingers check their pistols at the movie-house door.

Checking out coming attractions at the Omar, West Virginia, movie house

TUESDAYS ADM 10¢

"Movies helped audiences forget hard times and escape, for an hour or two."

27   Along with the enormously popular westerns, children of the 1930s enjoyed certain movies that have been recognized as classics and are still being shown today. Walt Disney's *Snow White and the Seven Dwarfs* (1937) was the first full-length animated feature. It contained 250,000 individual drawings, broke all attendance records, and was translated into ten languages. Another perennial favorite, *The Wizard of Oz* (1939), begins as a black-and-white film. When Dorothy, played by sixteen-year-old Judy Garland, is swept up by a Kansas tornado to the magical land of Oz, the film's sudden switch to breathtaking color (at that time, a recent film innovation) always made audiences gasp.

28   Hollywood's top box-office star during the 1930s was a child, Shirley Temple. She made her first film in 1934, when she was five years old. By the time she was six, her films were taking in millions of dollars a year. She was often featured as an orphan who overcomes poverty and hardship through pluck and luck. Her rags-to-riches stories with their Hollywood-style happy endings helped Depression audiences forget hard times and escape, for an hour or two, to a world where everything was bound to turn out all right.

Judy Garland portrays Dorothy in *The Wizard of Oz.*

Child star Shirley Temple meets one of her fans, First Lady Eleanor Roosevelt, July 1938.

perennial   If something is perennial, it is permanent, constant, or repeated over time.

29   Kids who didn't have a dime for the movies could listen to the radio, the most popular form of home entertainment during the 1930s (commercial television didn't arrive until the late 1940s). Back then, radio offered a much greater variety of programs than it does today. Hundreds of stations across the country broadcast soap operas, talent shows, serious dramas, comedy shows, mysteries, quizzes, sports events (especially baseball), and both classical and popular music programs.

30   Music was as important in the lives of young people then as it is now. The top bandleaders and vocalists of the era were as famous as movie stars. Fans drew a sharp distinction between "sweet" bands, popularized by leaders such as Guy Lombardo, which featured a dreamy, sentimental (some said schmaltzy) sound, and "swing" bands, led by Benny Goodman, Glenn Miller, Duke Ellington, and others, with their driving rhythm and improvised solos akin to jazz. Teenagers clustered around their radios to listen to their favorite bands on weekly broadcasts. On Saturday evenings—before disc jockeys and Top 40 charts were commonplace—kids tuned in to *Your Hit Parade*, which presented the top ten tunes of the week, saving the top three hits for the end of the show.

improvised   If something is improvised, it is done without any planning.

Some Hit Tunes of the 1930s
- And the Angels Sing
- A-Tisket A-Tasket
- Deep Purple
- Harbor Lights
- Love Walked In
- Moon over Miami
- Over the Rainbow
- Pennies from Heaven
- Red Sails in the Sunset
- The Way You Look Tonight
- You Must Have Been a Beautiful Baby

Listening to the radio in Aberdeen, South Dakota

31   Weekday evenings between five and six o'clock were known as "the children's hour" on radio. While dinner was being prepared, kids sat glued to the radio listening to a parade of suspenseful fifteen-minute radio serials, one after another. Many of these shows had kids as their main characters or as assistants to the adult hero. *Jack Armstrong, the All-American Boy* told the story of a brainy, brawny teenage athlete who plunged headlong into thrilling adventures all over the world with his friends Betty and Billy Fairfield, and their wise and witty Uncle Jim. Introduced in 1933 and broadcast regularly until 1951, this was one of the longest-running programs aimed at kids.

32   Westerns were as popular on the radio as they were on movie screens. *The Lone Ranger*, also introduced in 1933, was heard in at least twenty million homes, and the words "Hi-yo, Silver! Away!" shouted by the Lone Ranger as he mounted his Arabian stallion, Silver, were familiar to every kid in America. Parents liked the show because the Lone Ranger spoke perfect English and never shot to kill, although the outlaws he fought sometimes killed each other. He drew his pistols only in self-defense or to protect another's life, and when he did shoot, he fired silver bullets. He appeared in a radio serial, a movie serial, in feature-length films, in a 1950s television series, and in comic books.

Clayton Moore in character as the Lone Ranger. Moore was the best known of several actors who played the role on radio, in films, and on television.

33   *Captain Midnight*, another popular radio serial, followed the adventures of an undercover agent and airplane pilot who was constantly battling the evil plots of Ivan Shark and his nasty daughter, Fury. The captain was aided in his efforts by his teenage friends Joyce and Chuck, who were members of his Secret Squadron. Young listeners could join the Secret Squadron by sending in a dime and the label from a jar of Ovaltine, one of the show's sponsors. In return, they received a special decoder badge, the Mystery Dial Code-O-Graph, which enabled them to decode the secret message broadcast at the end of each episode. *Captain Midnight*, which began in 1938, also moved to film and later to television.

"With radio, you could imagine everything."

34   *The Aldrich Family*, a weekly comedy show, centered on the adolescent mishaps of Henry Aldrich and appealed especially to teenagers. Henry was sixteen when the program began in 1939. He was still sixteen when it ended in 1953.

35   Radio shows had one big difference from television: Listeners had to use their imaginations in order to "see" the characters, the settings, and the action. "Mother would come to the door and holler, 'It's time for Jack Armstrong,'" one listener recalled. "And we would come in the living room. It was radio, so Jack Armstrong looked like whatever you wanted him to. You could imagine everything."

36   Imaginations were aided by the ingenious men and women who created radio sound effects. A wooden match snapped near the microphone sounded like a bat hitting a baseball. Horses galloping could be imitated by beating coconut shells on an old board. Twisting cellophane sounded like a crackling fire. Squeezing a box of cornstarch suggested footsteps in the snow. Sounds made manually on the spot were supplemented by recorded sounds—a speeding train, a barking dog, a roaring lion, a cheering crowd.

37   Most children growing up in the Great Depression didn't have a lot of money to spend on toys and games. Radio shows offered them a chance to obtain popular toys cheaply. Many of the shows were sponsored by cereal companies.

By sending in cereal box tops and a coin or two—often a dime—kids could order kites, whistles, badges, tops, and hundreds of other wonderful treasures. The Hike-O-Meter, hooked to your belt, registered how many miles you hiked. The 5-Way-Detect-O-Scope was a cardboard-and-metal device for sighting objects and estimating their distance.

38   *Jack Armstrong* fans sent away for whistle rings like the one Jack wore. The ring arrived in the mail with a copy of Jack's secret whistle code. Other shows offered rings outfitted with secret compartments, with compasses, magnets, flashlights, and sirens, and with mirrors that allowed you to see behind you without turning your head. Some rings glowed in the dark. Because the rings were made of cheap metal, most of them turned the wearer's finger green after a few days.

39   Some families could not afford to buy the packaged breakfast cereals and other products that sponsored radio shows. When it came to box tops and the toys and gadgets you could get with them, many poor kids were out of luck. But they could always make their own toys. One of the most popular homemade toys during the 1930s was the rubber-band gun, made from a piece of wood, a clothespin, and a rubber band. Kids pretending to be cowboys or detectives could shoot a rubber band ten feet or more with one of these. With a crayon or a bit of paint, wooden clothespins could also be transformed into dolls, soldiers, and other make-believe people.

Chidren playing simple, imaginative games.

40   Two tin cans, connected by a long string, served as a kind of primitive walkie-talkie. By speaking into one can, you could communicate with a distant friend who was holding the open end of the other can against one ear.

41   Boys held racing contests with homemade "push-mobiles" or "sidewalk racers." All that was needed to build one was a discarded milk box or crate from the grocery store, a long wooden plank from a construction site, and a pair of old clamp-on steel roller skates. (Rollerblades and skateboards were in the distant future.) A kid would nail the skates to either end of the plank as wheels. The crate was nailed to the top of the plank, up front. Tin cans might be added as "headlights" or "taillights," along with an old license plate or automobile hood ornament. Standing on the wooden plank with one foot, and holding on to the sides of the crate, a boy would power his racer with his free foot and a helping push at the top of a steep hill. These simple Depression-era racers, built with scavenged materials, developed into the Soapbox Derby competitions held nationally today.

Children prepare for a racing contest.

A child proudly poses with his race entry.

Collaborative Discussion

Look back at what you wrote on page 336. Tell a partner two things that surprised you as you read this text. Then work with a group to discuss the questions below. Refer to details and examples in *Children of the Great Depression* to explain your answers. Take notes for your responses. When you speak, use your notes.

1   Why did so many children have to quit school during the Great Depression?

2   How did Eleanor Roosevelt help the children of the Great Depression? Use details from the text to explain.

3   How was life for children during the Great Depression different from today? How was it the same? List one example of each.

Listening Tip

If you can't hear someone in your group easily, politely ask that person to speak a little louder.

Speaking Tip

When speaking, say each word clearly and at a pace that isn't too fast or too slow so your listeners can understand you.

Write a Letter

PROMPT

In *Children of the Great Depression*, you read about what it was like to grow up during the Great Depression. The text described the hardships of the time, but it also included information about what children did for fun.

Imagine you were a child who lived during the Great Depression. What would you want future generations to understand about the hardships you faced—and the fun you had? Write an imaginary letter to future generations to tell them about your experiences.

PLAN

Review the text and record two details about hard times and one detail about good times that children had during the Great Depression.

WRITE

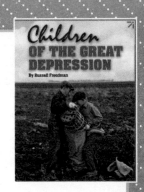

Now write your letter about children's hardships and good times from *Children of the Great Depression.*

Make sure your letter

☐	addresses future generations and focuses on this audience.
☐	is told from the point of view of someone who lived during the Great Depression.
☐	includes text evidence, including two details about hardships and one detail about good times.
☐	ends with a concluding message to future generations.
☐	uses transition words to connect ideas.

Essential Question

What in our American spirit helps us survive tough times?

Write an Informational Article

PROMPT Think about what you learned about the Great Depression in this module.

Look through the photographs that accompany the selection *Children of the Great Depression*. Choose one of the photographs to use as a basis for an informational article about the hardships children faced during the Great Depression and how they survived these hardships. Include facts and details from two or more of the texts in this module to support your ideas.

I will write about the photograph that shows _____.

✓ Make sure your informational article

- ☐ begins with an introduction that identifies the topic, which should relate to the chosen photograph.

- ☐ is organized into paragraphs with clear main ideas and supporting details.

- ☐ includes text evidence and details from two or more texts.

- ☐ uses transition words to connect ideas.

- ☐ ends with a conclusion that summarizes your key ideas.

What hardships did children face during the Great Depression and how did they overcome them? Study the photograph you have chosen and read its caption. Look back at your notes and revisit the texts and video as necessary.

Below, write the topic of your article. Then, in the chart, write the main idea of your informational article based on what you have learned about the Great Depression and what is shown in the photograph. Then use evidence from the texts and video to write details that you want to include in your article about the hardships children faced and how these hardships were overcome.

My Topic: _____

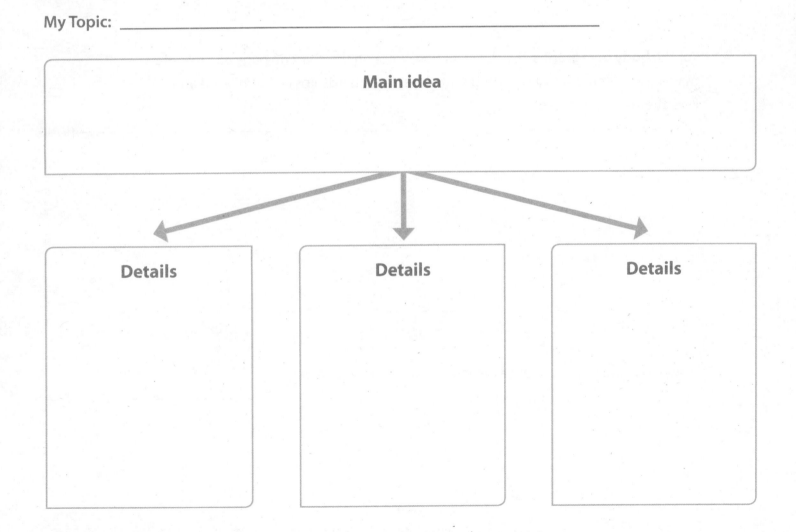

Main idea

Details

Details

Details

DRAFT ·· Write your informational article.

Write an **introduction** that will grab your readers' attention and clearly states your overall main idea, which should be related to the photograph.

For the **body paragraphs**, use the ideas you wrote on the chart on page 357 to write a main idea sentence and supporting sentences about hardships children faced and how they overcame them.

In your **conclusion**, summarize the information in your article.

The revision and editing steps give you a chance to look carefully at your writing and make changes. Work with a partner to determine whether you have explained your ideas clearly to readers. Use these questions to help you evaluate and improve your newspaper article.

✓ PURPOSE/ FOCUS	ORGANIZATION	EVIDENCE	LANGUAGE/ VOCABULARY	CONVENTIONS
☐ Does my article have a clear main idea? ☐ Does the topic of my article relate to the photograph I chose?	☐ Does my introduction grab readers' attention? ☐ Are my paragraphs in the best logical order?	☐ Does my main idea relate to the photograph? ☐ Does the text evidence I provided support my main idea?	☐ Have I used transition words to connect ideas and provide a smooth flow from paragraph to paragraph?	☐ Are all words spelled correctly? ☐ Have I used a variety of words to make my writing more interesting to readers? ☐ Did I use appropriate capitalization of proper nouns?

PUBLISH .... Share your work.

Create a Finished Copy Make a final copy of your newspaper article. Be sure to include the photograph you chose. Consider these options to share your article.

① Collect the articles and combine them to create a newspaper about the Great Depression.

② Display your photograph as you read your article aloud to the rest of your class.

③ Gather together with other students who chose the same photograph and compare and contrast the information you included in your articles.

Glossary

This glossary contains meanings and pronunciations for some of the words in this book. The Full Pronunciation Key shows how to pronounce each consonant and vowel in a special spelling. At the bottom of the glossary pages is a shortened form of the full key.

Full Pronunciation Key

CONSONANT SOUNDS

b	**b**i**b**, ca**bb**age	r	**r**oar, **rh**yme	
ch	**ch**urch, sti**tch**	s	mi**ss**, **s**au**c**e, **sc**ene, **s**ee	
d	**d**ee**d**, maile**d**, pu**dd**le	sh	**di**sh, **sh**ip, **s**ugar, ti**ss**ue	
f	**f**ast, **f**i**fe**, o**ff**, **ph**rase, rou**gh**	t	**t**igh**t**, stopp**ed**	
g	**g**a**g**, **g**et, fin**g**er	th	ba**th**, **th**in	
h	**h**at, **wh**o	th	ba**the**, **th**is	
hw	**wh**ich, **wh**ere	v	ca**v**e, **v**al**v**e, **v**ine	
j	**j**u**dg**e, **g**em	w	**w**ith, **w**olf	
k	**c**at, **k**ick, s**ch**ool	y	**y**es, **y**olk, on**i**on	
kw	**ch**oir, **qu**ick	z	ro**s**e, si**z**e, **x**ylophone, **z**ebra	
l	**l**id, need**l**e, ta**ll**	zh	gara**g**e, plea**s**ure, vi**s**ion	
m	a**m**, **m**an, du**mb**			
n	**n**o, sudd**en**			
ng	thi**ng**, i**nk**			
p	**p**op, ha**pp**y			

VOWEL SOUNDS

ă	p**a**t, l**au**gh	o͞o	b**oo**t, r**u**de, fr**ui**t, fl**ew**
ā	**a**pe, **ai**d, p**ay**	ŭ	c**u**t, fl**oo**d, r**ou**gh, s**o**me
â	**ai**r, c**a**re, w**ea**r	û	c**i**rcle, f**u**r, h**ea**rd, t**e**rm, w**o**rd
ä	f**a**ther, k**oa**la, y**a**rd		
ě	p**e**t, pl**ea**sure, **a**ny		
ē	b**e**, b**ee**, **ea**sy, p**ia**no	yo͝o	c**u**re, p**u**re
ĭ	**i**f, p**i**t, b**u**sy	yo͞o	c**u**be, m**u**sic, f**ew**, c**ue**
ī	r**i**de, b**y**, p**ie**, h**igh**		
î	d**ea**r, d**ee**r, f**ie**rce, m**e**re	ə	**a**go, sil**e**nt, penc**i**l, lem**o**n, circ**u**s
ŏ	d**o**t, **o**n		
ō	g**o**, r**ow**, t**oe**, th**ough**		
ô	**a**ll, c**augh**t, p**aw**		
ô	c**o**re, f**o**r, r**oar**		
oi	b**oy**, n**oi**se, **oi**l		
ou	c**ow**, **ou**t		
o͝o	f**u**ll, b**oo**k, w**o**lf		

STRESS MARKS

Primary Stress ´: biology [bī•ŏl´•ə•jē]

Secondary Stress ´: biological [bī´•ə•lŏj´•ĭ•kəl]

A

abdomen (ăb′·də·mən) *n.* The abdomen is the part of the body that contains the stomach and digestive organs. In a human body, the abdomen is the area between the chest and hips that contains the stomach, small intestine, large intestine, liver, gallbladder, pancreas, and spleen.

abundance (ə·bŭn′·dəns) *n.* If you have an abundance of something, you have a lot of it. There is an abundance of fruit to choose from at the supermarket.

administer (ăd·mĭn′·ĭ·stər) *v.* When you administer something, you take responsibility for supervising or managing it. The three volunteers on the left administer a program that places foreign exchange students with American families.

advances (əd·văns′·əs) *n.* Advances in a particular area of study, such as technology or medicine, are improvements in that area. Huge advances in information technology, such as laptop computers and smartphones, were made during the 1990s and 2000s.

adversity (ăd·vûrs′·sĭ·tē) *n.* Adversity is hardship or a difficult situation. He is not sure how he will deal with the adversity of losing his home.

amateur (ăm′·ə·chər or ăm′·ə·tər) *n.* An amateur does something as a hobby and not as a job. In his free time, my brother is an amateur photographer.

analysis (ə·năl′·ĭ·sĭs) *n.* An analysis is a detailed study of something. The principal prepared an analysis of the school's test results, which showed that student grades are up and student absences are down.

appealing (ə·pē′·ling) *adj.* Something that is appealing has qualities that people find pleasing and attractive. Using virtual reality to learn complex educational topics is appealing to most students.

artery (är′·tə·rē) *n.* An artery is a blood vessel (one of many) that carries oxygen-filled blood from the heart to every part of the body. The largest artery is the aorta, the main high-pressure pipeline connected to the heart's left chamber.

Word Origins

artery The word *artery* is from the Greek word *arteria*, which originally applied to arteries, veins, and bronchial tubes. Advances in medicine showed that arteries carry blood and bronchial tubes carry air. Thus, the meaning of the word *artery* changed.

---

o͞o b**oo**t / ou **ou**t / ŭ c**u**t / û f**u**r / hw **wh**ich / th **th**in / *th* **th**is / zh vi**s**ion / ə **a**go, sil**e**nt, penc**i**l, lem**o**n, circ**u**s

ascending (ə·**sĕn′**·dĭng) *v.* If you are ascending a hill or cliff, you are climbing it. She was proud of herself for overcoming her fear of heights and ascending the climbing wall.

ascending

associate (ə·**sō′**·sē·āt′) *v.* If you associate one idea with another idea, you are connecting the two ideas. We associate sledding with the winter months.

atmosphere (**ăt′**·mə·sfîr′) *n.* Atmosphere is the overall tone or mood of a place or situation. There is always a cheerful atmosphere when we get together for celebrations.

attain (ə·**tān′**) *v.* When you attain something, you achieve it. My little sister was happy to attain her goal of school spelling champion.

B

banished (**băn′**·ĭshd) *v.* If something is banished, it is chased away. She was banished from the classroom for the day because she was behaving badly.

belfry (**bĕl′**·frē) *n.* A belfry is a bell tower, sometimes part of a church, where bells are housed. We quickly spotted Independence Hall in Philadelphia, Pennsylvania, because of its tall belfry.

> ### Word Origins
>
> **belfry** The words *belfry* and *bell* were not always related. Originally, *belfry* came from *berg-frithu*, an ancient Germanic compound word, meaning "a high place of peace, safety."

blueprint (**blōō′**·prĭnt′) *n.* A blueprint is a plan or model of something. A 3D printer requires a digital blueprint before it can create a product.

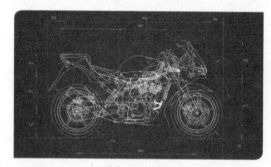
blueprint

bombarded (bŏm·**bär′**·dĭd) *v.* If you bombard someone with questions, you keep asking them a lot of questions. He was bombarded with questions by the news reporter.

C

captivated (kăp′·tə·**vā′**·tĭd) *v.* If you are captivated by someone or something, you find that person or thing fascinating. The audience was captivated by the juggler's amazing performance.

ă r**a**t / ā p**ay** / â c**a**re / ä f**a**ther / ĕ p**e**t / ē b**e** / ĭ p**i**t / ī p**ie** / î f**ie**rce / ŏ p**o**t / ō g**o** / ô p**aw** / ôr f**or** / oi **oi**l / ōō b**oo**k /

cipher (sī′•fər) *n.* A cipher is a secret system of writing that you use to send messages. You can use a simple cipher like this one to write and send secret messages.

civilized (**sĭv′•ə•**līzd′) *adj.* Something that is civilized is considered advanced in its development and customs. The Inca society in ancient Peru was considered civilized for its time because of its sophisticated architecture, roads, and canals for agriculture.

confided (kən•**fī′•**dĭd) *v.* If you confided in someone, you told that person something personal or secret. My sister confided her secrets to me.

confided

congestion (kən•**jĕs′•**chən) *n.* Congestion is crowding. In big cities, you have to leave home early in the morning to avoid the automobile congestion during rush hour.

considerate (kən•**sĭd′•**ər•ĭt) *adj.* To be considerate is to think of the feelings and needs of others. It is considerate to help older people when they are in need.

conspiring (kən•**spīr′•**ĭng) *v.* Conspiring is teaming up with someone to make a plan against someone else. They are conspiring against their classmate in the lunchroom.

coordination (kō•ôr′•dn•**ā′•**shən) *n.* If you have good coordination, you are able to move smoothly and efficiently. You need good hand-eye coordination to play tennis.

craft (krăft) *n.* You can refer to a boat as a craft. The sleek craft sails smoothly through the waves.

craft

crude (kro͞od) *adj.* If you describe something as crude, it means it is not exact or detailed but may be useful in a rough, general way. She made a crude sketch before deciding how to draw her final art piece.

crusade (kro͞o•**sād′**) *v.* If you crusade for something, you work hard to make sure it succeeds. The students joined together to crusade for more recycling at their school.

---

o͞o b**oo**t / ou **ou**t / ŭ c**u**t / û f**u**r / hw **wh**ich / th **th**in / *th* **th**is / zh vi**si**on / ə **a**go, sil**e**nt, penc**i**l, lem**o**n, circ**u**s

D

dedication (dĕd′•ĭ•kā′•shən) *n.* Dedication is extreme devotion or commitment to a task or purpose. Our drama teacher won a teaching award for her dedication to her students.

dejected (dĭ•jĕk′•tĭd) *adj.* To feel dejected is to feel sad and hopeless. She felt dejected after the exams and wished she had studied harder.

demeaning (dĭ•mēn′•ĭng) *adj.* Behaving in a demeaning way may show a lack of self-respect. My sister made demeaning comments after I lost the game.

democratic (dĕm′•ə•krăt′•ĭk) *adj.* Something that is democratic is available to everyone. The voting for the class trip was done in a democratic way.

deplorable (dĭ•plôr′•ə•bəl) *adj.* A deplorable situation is terrible and unacceptable. The beach is in a deplorable state, with garbage everywhere.

deport (dĭ•pôrt′) *v.* Governments deport people by removing them from the country in which they are living. The government will deport tourists and other foreigners who break the law.

Word Origins

deport The word *deport* is from the Latin word *deportare*, meaning "to carry away."

---

descend (dĭ•sĕnd′) *v.* To descend means to move from a higher point to a lower point. For many hikers, the most challenging part is when they descend.

descent (dĭ•sĕnt′) *n.* A person's descent is his or her family background or ancestors. These are old photographs of my ancestors from Germany, so I am of German descent.

destination (dĕs′•tə•nā′•shən) *n.* The destination is the place where you are going or are being sent. Last year, we visited the twin Wailua waterfalls on Kauai, Hawaii, which is a popular tourist destination.

discipline (dĭs′•ə•plĭn) *n.* Discipline is self-control. My cousin has the discipline to write in his journal each evening.

disposal (dĭ•spō′•zəl) *n.* If you have something at your disposal, you can use it however and whenever you want. When my mom wraps gifts, she has plenty of wrapping paper close by at her disposal.

ă rat / ā pay / â care / ä father / ĕ pet / ē be / ĭ pit / ī pie / î fierce / ŏ pot / ō go / ô paw / ôr for / oi oil / ŏŏ book /

dissect (dĭ·sĕkt′ or dī·sĕkt′) *v.* If you dissect something, you carefully cut it up to examine it scientifically. The students are working together to dissect a frog and learn more about the parts of its body.

downturn (dŏŭn′·tûrn′) *n.* A downturn is a decline in the economy or a business. When there is a downturn, some stores go out of business.

drenched (drĕnchd) *adj.* If something is drenched, it is soaking wet. The dog was drenched after his bath.

drenched

dubious (dōō′·bē·əs) *adj.* If you are dubious, you are doubtful and disbelieving. She was dubious of the news she was reading because the story was so outrageous.

E

ease (ēz) *v.* When something eases, its impact decreases. When he hurt his knee playing soccer, he used ice to ease his pain.

efficacy (ĭ·fĭsh′·ən·sē) *n.* The efficacy of something is its effectiveness and ability to do what it should. Once we finished our new invention, we needed to test the efficacy of the product.

elope (ĭ·lōp′) *v.* To elope means to run away secretly to get married. The couple decided to elope because their parents were against the marriage.

eminent (ĕm′·ə·nənt) *adj.* An eminent person is well known and respected. Jane Goodall is an eminent animal scientist who is best known for her work with chimpanzees.

> **Word Origins**
>
> **eminent** The word *eminent* comes from the Latin verb *eminere*, meaning "to stand out."

endorsement (ĕn·dôrs′·mənt) *n.* A person who signs endorsement deal, agrees to publicly say that he or she likes a product or service in exchange for money. She is a track athlete who has an endorsement deal with a sports drink company.

equipped (ĭ·kwĭpd′) *v.* If you equip yourself for a job or an experience, you make sure you have what is necessary to do it well. The builder made sure he was equipped with the correct safety gear before performing the job.

ōō b**oo**t / ou **ou**t / ŭ c**u**t / û f**u**r / hw **wh**ich / th **th**in / *th* **th**is / zh vi**si**on / ə **a**go, sil**e**nt, penc**i**l, lem**o**n, circ**u**s

erosion (ĭ•rō′•zhən) *n.* Erosion is the process of wearing away something by wind, water, or other natural agents. Years of wind and water erosion have worn away the parking lot by the ocean.

erosion

escorting (ĕs′•kôr′•tĭng) *v.* If you are escorting someone, you are going somewhere with that person. The father is escorting the bride down the aisle at her wedding.

executive (ĭg•zĕk′•yə•tĭv) *n.* An executive in a business decides what should be done. An executive in the company meets with the employees to discuss their ideas.

exhaled (ĕks•hāld′) *v.* If you exhaled, you breathed out. It was so cold she could see her breath when she exhaled.

expedition (ĕk′•spĭ•dĭsh′•ən) *n.* An expedition is a journey organized for a particular purpose, such as exploration. We went on a cave expedition throughout the world.

extensive (ĭk•stĕn′•sĭv) *adj.* Something that is extensive is far-reaching or covers a large area. The store had an extensive selection of shoes.

F

fleet (flēt) *adj.* When something is fleet, it is fast and nimble. The cheetah, fleet of foot, is considered the world's fastest land animal.

fleeting (flē′•tĭng) *adj.* Something that is fleeting passes by very quickly. I got a fleeting look at the hummingbird before it quickly flew away.

foster (fô′•stər) *adj.* Foster parents take a child into their family for a period of time. His foster mom makes sure he has everything he needs while he is living in her home.

Word Origins

foster The word *foster* comes from the Old English word *fostrian*, meaning "to nourish or feed."

frail (frāl) *adj.* Something frail is weak and easily broken. The frail eggshells easily cracked even though they were inside the carton.

frets (frĕtz) *v.* Someone who frets about something worries about it. He frets whenever he is about to take a test.

ă **r**at / ā **p**ay / â **c**are / ä **f**ather / ĕ **p**et / ē **b**e / ĭ **p**it / ī **p**ie / î **fie**rce / ŏ **p**ot / ō **g**o / ô **p**aw / ôr **f**or / oi **oil** / ŏŏ **b**oo**k** /

fumed (fyo͞omd) *v.* A person who fumed was very angry. My teacher fumed after hearing how badly I behaved during her absence.

fundamentals (fŭn'•də•měn'•tls) *n.* Fundamentals are the simplest ideas or parts of something. Our gym teacher showed us the fundamentals of tennis.

G

gait (gāt) *n.* A gait is a way of walking. He speeds up his gait so he can catch the bus.

gait

garland (gär'•lənd) *n.* A garland is a wreath of leaves and flowers worn on the head or around the neck. She is wearing a garland of lavender flowers on the top of her head.

garland

graces (grā'•səs) *n.* The graces of neighbors is the kindness of neighbors. The new residents were grateful for the graces of their neighbors, who made them feel welcomed.

> **Word Origins**
>
> **graces** The word *graces* is from the Latin word *gratus*, meaning "pleasing."

H

habitually (hə•bĭch'•o͞o•əl•lē) *adv.* To do something habitually is to do it repeatedly, out of habit. She habitually bites her nails when she is nervous.

haphazardly (hăp•hăz'•ərd•lē) *adv.* Things that are arranged haphazardly are not organized and are perhaps out of order. She put away her clothes haphazardly instead of hanging them up neatly.

harnesses (här'•nĭ•səs) *n.* A harness is a strap used to fasten or control something. Our van is equipped with safety harnesses for my chair.

households (hous'•hōlds') *n.* A household is all the people who live together in a house. The members of this household enjoy spending time together as a family.

---

o͞o b**oo**t / ou **ou**t / ŭ c**u**t / û f**u**r / hw **wh**ich / th **th**in / *th* **th**is / zh vi**si**on / ə **a**go, sil**e**nt, penc**i**l, lem**o**n, circ**u**s

hurdle (hûr′•dl) *n.* Hurdles are barriers or obstacles to success. The French student had to spend extra time studying after school in order to overcome the hurdle of learning English.

I

imitation (ĭm′•ĭ•tā′•shən) *adj.* Something described as imitation looks like the real thing but is only a copy. A jeweler can tell if your jewelry is genuine or if it is imitation jewelry.

improvised (ĭm′•prə•vīzd′) *v.* If something is improvised, it is done without any planning. They improvised a tent out of chairs and a blanket.

impulsive (ĭm•pŭl′•sĭv) *adj.* Someone who is impulsive does things without thinking about them carefully first. She is an impulsive shopper who buys things on a whim.

indifference (ĭn•dĭf′•ər•əns or ĭn•dĭf′•rəns) *n.* Indifference is a lack of interest. She had a look of indifference as her mother tried to explain why she needed to study harder.

indigenous (ĭn•dĭj′•ə•nəs) *adj.* Indigenous people are native to an area. The people of the indigenous Tupi-Guarani tribe are native to Brazil.

industry (ĭn′•də•strē) *n.* Industry is the work involved in the processing of raw materials and then making them into products in factories. Almost everyone growing up in our small town had a job in the coal industry.

initiatives (ĭ•nĭsh′•ə•tĭvs) *n.* An initiative is an important program or plan that's intended to solve a problem. The recycling initiative at school has resulted in fewer items going into the garbage.

innovations (ĭn′•ə•vā′•shəns) *n.* An innovation is a new idea or way of doing something. In the late 1940s, the television and the LP record were considered innovations.

insisted (ĭn•sĭs′•tĭd) *v.* If you insisted that something should be done, you said so firmly and refused to give up. His mom insisted that he do his chores before meeting up with friends.

integrated (ĭn′•tĭ•grā′•tĭd) *v.* If you have integrated one thing with another, the two have been closely linked or form part of the same system. She has integrated her cell phone and her computer to work together.

Word Origins

integrated The word *integrated* is from the Latin word *integrare*, meaning "to make whole."

ă **r**at / ā **p**ay / â **c**are / ä **f**ather / ě **p**et / ē **b**e / ĭ **p**it / ī **p**ie / î **f**ierce / ŏ **p**ot / ō **g**o / ô **p**aw / ôr **f**or / oi **o**il / ŏŏ **b**ook /

intrepid (ĭn•**trĕp′**•ĭd) *adj.* An intrepid person is fearless and adventurous. My cousin and her family are intrepid travelers who love hiking trails during any season—even winter.

investors (ĭn•**vĕs′**•tərz) *n.* Investors are people or organizations that buy stocks or shares to receive a profit. In the 1980s, investors were excited to buy stocks in a new computer company that offered popular gaming systems.

L

labor (**lā′**•bər) *n.* Labor is work— especially hard, physical work. It takes a lot of physical labor to plant trees.

lax (lăks) *adj.* If something is lax, it has been done in a lazy way instead of being done carefully. She was in a rush to get to school and made her bed in a very lax way.

liable (**lī′**•ə•bəl) *adj.* If you are liable for something, you are responsible or accountable for it. When my mother saw what the dog had done, she said my brother was liable for the mess because he was supposed to be watching the dog.

Word Origins

liable The word *liable* is from the Old French word *lier*, meaning "to bind."

---

livestock (**līv′**•stŏk′) *n.* Livestock are animals, such as cattle and sheep, that are kept on a farm. The two ranchers take care of the livestock on the cattle farm.

M

mandatory (**măn′**•də•tôr′•ē) *adj.* Something that is mandatory is required by rules or the law. It is mandatory that all students exit the building during a school fire drill.

manufacturer (măn′•yə•**făk′**•chər•ər) *n.* A manufacturer is a business that makes goods for sale. A textile manufacturer makes cloth for clothing and furniture.

matrimonial (**măt′**•rə•mō′•nē•əl) *adj.* Matrimonial issues have to do with marriage. A wedding is a matrimonial event that celebrates a marriage.

matrimonial

metropolitan (mĕt′•rə•**pŏl′**•ĭ•tən) *adj.* If you describe a place as metropolitan, you mean that the place has the characteristics of a large city. The streets of the metropolitan community were filled with people and towering skyscrapers.

---

o͞o b**oo**t / ou **ou**t / ŭ c**u**t / û f**u**r / hw **wh**ich / th **th**in / *th* **th**is / zh vi**s**ion / ə **a**go, sil**e**nt, penc**i**l, lem**o**n, circ**u**s

miscellaneous (mĭs′•ə•lā′•nē•əs) *adj.* A miscellaneous group is made up of different types of things that are difficult to put into one category. His grandfather keeps a miscellaneous group of objects in his office.

miserable (mĭz′•ər•ə•bəl) *adj.* Someone who is miserable is very unhappy. She looked miserable sitting alone in the park.

mission (mĭsh′•ən) *n.* A mission is an organization that helps people in need. Families at the mission serve food to people who are homeless.

motley (mŏt′•lē) *adj.* A motley group seems strange because its members are all very different from one another. A motley group of bystanders gathered to watch the parade.

muster (mŭs′•tər) *n.* A muster is a formal gathering of soldiers, especially for inspection or exercise. The troops gathered for muster every morning at six o'clock.

mystifies (mĭs′•tə•fīz′) *v.* If something mystifies you, you find it impossible to explain or understand. The meaning and construction of the massive stone monument Stonehenge still mystifies people today.

O

orderly (ôr′•dər•lē) *adj.* When something is done in an orderly manner, it is done in an organized and controlled way. They waited in line in an orderly fashion to purchase their meals from the restaurant.

outraged (out′•rājd′) *adj.* If you are outraged about something, you're angry and shocked. She is outraged that her friend posted an unflattering picture of her on her blog.

overcome (ō′•vər•kŭm′) *v.* Someone who is overcome is experiencing a deep level of emotion. Upon hearing the bad news, she was overcome with sadness.

P

passage (păs′•ĭj) *n.* A passage is a journey by ship. We booked a passage on a cruise to Northern Europe.

passage

perennial (pə•rĕn′•ē•əl) *adj.* If something is perennial, it is permanent, constant, or repeated over time. Perennial flowers border the pond in the park.

Word Origins
perennial The word *perennial* is from the Latin word *perennis*, meaning "lasting throughout the year."

ă **r**at / ā p**ay** / â c**are** / ä f**a**ther / ĕ p**e**t / ē b**e** / ĭ p**i**t / ī p**ie** / î f**ie**rce / ŏ p**o**t / ō g**o** / ô p**aw** / ôr f**or** / oi **oi**l / o͝o b**oo**k /

peril (**pĕr′**·əl) *n.* Peril is a state of risk or danger. Some might say that people who engage in hang-gliding put their lives in great peril.

persevere (pûr′·sə·**vîr′**) *v.* When you persevere with something, you continue to do it even when there is little hope of success. The runners persevere through the muddy conditions to finish the race.

persisted (pər·**sĭs′**·tĭd) *v.* If something persists, it continues to exist. We moved our picnic blanket, but the ants persisted in crawling toward our food.

Word Origins

persisted The word *persist* is from the Latin word *persistere:* *per-,* meaning "through" or "forward," plus the word *sistere,* meaning "to stand or last."

---

phenomenon (fĭ·**nŏm′**·ə·nŏn′) *n.* A phenomenon is someone who is very impressive because of a special ability or wide popularity. She is a phenomenon among musicians for her piano-playing ability.

pondered (**pŏn′**·dərd) *v.* If you pondered something, you thought deeply about it. He pondered the answer to the essay question on his test.

pondered

practicable (**prăk′**·tĭ·kə·bəl) *adj.* A practicable plan is possible to carry out. When practicable, students go on field trips by bus.

precision (prĭ·**sĭzh′**·ən) *n.* When you do something with precision, you do it exactly the way it should be done. An archer shows precision by shooting arrows in the yellow circle—the very center of the target.

principles (**prĭn′**·sə·pəls) *n.* The principles of a game are its basic rules. Our teacher explained the principles of playing chess.

propaganda (prŏp′·ə·**găn′**·də) *n.* Propaganda is information, especially of a misleading nature, used to promote a particular point of view. Sometimes on social media sites, there is political propaganda that looks similar to factual news stories.

prosthetics (prŏs·**thĕt′**·ĭks) *n.* Prosthetics are parts of the body that are artificial and are used to replace natural ones. With the advancement in prosthetics, the man is active again with his new prosthetic leg.

ōō b**oo**t / ou **ou**t / ŭ c**u**t / û f**u**r / hw **wh**ich / th **th**in / *th* **th**is / zh vi**s**ion / ə **a**go, sil**e**nt, penc**i**l, lem**o**n, circ**u**s

pursuers (pûr·**soo**'·ərz) *n.* The people who are chasing or searching for you are your pursuers. The cheetahs are pursuers of their prey.

R

rafters (**răf**'·tərs) *n.* Rafters are the sloping pieces of wood that support a roof. The attic was small, but the high wooden rafters made the room seem spacious.

rafters

rank (răngk) *v.* If you rank something, you give it a position or grade in relation to others of its type. The judges at the county fair rank the sheep best in breed, as well as first place for its muscle tone and style.

replicate (**rĕp**'·lĭ·**kāt**') *v.* If you replicate something, you do or make it in the exact same way as the original. The students tried to replicate the experiment that the teacher had demonstrated.

represent (**rĕp**'·rĭ·**zĕnt**') *v.* If you represent your country in a competition, you participate in it on behalf of the country. He hopes to represent the U.S. for snowboarding in the next Olympic competition.

resilient (rĭ·**zĭl**'·yənt) *adj.* Something that is resilient is strong and recovers quickly. Plants that grow in the desert have to be resilient to the hot, dry weather conditions and to limited water resources.

revolutionary (**rĕv**'·ə·**loo**'·shə·**nĕr**'·ē) *adj.* Revolutionary ideas involve great changes in the way that something is done or made. Smartphones were a revolutionary idea because they changed the way people communicate across the world.

rigid (**rĭj**'·ĭd) *adj.* Something that is rigid is unable to adapt and difficult to change. His dad is very rigid about the amount of time he can spend watching television.

S

savagely (**săv**'·ĭj·lē) *adv.* To do something savagely is to do it in a forceful and unfriendly way. The male tigers are savagely attacking each other.

scraggly (**skrăg**'·lē) *adj.* Something that is scraggly is messy or raggedy-looking. The dog has scraggly fur and needs a bath and haircut.

scraggly

ă r**at** / ā **pay** / â c**are** / ä f**a**ther / ĕ p**et** / ē b**e** / ĭ p**it** / ī p**ie** / î f**ie**rce / ŏ p**ot** / ō g**o** / ô p**aw** / ôr **for** / oi **oil** / o͞o b**oo**k /

sheer (shîr) *adj.* A sheer cliff is extremely steep or completely vertical. It is very difficult to climb the cliff's sheer walls.

sheer

skirt (skûrt) *v.* Things that skirt an area form its border or edge. The flowers and shrubs skirt the edge of the lawn.

slackening (slăk'•ən•ĭng) *v.* Something that is slackening is slowing down. The biker's pace started slackening as he went uphill.

slew (slo͞o) *n.* A slew is a lot of something. Our dog has a slew of tennis balls to play with.

slum (slŭm) *n.* A slum is an overcrowded, impoverished urban area. Many residents in a slum live in unhealthy conditions.

sophisticated (sə•fĭsh'•tĭ•kā'•tĭd) *adj.* A sophisticated machine or method is more complex than others. The James Webb Space Telescope is a sophisticated instrument that allows scientists to look deeper into our universe than a traditional telescope.

spitefully (spīt'•fəl•lē) *adv.* To do something spitefully is to do it in a deliberately mean, hurtful way. He spitefully played a trick on his classmate by scaring her with a fake spider.

stabilizing (stā'•bə•līz'•ĭng) *adj.* Something that's stabilizing keeps other things steady. If he removes the stabilizing block, the tower will fall over.

sterile (stĕr'•əl or stĕr'•ĭl') *adj.* Something that is totally sterile is very clean and free from bacteria. Dentists use sterile medical instruments during dental procedures.

stimulated (stĭm'•yə•lā•tĭd) *v.* If something stimulated you, it made you feel full of ideas and enthusiasm. Sewing class stimulated her interest in becoming a fashion designer.

stocks (stŏks) *n.* If you own stocks in a company, you are entitled to a share in the company's profits. Dad checks the newspaper every day to see if the price of his stocks is increasing.

stricken (strĭk'•ən) *adj.* To be stricken is to be deeply affected by something. She was stricken when she found out what happened to her friend.

surmised (sər•mīzd') *v.* If you surmised, you guessed it was true. By the excited look on her face, we surmised that the gift was exactly what she wanted.

---

o͞o b**oo**t / ou **ou**t / ŭ c**u**t / û f**u**r / hw **wh**ich / th **th**in / *th* **th**is / zh vi**si**on / ə **a**go, sil**e**nt, penc**i**l, lem**o**n, circ**u**s

surveying (sər•**vā**'•ĭng or **sûr**'•vā'•ĭng) *v.* If you are surveying land, you are finding its shape, area, and boundaries by measuring. The contractor is surveying the land before construction of the building begins.

T

theory (**thē**'•ə•rē) *n.* The theory of a subject is the set of rules that form the basis of it. "String theory" is a theory in physics. Sir Isaac Newton came up with the theory of gravity to explain why objects such as apples fall toward the ground.

Word Origins

theory The word *theory* is from the Greek word *theoria*, meaning "contemplation or speculation."

---

tragedy (**trăj**'•ĭ•dē) *n.* A tragedy is a very sad event. When wildfires destroy communities, it is a tragedy for the people who live there.

tranquil (**trăng**'•kwĭl) *adj.* Something that is tranquil is calm and peaceful. A tranquil view of the lake could be seen at sunset.

tranquil

transformed (trăns•**fôrmd**') *v.* Something that is transformed is changed in a meaningful way. The park was transformed after the volunteers cleaned up all the trash.

tread (trĕd) *n.* A tread is the sound of a person's footsteps. We heard my dad's heavy tread as he was coming up the stairs.

trial (**trī**'•əl) *adj.* When you take a trial run, you test or practice something before you actually do it. The director of the school band had a trial run before the first performance.

U

undertaking (ŭn'•dər•**tāk**'•ĭng) *n.* An undertaking is a large or difficult task or job. It will be an undertaking to wash all the dirty dishes.

usurped (yo͞o•**sûrpd**' or yo͞o•**zûrpd**') *v.* If someone usurped a job or position, he or she took it illegally or by force. Our cat usurped Dad's place in the bed.

V

vanquished (**văng**'•kwĭshd or **văn**'•kwĭshd) *v.* Vanquished means defeated. The chess player vanquished all of his opponents to win the competition.

ă r**a**t / ā p**ay** / â c**a**re / ä f**a**ther / ĕ p**e**t / ē b**e** / ĭ p**i**t / ī p**ie** / î f**ie**rce / ŏ p**o**t / ō g**o** / ô p**aw** / ôr f**or** / oi **oi**l / o͝o b**oo**k /

variations (vâr′•ē•**ā**′•shənz) *n.* Variations are changes in the condition, level, or quantity of something. The cat's fur had many variations in color and patterns.

Victorian (vĭk•**tôr**′•ē•ən) *adj.* If something is Victorian, it is in the romantic style of England's 19th-century Victorian era. This Victorian-style house in our neighborhood has decorative trim, textured walls, vibrant colors, and a pointed roof.

Victorian

viewpoints (**vyōō**′•points′) *n.* Viewpoints are ways of looking at things. Students respectfully express their viewpoints during a group discussion.

vocational (vō•**kā**′•shə•nəl) *adj.* Vocational schools train students to do various jobs. Students at some vocational schools learn how to fix cars.

voracious (vô•**rā**′•shəs or və•**rā**′•shəs) *adj.* If you describe a person as a voracious reader, you mean that the person is extremely eager about reading. A voracious reader can read two books or more a month.

W

warping (wôrp•ĭng) *v.* If something is warping something, it is distorting it or twisting it out of shape. The funhouse mirror is warping their reflections.

wringer (**rĭng**′•ər) *n.* A wringer is a device that squeezes water out of laundry. Water is squeezed out as the clothes pass between the two rollers on the wringer.

wringer

---

o͞o b**oo**t / ou **ou**t / ŭ c**u**t / û f**u**r / hw **wh**ich / th **th**in / *th* **th**is / zh vi**si**on / ə **a**go, sil**e**nt, penc**i**l, lem**o**n, circ**u**s

Index of Titles and Authors

Acknowledgments

"All Summer in a Day" from *A Medicine for Melancholy and Other Stories* by Ray Bradbury. Text copyright © 1954, renewed 1982 by Ray Bradbury. Reprinted by permission of Don Congdon Associates, Inc.

"And the Market Crashes" by Eric Arnesen from *Cobblestone* magazine, April 2006. Text copyright © 2006 by Carus Publishing Company. Reprinted by permission of Cricket Media. All Cricket Media material is copyrighted by Carus Publishing Company d/b/a Cricket Media, and/or various authors and illustrators. Any commercial use or distribution of material without permission is strictly prohibited. Please visit http://www.cricketmedia.com/licensing for licensing and http://www.cricketmedia.com for subscriptions.

"Excerpt from *The Boy Who Invented TV: The Story of Philo Farnsworth* by Kathleen Krull, illustrated by Greg Couch. Text copyright © 2009 by Kathleen Krull. Illustrations copyright © 2009 by Greg Couch. Reprinted by permission of Alfred A. Knopf, an imprint of Random House Children's Books, a division of Penguin Random House LLC, and Writers House, LLC. All rights reserved.

Excerpt from *Bud, Not Buddy* by Christopher Paul Curtis. Text copyright © 1999 by Christopher Paul Curtis. Reprinted by permission of Delacorte Press, an imprint of Random House Children's Books, a division of Penguin Random House LLC, Random House Group Limited, and Lectorum Publications. All rights reserved.

Excerpt from *Children of the Great Depression* by Russell Freedman. Text copyright © 2005 by Russell Freedman. Reprinted by permission of Houghton Mifflin Harcourt Publishing Company.

"Garrett Morgan to the Rescue!" by Paula Morrow from *Ask* magazine, January 2015. Text copyright © 2015 by Carus Publishing Company. Reprinted by permission of Cricket Media. All Cricket Media material is copyrighted by Carus Publishing Company d/b/a Cricket Media, and/or various authors and illustrators. Any commercial use or distribution of material without permission is strictly prohibited. Please visit http://www.cricketmedia.com/licensing for licensing and http://www.cricketmedia.com for subscriptions.

"Hamadryad at Midwinter" by Elizabeth Creith, illustrated by Ryan Durney from *Odyssey* magazine. Text copyright © 2011 by Carus Publishing Company. Illustrations copyright © 2011 by Ryan Durney. Reprinted by permission of Cricket Media. All Cricket Media material is copyrighted by Carus Publishing Company d/b/a Cricket Media, and/or various authors and illustrators. Any commercial use or distribution of material without permission is strictly prohibited. Please visit http://www.cricketmedia.com/licensing for licensing and http://www.cricketmedia.com for subscriptions.

Excerpt from "Identity Theft" from *Facts of Life: Stories* by Gary Soto. Text copyright © 2008 by Gary Soto. Reprinted by permission of Houghton Mifflin Harcourt Publishing Company.

Excerpt from "It's More Than Just Rain or Snow or Springtime" from *How to Read Literature Like a Professor: For Kids* by Thomas C. Foster. Text copyright © 2003, 2013 by Thomas C. Foster. Reprinted by permission of HarperCollins Publishers and Sanford J. Greenburger Associates, Inc.

"Lions No Match for Young Boy and His Invention: Richard Turere at TED" by Andrew J. Howley. Text copyright © 2013 by Andrew Howley. Reprinted by permission of Andrew J. Howley.

Excerpt from "Malala Yousafzai Peter J. Gomes Humanitarian of the Year Award Speech at Harvard University." Text copyright © 2013 by Malala Yousafzai. Reprinted by permission of Curtis Brown Group, Ltd, on behalf of Malala Yousafzai.

"Racing with the Wind Around the World" by Valerie Biebuyck and Marcia Lusted from *Appleseeds* magazine, July 2012. Text copyright © 2012 by Carus Publishing Company. Reprinted by permission of Cricket Media. All Cricket Media material is copyrighted by Carus Publishing Company d/b/a Cricket Media, and/or various authors and illustrators. Any commercial use or distribution of material without permission is strictly prohibited. Please visit http://www.cricketmedia.com/licensing for licensing and http://www.cricketmedia.com for subscriptions.

Adapted from *The Real Story of Paul Revere's Ride*. Copyright © 2017 by the Paul Revere House. Reprinted by permission of the

Credits